T0212437

Lecture Notes in Computer Science 12017

Founding Editors

Gerhard Goos
Karlsruhe Institute of Technology, Karlsruhe, Germany
Juris Hartmanis
Cornell University, Ithaca, NY, USA

Editorial Board Members

Elisa Bertino
Purdue University, West Lafayette, IN, USA
Wen Gao
Peking University, Beijing, China
Bernhard Steffen
TU Dortmund University, Dortmund, Germany
Gerhard Woeginger
RWTH Aachen, Aachen, Germany
Moti Yung
Columbia University, New York, NY, USA

More information about this series at http://www.springer.com/series/7408

Sandra Wienke · Sridutt Bhalachandra (Eds.)

Accelerator Programming Using Directives

6th International Workshop, WACCPD 2019
Denver, CO, USA, November 18, 2019
Revised Selected Papers

 Springer

Editors
Sandra Wienke ⓘ
RWTH Aachen University
Aachen, Germany

Sridutt Bhalachandra ⓘ
Lawrence Berkeley National Laboratory
Berkeley, CA, USA

ISSN 0302-9743   ISSN 1611-3349   (electronic)
Lecture Notes in Computer Science
ISBN 978-3-030-49942-6   ISBN 978-3-030-49943-3   (eBook)
https://doi.org/10.1007/978-3-030-49943-3

LNCS Sublibrary: SL2 – Programming and Software Engineering

© Springer Nature Switzerland AG 2020
This work is subject to copyright. All rights are reserved by the Publisher, whether the whole or part of the material is concerned, specifically the rights of translation, reprinting, reuse of illustrations, recitation, broadcasting, reproduction on microfilms or in any other physical way, and transmission or information storage and retrieval, electronic adaptation, computer software, or by similar or dissimilar methodology now known or hereafter developed.
The use of general descriptive names, registered names, trademarks, service marks, etc. in this publication does not imply, even in the absence of a specific statement, that such names are exempt from the relevant protective laws and regulations and therefore free for general use.
The publisher, the authors and the editors are safe to assume that the advice and information in this book are believed to be true and accurate at the date of publication. Neither the publisher nor the authors or the editors give a warranty, express or implied, with respect to the material contained herein or for any errors or omissions that may have been made. The publisher remains neutral with regard to jurisdictional claims in published maps and institutional affiliations.

This Springer imprint is published by the registered company Springer Nature Switzerland AG
The registered company address is: Gewerbestrasse 11, 6330 Cham, Switzerland

Preface

The ever-increasing heterogeneity in supercomputing applications has given rise to complex compute node architectures offering multiple, heterogeneous levels of massive parallelism. As a result, the 'X' in MPI+X demands more focus. Exploiting the maximum available parallelism out of such systems necessitates sophisticated programming approaches that can provide scalable as well as portable solutions without compromising on performance. A programmer's expectation from the scientific community is to deliver solutions that would allow maintenance of a single code base whenever possible avoiding duplicate effort.

Raising the abstraction of the code is one of the effective methodologies to reduce the burden on the programmer while improving productivity. Software abstraction-based programming models, such as OpenMP and OpenACC, have been serving this purpose over the past several years as the compiler technology steadily improves. These programming models address the 'X' component by providing programmers with high-level directive-based approaches to accelerate and port scientific applications to heterogeneous platforms.

These proceedings contain the papers accepted for presentation at the 6th Workshop on Accelerator Programming using Directives (WACCPD 2019) – http://waccpd.org/. WACCPD is one of the major forums for bringing together users, developers, and the software and tools community to share knowledge and experiences when programming emerging complex parallel computing systems.

Recent architectural trends indicate a heavy reliance of future exascale machines on accelerators for performance. Toward this end, the workshop highlighted improvements to the state of the art through the accepted papers and prompted discussion through keynotes/panels that drew the community's attention to key areas that will facilitate the transition to accelerator-based high-performance computing (HPC). The workshop aimed to showcase all aspects of heterogeneous systems discussing innovative high-level language features, lessons learned while using directives to migrate scientific legacy code to parallel processors, compilation and runtime scheduling techniques, among others.

The WACCPD 2019 workshop received 13 submissions out of which 7 were accepted to be presented at the workshop and published in these proceedings. The Program Committee of the workshop comprised 24 members spanning universities, national laboratories, and industries. Each paper received an average of five reviews.

For 2019, we encouraged all authors to add the Artifact Description (AD) to their submissions. Two additional pages were made available to authors (however without obligations) to make their code and data publicly available (e.g. on GitHub, Zenodo, Code Ocean, etc.) in support of the reproducibility initiative. As a further push, only papers with AD were considered for the Best Paper Award.

Of the 7 accepted papers, 86% had reproducibility information and these manuscripts are highlighted with an 'artifacts available' logo in this book.

The program co-chairs invited Dr. Nicholas James Wright from Lawrence Berkeley National Laboratory (LBL) to give a keynote address on "Perlmutter – A 2020 Pre-Exascale GPU-accelerated System for NERSC: Architecture and Application Performance Optimization." Dr. Nicholas J. Wright is the Perlmutter chief architect and the Advanced Technologies Group lead in the National Energy Research Scientific Computing (NERSC) center at LBL. He led the effort to optimize the architecture of the Perlmutter machine, the first NERSC platform designed to meet the needs of both large-scale simulation and data analysis from experimental facilities. Nicholas has a PhD from the University of Durham in computational chemistry and has been with NERSC since 2009.

Robert Henschel from Indiana University gave an invited talk titled "The SPEC ACCEL Benchmark – Results and Lessons Learned." Robert Henschel is the director of Research Software and Solutions at Indiana University. He is responsible for providing advanced scientific applications to researchers at Indiana University and national partners as well as providing support for computational research to the Indiana University School of Medicine. Henschel serves as the chair of the Standard Performance Evaluation Corporation (SPEC) High-Performance Group and in this role leads the development of production quality benchmarks for HPC systems. He also serves as the treasurer of the OpenACC organization. Henschel has a deep background in HPC and his research interests focus on performance analysis of parallel applications.

The workshop concluded with a panel "Convergence, Divergence, or New Approaches? – The Future of Software-Based Abstractions for Heterogeneous Supercomputing" moderated by Fernanda Foertter from NVIDIA. The panelists included:

- Christian Trott, Sandia National Laboratories, USA
- Michael Wolfe, Nvidia, USA
- Jack Deslippe, Lawrence Berkeley National Laboratory, USA
- Jeff Hammond, Intel, USA
- Johannes Doerfert, Argonne National Laboratory, USA

Based on rigorous reviews and ranking scores of all papers reviewed, the following paper won the Best Paper Award. The authors of the Best Paper Award also included reproducibility results to their paper, which the WACCPD workshop organizers had indicated as a criteria to be eligible to compete for the Best Paper Award.

- Hongzhang Shan and Zhengji Zhao from Lawrence Berkeley National Laboratory, and Marcus Wagner from Cray: "Accelerating the Performance of Modal Aerosol Module of E3SM Using OpenACC"

Emphasizing the importance of using directives for legacy scientific applications, each keynote/invited speakers, panelists, and Best Paper Award winners were given a book on "OpenACC for Programmers: Concepts & Strategies."

April 2020   Sandra Wienke
                                                    Sridutt Bhalachandra

Organization

Steering Committee

Barbara Chapman	Stony Brook, USA
Duncan Poole	OpenACC, USA
Kuan-Ching Li	Providence University, Taiwan
Oscar Hernandez	ORNL, USA
Jeffrey Vetter	ORNL, USA

Program Co-chairs

Sandra Wienke	RWTH Aachen University, Germany
Sridutt Bhalachandra	Lawrence Berkeley National Laboratory, USA

Publicity Chair

Neelima Bayyapu	NMAM Institute of Technology, Karnataka, India

Web Chair

Shu-Mei Tseng	University of California, Irvine, USA

Program Committee

Adrian Jackson	Edinburgh Parallel Computing Centre, University of Edinburgh, UK
Andreas Herten	Forschungszentrum Jülich, Germany
Arpith Jacob	Google, USA
Cheng Wang	Microsoft, USA
Christian Iwainsky	Technische Universität Darmstadt, Germany
Christian Terboven	RWTH Aachen University, Germany
Christopher Daley	Lawrence Berkeley National Laboratory, USA
C. J. Newburn	NVIDIA, USA
David Bernholdt	Oak Ridge National Laboratory, USA
Giuseppe Congiu	Argonne National Laboratory, USA
Haoqiang Jin	NASA Ames Research Center, USA
Jeff Larkin	NVIDIA, USA
Kelvin Li	IBM, USA
Manisha Gajbe	Intel, USA
Michael Wolfe	NVIDIA/PGI, USA
Ray Sheppard	Indiana University, USA
Ron Lieberman	AMD, USA

Ronan Keryell	Xilinx, USA
Seyong Lee	Oak Ridge National Laboratory, USA
Simon Hammond	Sandia National Laboratories, USA
Sameer Shende	University of Oregon, USA
Thomas Schwinge	Mentor Graphics, Germany
Tom Scogland	Lawrence Livermore National Laboratory, USA
William Sawyer	Swiss National Supercomputing Centre, Switzerland

Held in conjunction with the International Conference for High Performance Computing, Networking, Storage and Analysis (SC 2019), Denver, USA:

Contents

Porting Scientific Applications to Heterogeneous Architectures Using Directives

GPU Implementation of a Sophisticated Implicit Low-Order Finite Element Solver with FP21-32-64 Computation Using OpenACC

Takuma Yamaguchi[1]([✉]), Kohei Fujita[1,2], Tsuyoshi Ichimura[1], Akira Naruse[3], Maddegedara Lalith[1], and Muneo Hori[4]

[1] The University of Tokyo, Yayoi, Bunkyo, Tokyo, Japan
[2] Center for Computational Science, RIKEN, Minatojima-minamimachi, Chuo, Kobe, Japan
{yamaguchi,fujita,ichimura,lalith}@eri.u-tokyo.ac.jp
[3] NVIDIA Corporation, Akasaka, Minato, Tokyo, Japan
anaruse@nvidia.com
[4] Japan Agency for Marine-Earth Science and Technology, Kanazawa, Yokohama, Kanagawa, Japan
horimune@jamstec.go.jp

Abstract. Accelerating applications with portability and maintainability is one of the big challenges in science and engineering. Previously, we have developed a fast implicit low-order three-dimensional finite element solver, which has a complicated algorithm including artificial intelligence and transprecision computing. In addition, all possible tunings for the target architecture were implemented; accordingly, the solver has inferior portability and maintainability. In this paper, we apply OpenACC to the solver. The directive-based implementation of OpenACC enables GPU computation to be introduced with a smaller developmental cost even for complex codes. In performance measurements on AI Bridging Cloud Infrastructure (ABCI), we evaluated that a reasonable speedup was attained on GPUs, given that the elapsed time of the entire solver was reduced to 1/14 of that on CPUs based on the original CPU implementation. Our proposed template to use transprecision computing with our custom FP21 data type is available to the public; therefore, it can provide a successful example for other scientific computing applications.

Keywords: OpenACC · Finite element analysis · Conjugate gradient solver · Transprecision computing · Lower-Precision data types

1 Introduction

Nowadays, computer architectures are becoming increasingly diverse and new hardware, including heterogeneous systems, is released every year. Software

Electronic supplementary material The online version of this chapter (https://doi.org/10.1007/978-3-030-49943-3_1) contains supplementary material, which is available to authorized users.

© Springer Nature Switzerland AG 2020
S. Wienke and S. Bhalachandra (Eds.): WACCPD 2019, LNCS 12017, pp. 3–24, 2020.
https://doi.org/10.1007/978-3-030-49943-3_1

needs to keep up with this rapid development of hardware. Unfortunately, developing codes for every type of architecture leads to huge developmental costs. In addition, handling all the maintenance in such a case becomes increasingly difficult. These two factors in particular have a marked influence on sophisticated algorithms, which leads to long lines of codes.

Reflecting this situation, OpenACC [20] is in widespread use. OpenACC is a programming model that offloads computations onto GPUs or multi-core CPUs by inserting a few directives. Reference [3] demonstrated that simple codes can easily be ported using OpenACC. For various scientific applications, porting more complex algorithms to GPUs using OpenACC can be a successful example.

In this paper, we target a finite element analysis. We use implicit time integration for stability and low-order elements for complicated geometries; therefore, the code tends to be complex and the performance decreases due to random memory accesses. This analysis is regarded as a de-facto standard for manufacturing and Earth sciences; therefore, its acceleration is beneficial to these fields. We demonstrated in WACCPD 2016 [5] and WACCPD 2017 [25] that finite element solvers designed for CPU-based computers can be ported using OpenACC and that such ported solvers exhibit reasonable performances.

Meanwhile, a solver extremely tuned for better performance on GPU-based supercomputers was proposed [8]. Hereafter, we refer to this solver as the SC18-GBF solver. It has a sophisticated algorithm including artificial intelligence (AI) and transprecision computing with lower-precision data types. Moreover, its performance is thoroughly optimized when using specialized hardware in the targeted architecture, e.g., two-way packed half-precision computations on NVIDIA Tesla V100 GPUs [19]. Therefore, the developed code lacks portability and maintainability.

We apply OpenACC to the SC18GBF solver to improve its compatibility for portability and its performance. We show that our target application achieves a reasonable speedup with a smaller developmental cost in a directive-based method even though our solver includes a non-standard data type. Our sample codes to use the lower-precision data type FP21 are available to the public [26]; thus, it could prove beneficial to other scientific computing applications.

The remainder of this paper is organized as follows. Section 2 describes the baseline solver on CPU-based computers, and Sect. 3 describes the GPU implementation with FP21-32-64 data types using OpenACC. In Sect. 4, we show the effectiveness of our proposed method via performance measurements on AI Bridging Cloud Infrastructure (ABCI). In addition, we show an application example on the supercomputer Summit. Section 5 provides our conclusions.

2   Baseline Solver on CPU-based Computers

In this paper, we target a low-order unstructured implicit finite element method used for solving complex shaped three-dimensional (3D) domains. When solving this type of problem, solver programs often become complex due to the use of sophisticated preconditioners in iterative solvers. Further, it is difficult to attain a good computational performance because the computation of unstructured elements requires a large amount of random memory accesses. The target SC18GBF solver is further complicated compared to standard solvers due to its use of AI and transprecision arithmetic in its preconditioner. Below we pose the target problem and explain the solver algorithm and its CPU implementation.

2.1   The Target Problem

Earthquake simulations involve large-domain nonlinear time-evolution problems with locally complex structures. Therefore, we solve the target dynamic nonlinear continuum mechanics problem using a nonlinear dynamic 3D finite element method with second-order tetrahedral elements because such a method is suitable for modeling complex geometries and analytically satisfies the traction-free boundary condition at the surface. The target equation using the Newmark-β method ($\beta = 1/4$, $\delta = 1/2$) for time integration is

$$\mathbf{A}_n \, \delta\mathbf{u}_n = \mathbf{b}_n, \tag{1}$$

where

$$\begin{cases} \mathbf{A}_n = \frac{4}{dt^2}\mathbf{M} + \frac{2}{dt}\mathbf{C}_n + \mathbf{K}_n, \\ \mathbf{b}_n = \mathbf{f}_n - \mathbf{q}_{n-1} + \mathbf{C}_n\mathbf{v}_{n-1} + \mathbf{M}\left(\mathbf{a}_{n-1} + \frac{4}{dt}\mathbf{v}_{n-1}\right). \end{cases}$$

Here, $\delta\mathbf{u}$, $\mathbf{u}$, $\mathbf{v}$, $\mathbf{a}$, $\mathbf{q}$, and $\mathbf{f}$ are the incremental displacement, displacement, velocity, acceleration, internal force, and external force vectors, respectively, $\mathbf{M}$, $\mathbf{C}$, and $\mathbf{K}$ are the consistent mass, damping, and stiffness matrices, respectively, dt is the time increment, and n is the time step. We use Rayleigh damping [1] for $\mathbf{C}$. After solving Eq. 1, $\mathbf{q}$, $\mathbf{u}$, $\mathbf{v}$, and $\mathbf{a}$ are updated using

$$\begin{cases} \mathbf{q}_n = \mathbf{q}_{n-1} + \mathbf{K}_n\delta\mathbf{u}_n, \\ \mathbf{u}_n = \mathbf{u}_{n-1} + \delta\mathbf{u}_n, \\ \mathbf{v}_n = -\mathbf{v}_{n-1} + \frac{2}{dt}\delta\mathbf{u}_n, \\ \mathbf{a}_n = -\mathbf{a}_{n-1} - \frac{4}{dt}\mathbf{v}_{n-1} + \frac{4}{dt^2}\delta\mathbf{u}_n. \end{cases} \tag{2}$$

In summary, the time-history response $\mathbf{u}^n$ is computed by repeating the following steps.

1. Read the boundary conditions.
2. Evaluate $\mathbf{C}_n$ and $\mathbf{K}_n$ based on the constitutive relationships and the strain at the time step $n - 1$.
3. Obtain $\delta\mathbf{u}_n$ by solving Eq. 1.
4. Update Eq. 2 using $\delta\mathbf{u}_n$.

Because most of the computational cost is incurred when solving Eq. 1, we explain the details of the linear equation solver in the next subsection.

2.2 The Solver Algorithm

Although it is sparse, the symmetric positive definite matrix $\mathbf{A}$ in Eq. 1 becomes large in scale. Therefore, it is difficult to store $\mathbf{A}$ or variants of $\mathbf{A}$ directly in fast memory; consequently, matrix-free matrix-vector products are often used in iterative solvers for solving Eq. 1. For example, the PCGE method, which combines a matrix-free matrix-vector product [24] with 3×3 block diagonal preconditioned conjugate gradient solver is often used. This method solves the entire target domain uniformly in double precision and, therefore, is robust for solving a wide range of problems. However, its convergence rate is often slow, which makes it computationally expensive. The efficiency of the conjugate gradient solver is improved in the SC18GBF solver by changing the intensity of the computation according to the mathematical properties of the target problem and, further, by using AI methods considering the convergence characteristics. Below, we explain the solver algorithm in detail following Algorithm 1.

1. Use of an adaptive conjugate gradient method

   We first use an adaptive conjugate gradient method [6]. Instead of using a fixed matrix approximating the inverse matrix $\mathbf{A}^{-1}$ in the preconditioner of each conjugate gradient iteration, the preconditioning equation $\mathbf{z} = \mathbf{Ar}$ is solved using another conjugate gradient solver. We refer to the solving of the preconditioning equation as the inner iteration (Algorithm 1, lines 5–17), while we refer to the original conjugate gradient iteration as the outer iteration (Algorithm 1, lines 18–28). By setting suitable thresholds for the tolerances of the preconditioning solvers, we can shift most of the computational cost to the inner iterations. Because the preconditioning equation only needs to be roughly solved, this allows for flexibility in the algorithm design combining different methods with varying accuracies and computational costs in the preconditioner.

2. Use of AI in a preconditioner

   Data analytics exemplified by AI is often faster in inference than equation-based methods; however, its accuracy is often not as high [11]. Therefore, the direct use of data analytics in equation-based methods may lead to a degradation of the accuracy of the result or a divergence in the solution. Therefore, to use AI in linear equation solvers, an algorithm design considering the solver robustness is required. Here we focus on the heterogeneity of the convergence characteristics of a target matrix $\mathbf{A}$; that is, we develop a preconditioner algorithm that can coarsen or refine the solving process according to the convergence characteristics at each local domain and consider using AI to guess these convergence characteristics. Using this approach, even if the inference of the convergence characteristics is not perfectly accurate, it is only used in the preconditioner; therefore, the robustness of the solver and the accuracy of the solution are maintained and only the computational performance is affected.

   First, in preparation for the training with AI, we uniformly coarsen the target second-order tetrahedral finite element model (FEMmodel shown in Fig. 1a)

Algorithm 1. SC18GBF solver algorithm for solving $\mathbf{Ax} = \mathbf{b}$ on FEMmodel. The matrix vector product $\mathbf{Ay} = (\frac{4}{dt^2}\mathbf{M} + \frac{2}{dt}\mathbf{C} + \mathbf{K})\mathbf{y}$ is computed using matrix-free matrix-vector products (i.e., element-by-element method): $\sum_i^N (\frac{4}{dt^2}\mathbf{M}_i + \frac{2}{dt}\mathbf{C}_i + \mathbf{K}_i)\mathbf{y}_i$, where dt is the time increment, $\mathbf{M}$, $\mathbf{C}$, and $\mathbf{K}$ are the consistent mass, damping, and stiffness matrices, respectively, and subscript i indicates the i-th element. $diag[~]$, $(^-)$, and ϵ indicate the 3×3 block Jacobi of [ ], single-precision variable, and tolerance for relative error, respectively. $(~)_c$ and $(~)_{cp}$ indicates the calculation related to FEMmodel$_c$ and FEMmodel$_{cp}$, respectively, while the other is the related calculation of the FEMmodel. $\bar{\mathbf{P}}$ is a mapping matrix, from FEMmodel$_c$ to FEMmodel, which is defined by interpolating the displacement in each element of FEMmodel$_c$. $\mathbf{p}$, $\mathbf{q}$, $\mathbf{r}$, and $\mathbf{z}$ are temporal vectors and α, β, and ρ are scalars in conjugate gradient method and i denotes the number of iteration.

1: $\mathbf{r} \Leftarrow \mathbf{b} - \mathbf{Ax}$, where $\mathbf{x}$ is initial solution
2: $\beta \Leftarrow 0, i \Leftarrow 1$
3: (* outer loop start *)
4: **while** $\|\mathbf{r}\|_2/\|\mathbf{b}\|_2 \geq \epsilon$ **do**
5:      (* inner loop start *)
6:      $\bar{\mathbf{r}} \Leftarrow \mathbf{r}$
7:      $\bar{\mathbf{z}} \Leftarrow diag[\mathbf{A}]^{-1}\mathbf{r}$
8:      $\bar{\mathbf{r}}_c \Leftarrow \bar{\mathbf{P}}^T\bar{\mathbf{r}}$
9:      $\bar{\mathbf{z}}_c \Leftarrow \bar{\mathbf{P}}^T\bar{\mathbf{z}}$
10:     Solve $\bar{\mathbf{r}}_c = \bar{\mathbf{A}}_c\bar{\mathbf{z}}_c$ (* $PreCG_c$: solved on FEMmodel$_c$ by PCGE with ϵ_c^{in} and initial solution $\bar{\mathbf{z}}_c$ *)
11:     Extract $\bar{\mathbf{z}}_{cp}$ from $\bar{\mathbf{z}}_c$ and $\bar{\mathbf{r}}_{cp}$ from $\bar{\mathbf{r}}_c$
12:     Solve $\bar{\mathbf{r}}_{cp} = \bar{\mathbf{A}}_{cp}\bar{\mathbf{z}}_{cp}$ (* $PreCG_{cp}$: solved on FEMmodel$_{cp}$ by PCGE with ϵ_{cp}^{in} and initial solution $\bar{\mathbf{z}}_{cp}$ with Dirichlet boundary condition of $\bar{\mathbf{z}}_c$ at boundary *)
13:     Update $\bar{\mathbf{z}}_c$ with $\bar{\mathbf{z}}_{cp}$
14:     $\bar{\mathbf{z}} \Leftarrow \bar{\mathbf{P}}\bar{\mathbf{z}}_c$
15:     Solve $\bar{\mathbf{r}} = \bar{\mathbf{A}}\bar{\mathbf{z}}$ (* $PreCG$: solved on FEMmodel by PCGE with ϵ^{in} and initial solution $\bar{\mathbf{z}}$ *)
16:     $\mathbf{z} \Leftarrow \bar{\mathbf{z}}$
17:     (* inner loop end *)
18:     **if** $i > 1$ **then**
19:         $\beta \Leftarrow (\mathbf{z}, \mathbf{q})/\rho$
20:     **end if**
21:     $\mathbf{p} \Leftarrow \mathbf{z} + \beta\mathbf{p}$
22:     $\mathbf{q} \Leftarrow \mathbf{Ap}$ (* computed by matrix-free matrix-vector multiplication *)
23:     $\rho \Leftarrow (\mathbf{z}, \mathbf{r})$
24:     $\alpha \Leftarrow \rho/(\mathbf{p}, \mathbf{q})$
25:     $\mathbf{q} \Leftarrow -\alpha\mathbf{q}$
26:     $\mathbf{r} \Leftarrow \mathbf{r} + \mathbf{q}$
27:     $\mathbf{x} \Leftarrow \mathbf{x} + \alpha\mathbf{p}$
28:     $i \Leftarrow i + 1$
29: **end while**
30: (* outer loop end *)

Algorithm 2. Standard time-integration algorithm for solving $\mathbf{A}_i\mathbf{x}_i = \mathbf{b}_i(i = 0, ..., n-1)$. Values with over bars ($^-$) indicate approximate values, while values without over bars indicate exact values.

1: Set $\mathbf{x}_{-1} \Leftarrow 0$
2: **for** $i = 0; i < n; i = i + 1$ **do**
3:    Guess $\bar{\mathbf{x}}_i$ using standard predictor
4:    Set $\mathbf{A}_i$ and $\mathbf{b}_i$ using $\mathbf{x}_{i-1}$
5:    Solve $\mathbf{A}_i\mathbf{x}_i = \mathbf{b}_i$ with error tolerance $\dfrac{|\mathbf{A}_i\mathbf{x}_i - \mathbf{b}_i|}{|\mathbf{b}_i|} \leq \epsilon$ using initial solution $\bar{\mathbf{x}}_i$:
      Computed using iterative solver with matrix-free matrix-vector multiplication kernel (1 vector)
6: **end for**

Algorithm 3. Time-parallel time-integration algorithm for solving $\mathbf{A}_i\mathbf{x}_i = \mathbf{b}_i(i = 0, ..., n-1)$. Values with over bars ($^-$) indicate approximate values, while values without over bars indicate exact values. Algorithm 1 is used to solve m sets of linear systems of equations in line 9 in parallel.

1: Set $\mathbf{x}_{-1} \Leftarrow 0$ and $\bar{\mathbf{x}}_i \Leftarrow 0(i = 0, ..., m-2)$
2: **for** $i = 0; i < n; i = i + 1$ **do**
3:    Guess $\bar{\mathbf{x}}_{i+m-1}$ using standard predictor
4:    Set $\mathbf{A}_i$ and $\mathbf{b}_i$ using $\mathbf{x}_{i-1}$
5:    $\bar{\mathbf{A}}_i \Leftarrow \mathbf{A}_i$
6:    $\bar{\mathbf{b}}_i \Leftarrow \mathbf{b}_i$
7:    **while** $\dfrac{|\mathbf{A}_i\bar{\mathbf{x}}_i - \mathbf{b}_i|}{|\mathbf{b}_i|} > \epsilon$ **do**
8:       Guess $\bar{\mathbf{A}}_j$ and $\bar{\mathbf{b}}_j$ using $\bar{\mathbf{x}}_{j-1}(j = i+1, ..., i+m-1)$
9:       Refine solution $\{\bar{\mathbf{A}}_i\bar{\mathbf{x}}_j = \bar{\mathbf{b}}_j\}$ with initial solution $\bar{\mathbf{x}}_j(j = i, ..., i+m-1)$:
         Computed using iterative solver with matrix-free matrix-vector multiplication kernel (m vectors)
10:    **end while**
11:    $\mathbf{x}_i \Leftarrow \bar{\mathbf{x}}_i$
12: **end for**

---

using a geometric multi-grid [21] to obtain a first-order tetrahedral finite element model (FEMmodel$_c$ shown in Fig. 1b). Next, we obtain the error history distribution of a small-scale problem with similar characteristics to the target large-scale problem using a standard PCGE solver. Using this error distribution data, we train an artificial neural network (ANN) that inputs mesh information at a target node (i.e., the element connectivity, material property, and element sizes) and outputs the level of error at that node. Using this ANN, we infer the error levels at each node of the large-scale target problem using the element connectivity, material property, and element size as input. The nodes that are guessed to have large error levels (i.e., bad convergence) are included in FEMmodel$_{cp}$, as shown in Fig. 1c. We use a solver on FEMmodel$_{cp}$ (Algorithm 1, lines 11–13) to refine the rough solution obtained by the solver on the uniformly coarsened FEMmodel$_c$ (Algorithm 1, line 10) in the preconditioner.

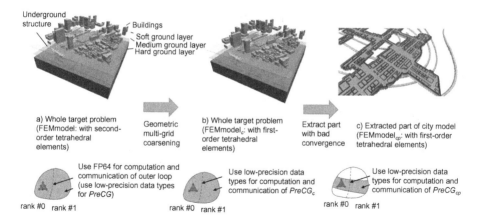

a) Whole target problem (FEMmodel: with second-order tetrahedral elements)

Geometric multi-grid coarsening

b) Whole target problem (FEMmodel$_c$: with first-order tetrahedral elements)

Extract part with bad convergence

c) Extracted part of city model (FEMmodel$_{cp}$: with first-order tetrahedral elements)

Use FP64 for computation and communication of outer loop (use low-precision data types for *PreCG*)

rank #0   rank #1

Use low-precision data types for computation and communication of *PreCG$_c$*

rank #0   rank #1

Use low-precision data types for computation and communication of *PreCG$_{cp}$*

rank #0   rank #1

Fig. 1. Extraction of part of the problem having bad convergence using AI.

Finally, we map this result to a second-order finite element model and use it as an initial solution for the solver on FEMmodel (Algorithm 1, line 15), and further use the results for the search direction **z** in the outer iteration.

By setting the tolerance of each preconditioning solver to a suitable value, we can solve parts of the problem with bad convergence extensively while solving most of the problem with good convergence less extensively. This leads to a reduction in the computational cost compared to a solver that solves the entire domain uniformly. Even if the selection of FEMmodel$_{cp}$ by ANN is slightly altered, the effects are absorbed by the other preconditioning solvers ($PreCG_c$ and $PreCG$); therefore, the solver becomes highly robust.

The training and reference of the AI for extracting FEMmodel$_{cp}$ are conducted offline using commercial neural network packages on a few GPUs, and are conducted only once prior to the time-history earthquake simulation .

3. Use of low-precision arithmetic in the preconditioner

While the solution of the entire solver is required in double precision, we can use transprecision computing [15] in the preconditioner because it is only used to obtain rough solutions. We can use not only FP32 but also other data types, such as FP21, which has an intermediate range and the accuracy of FP32 and FP16 to reduce the data transfer cost and the memory footprint. As mentioned later, all vectors can be in FP21 on CPUs while FP32 must be used for some vectors on GPUs. The introduction of FP21 data types in both CPU and GPU implementations makes maintenance of the entire code and performance evaluation more complex; thus, we use custom data type only in GPU implementation for simplicity.

4. Use of time-parallel time integration in the solver

Although AI with a transprecision-computing solver appears to be highly complicated, it is merely a combination of conjugate gradient-based solvers solved using simple PCGE methods. Therefore, the majority of its computational costs consist of matrix-vector products. However, because the computation of matrix-vector products becomes dominated by random memory accesses in unstructured finite element methods, it has become difficult to attain high performance on recent computational architectures regardless of the use of CPU or GPU. Using the fact that mesh connectivity is invariable in the time domain even for an unstructured finite element method, the SC18GBF solver uses a time-parallel time-integration algorithm [7] to improve the computational efficiency. In standard time integration, each step is solved step by step (Algorithm 2), while in the time-parallel solver, several steps, including future time steps, are solved simultaneously (Algorithm 3). When indicating the number of time steps solved simultaneously as m, the arithmetic count for computing a single iteration of the iterative solver becomes m times of that of a standard solver. However, the results obtained by the time-parallel solver can be used as high-precision initial solutions for future time steps; therefore, the total number of iterations is reduced by approximately $1/m$. Accordingly, the total arithmetic count becomes approximately the same as that of a standard time-integration method. The advantage of using a time-parallel method is that random accesses are reduced by $1/m$ compared to a standard solver by placing time-directional nodal variables consecutively in memory. This leads to the efficient use of single-instruction multiple-data (SIMD) units, which leads to a short time-to-solution for the entire solver. Typically, $m = 4$ is used because enlarging m leads to an increase in the total arithmetic count due to the degradation in the prediction accuracy of future time steps.

Because the approximated methods are only used in the preconditioner or are used to obtain the initial solutions of the iterative solver, the obtained solution $\delta \mathbf{u}_i (i = 1, 2, ...)$ is same as that of the double-precision PCGE method within the solver error tolerance ϵ. Further, because most of the computational cost is in matrix-vector products, we can maintain load balance by allocating an equal number of elements to each process/thread, which leads to high scalability for large-scale systems.

2.3   Implementation of Solver for CPU Systems

Because the innermost loop of the solver becomes the length $m = 4$ with consecutive data accesses, the current algorithm can be implemented using packed SIMD units with width 4. Furthermore, for systems with AVX-512 instruction units, loop blocking and splitting are applied for use of the 8-wide FP64 and the 16-wide FP32 SIMD units in the computation of matrix-vector products. We avoid data recurrence in multi-core computation of matrix-vector products by coloring of elements for each core. See Ref. [4] for details of the SIMD and multi-core implementation of matrix-vector products. This leads to an implementation of the solver with most of its computation using SIMD instructions on multi-cores. For simplicity of implementation, we use FP32 for the computations and communication in the inner loop solvers ($PreCG_c$, $PreCG_{cp}$, and $PreCG$) in the CPU version.

Using the SC18GBF solver algorithm, the FLOP count is reduced by 5.56-fold compared to the standard PGCE solver for an earthquake wave propagation problem in a ground region with a buried concrete structure. Because mixed-precision arithmetic and highly efficient SIMD arithmetic can be used, we expected an additional speedup from the reduction in the arithmetic count. Indeed, we obtained 9.09-fold speedup from the PCGE method [8] when measured on the CPU-based K computer system [18].

3   GPU Implementation Using OpenACC

Our solver algorithm, as described in the previous section, is suitable not only for CPUs but also for GPUs. For example, the introduction of time-parallel computation circumvents random accesses to the global vector in a matrix-vector multiplication kernel, which greatly improves the performance on GPUs. In addition, $PreCG_{cp}$ computation can reduce the data transfer size as well as the computational amount; accordingly, this solver is appropriate for GPUs because data transfer is a major bottleneck in GPU computations. We assume that our solver will be accelerated even by a straightforward implementation of GPU computations. In this section, we first describe a baseline OpenACC implementation and then optimize its performance using lower-precision data types and other tunings.

3.1   Baseline Implementation

We apply OpenACC to our CPU-based code following the general procedures given below.

1. Define where to apply OpenACC
   In our solver, all computations are computed for each node or each element and are easily parallelized by GPUs. Therefore, we target the entire solver to be ported to the GPUs. Conversely, the training and reference of the AI for extracting $FEMmodel_{cp}$ conducted only once and their computational cost is negligible. Accordingly, we do not port this part of the code.
2. Insert directive to parallelize loops
   We can compute targeting loops on GPUs by adding the corresponding directives, as shown in Fig. 2. OpenACC has three levels of parallelism: gang, worker, and vector. On NVIDIA GPUs, gang and vector correspond to block and thread, respectively, and usually the worker level is ignored. We insert directives so that the expected granularity of the parallelization can be attained. Figure 2 describes an outline of the implementation in a matrix-vector multiplication kernel. Loops for elements and time steps are collapsed to enable further parallelism. Each thread on the NVIDIA GPU is assigned to one element and its element-wise results are added to the global vector, which may cause data race conditions between threads. A previous study [5] showed that addition via atomic operations is much faster than explicit reordering

```
1  #pragma acc parallel loop collapse(2)
2  for(i_ele = 0; i_ele < (*n_element); i_ele++){
3    for(i_vec = 0; i_vec < (*n_vector); i_vec++){
4      cny0 = connect[i_ele][0];
5      cny1 = connect[i_ele][1];
6      …
7      cny9 = connect[i_ele][9];
8
9      u0x = u[cny0][0][i_vec];
10     u0y = u[cny0][1][i_vec];
11     u0z = u[cny0][2][i_vec];
12     …
13     u9z = u[cny9][2][i_vec];
14
15     Au0x = …
16     …
17     Au9z = …
18
19     #pragma acc atomic
20     r[cny0][0][cny0] += Au0x;
21     …
22     #pragma acc atomic
23     r[cny9][2][cny9] += Au9z;
24   }
25 }
```

Fig. 2. Porting example of the matrix-vector multiplication kernel on a tetrahedral second order mesh.

```
1  #pragma acc data present_or_copy(u, r, connect, err,…){
2    while(err < tolerance){
3
4      /* CG computation in GPU */
5
6      #pragma acc update host(err)
     }
7  }
```

Fig. 3. Example code for data transfer in a conjugate gradient loop.

via coloring; therefore, we use atomic operations for this part. As shown in Fig. 2, we can enable atomic operations by adding the option #pragma acc atomic.

3. Control data transfer between CPUs and GPUs

Without explicit instructions, OpenACC automatically transfers the necessary data from the CPUs to the GPUs prior to the GPU computation and from the GPUs to the CPUs following the GPU computation to obtain the expected results. When data are transferred too frequently, the performance greatly diminishes; therefore, we add directives to control the data transfer, as described in Fig. 3, to minimize these data transfer costs.

```
1  /* pack data in sendbuf */
2
3  #pragma acc host_data use_device(sendbuf, recvbuf){
4    ret = MPI_Irecv(recvbuf, mpicount, MPI_REAL,
                        source, tag, MPI_COMM_WORLD, &prequest[0]);
5    ret = MPI_Isend(sendbuf, mpicount, MPI_REAL,
                        dest, tag, MPI_COMM_WORLD, &prequest[1]);
6    ret = MPI_Waitall(commcount, prequest, pstatus)
7  }
8
9  /* unpack data in recvbuf */
```

Fig. 4. Example code for point-to-point communication.

In addition, original codes are designed for the MPI parallelization to allow us to use multiple GPUs and assign one GPU to each MPI process. Point-to-point communication requires data transfer between GPUs; we use GPUDirect. We issue MPI_Isend/Irecv to access GPU memory directly by adding the corresponding directives, as shown in Fig. 4.

We refer to these implementations as the baseline OpenACC implementation. To improve the performance, we introduce lower-precision data types and modify a few parts of the code that can decrease the performance.

3.2 Introduction of Lower-Precision Data Types

Our proposed solver can introduce transprecision computing to preconditioning conjugate gradient solvers. These solvers include many memory-bound computations. Therefore, we can reduce the computational cost simply by reducing the number of bits in each variable and reducing the footprint. In CPU-based implementations, a single-precision data type (FP32) is used in $PreCG_c$, $PreCG_{cp}$, and $PreCG$. Typical floating-point numbers including FP32 are standardized in IEEE 754 as $x = (-1)^{sign} \times (1.fraction) \times 2^{exponent-bias}$ for normalized numbers [13]. The sign bit determines the sign of the number, the exponent width influences the dynamic range of the number, and the fraction width defines the accuracy of the data type. Recently, data types with lower precision than FP32 have become widely supported on various types of hardware. The half-precision number, FP16, is a major example of such data types. It shortens the number of exponent bits and fraction bits compared to FP32 data types. It is not difficult to use FP16 for applications that do not require very high accuracy, e.g., deep learning [14]; however, using it for general scientific computations is challenging due to its narrow dynamic range. For our iterative solver, more exponent bits are required. Another data type, bfloat16, was proposed in Ref. [23]. It has the same width of exponent bits as FP32; therefore, it can avoid overflow/underflow in more general computations. However, it cuts down on the fraction bits by only 7 bits; accordingly, its machine epsilon becomes $1/2^7 = 1/128$. This low accuracy may lead to poor convergency.

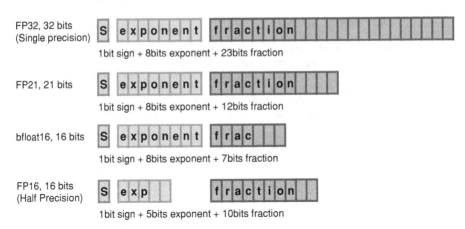

Fig. 5. Bit alignments for the sign, exponent, and fraction parts in each data type. Each cell describes one bit.

Therefore, we define our custom 21-bit data type in Fig. 5. Hereafter, we refer to this data type as FP21. FP21 has the advantage of the same dynamic range as FP32 and bfloat16 and a better accuracy than FP16 or bfloat16. In addition, the border between the sign bit and exponent bits and the border between the exponent bits and fraction bits in FP21 are the same as those in FP32 numbers; therefore, conversions between FP21 and FP32 are easier than conversions between other combinations of data types. To facilitate the bit operations, we store three FP21 numbers in one component of the 64-bit arrays and space 1-bit. Our proposed data type is not supported on our targeted hardware; therefore, we use it only when storing into memory. We convert the FP21 data types into FP32 prior to computation in FP32 and convert the results in FP32 into FP21 numbers following the computation. Figure 6 shows an implementation of the data type conversion. Only addition or subtraction operations and bit operations are required for this conversion, and they can be implemented entirely within OpenACC. If these functions are called with stack frames, they decrease the performance. Therefore, they have to be in-line in all related computations. When we convert FP32 data types into FP21, we can remove the lower 11-bits in the fraction parts; however, rounding to the nearest number can halve the rounding error compared to dropping the lower-bits. We obtain rounded numbers as follows. First, we remove the last 11 bits of the original FP32 number a and obtain the FP21 number $\bar{a}$. Then, we can obtain the result by removing the last 11 bits of $a + (a - \bar{a})$ in FP32.

Here, we are targeting a 3D problem; therefore, we have the three components of x, y, and z per node. Using FP21 for this problem enables us to assign one component in the 64-bit arrays to one node including the x, y, and z components in FP21; therefore, we can easily handle memory access to the FP21 numbers.

```
 1 static inline float conv_fp21_to_fp32(unsigned int fp21tmp)
 2 {
 3   fp21tmp <<= 11;
 4   float *b = reinterpret_cast<float*>(&fp21tmp);
 5   return b[0];
 6 }
 7
 8 static inline float conv_fp21x3_to_fp32_x(unsigned long fp21x3tmp)
 9 {
10   return conv_fp21_to_fp32(
            ((unsigned int)((fp21x3tmp >>  0) & 0x1fffff)));
11 }
12
13 static inline float conv_fp21x3_to_fp32_y(unsigned long fp21x3tmp)
14 {
15   return conv_fp21_to_fp32(
            ((unsigned int)((fp21x3tmp >> 21) & 0x1fffff)));
16 }
17
18 static inline float conv_fp21x3_to_fp32_z(unsigned long fp21x3tmp)
19 {
20   return conv_fp21_to_fp32(
            ((unsigned int)((fp21x3tmp >> 42) & 0x1fffff)));
21 }
```

Fig. 6. Mock code for the FP21 implementation. These functions convert FP21 numbers into FP32 numbers and are in-line for all computations requiring FP21 computations.

Note that atomic operations used in matrix-free matrix-vector multiplication are supported only for FP16/32/64 and that the output vector of this kernel must be in FP32. Therefore, vectors in FP21 and FP32 are mixed in the preconditioning solvers.

3.3 Miscellaneous Optimizations in the Solver

The introduction of FP21 data types is expected to reduce the computational time of memory bound computations compared to the baseline implementation using OpenACC; however, our solver algorithm includes several operations that greatly decrease the performance compared to the low-level description, e.g., CUDA. We avoid this performance decrease via the following modifications.

1. Dot product targeting multiple vectors
   Originally, dot products could be computed on OpenACC by adding the option reduction to the loop directive #pragma acc loop. However, the current version of OpenACC does not allow us to specify arrays for the target of the reduction, which prevents the parallelization of the inner loops for four time steps. We can compute dot products by creating multiple scalar variables and corresponding loops, as described in Fig. 7. However, such an implementation leads to strides in the memory accesses and a decline in the

```
1  #pragma acc parallel loop reduction(+:xy0, xy1, xy2, xy3)
2  for(i = 0; i < (*n_node); i++){
3    xy0 += (x[i][0][0]*y[i][0][0]+
             x[i][1][0]*y[i][1][0]+
             x[i][2][0]*y[i][2][0])*z[i];
4    …
5    xy3 += (x[i][0][3]*y[i][0][3]+
             x[i][1][3]*y[i][1][3]+
             x[i][2][3]*y[i][2][3])*z[i];
7  }
```

Fig. 7. Example code for computing dot products for multiple vectors in OpenACC.

```
1  __global__
2  void dotproduct(int *n, float *x, float *y, float *z, float *xy){
3    /* CUDA computation */
4  }
```

```
1  void dotproduct_wrapper(int *n, float *x, float *y, float *z, float *xy){
2    dotproduct<<<960,128>>>(n, x, y, z, xy);
3  }
```

```
1  #pragma acc host_data use_device(n, x, y, z, xy){
2    dotproduct_wrapper(n, x, y, z, xy);
3  }
```

Fig. 8. Example code to call the dot product kernel in CUDA from the OpenACC codes.

performance. Therefore, we use a CUDA kernel to compute dot products. We can call CUDA-based kernel from the OpenACC-based code via a wrapper, as shown in Fig. 8, and improve the performance of this computation.

2. Overheads for launching kernels
   OpenACC has larger overheads for launching kernels than CUDA. The degrees of freedom in $PreCG_c$ and $PreCG_{cp}$ in our solver become smaller than the original problem; therefore, the relative overhead cost increases for computations with shorter loop lengths. To reduce overhead costs, we modify several kernels. In particular, we add options `#pragma acc async(1)` and `#pragma acc wait(1)` for kernels that can be computed asynchronously to overlap the overhead cost. Moreover, local arrays in OpenACC loops are sometimes stored in local memory instead of in registers. When local memory is used, memory allocation is required and this increases the overhead for launching kernels; therefore, we redefine these local arrays as scalar variables.

4   Performance Measurement

In this section, we evaluate the performance of our proposed solver using GPU-based supercomputer ABCI [2], which is operated by the National Institute of

Advanced Industrial Science and Technology. Each compute node of ABCI has four NVIDIA Tesla V100 GPUs and two Intel Xeon Gold 6148 CPUs (20 cores). Its peak performance in double precision is 7.8 TFLOPS × 4 = 31.2 TFLOPS on the GPUs and 1.53 TFLOPS × 2 = 3.07 TFLOPS on the CPUs. In addition, its theoretical memory bandwidth is 900 GB/s × 4 = 3600 GB/s on the GPUs and 126 GB/s × 2 = 256 GB/s on the CPUs. The GPUs in each compute node are connected via NVLink, with a bandwidth of 50 GB/s bandwidth in each direction.

We generated a finite element model assuming a small-scale city problem. The problem settings were nearly the same as those of our previous performance measurement in Ref. [8] except for the domain size and the number of MPI processes. The target domain included two soil layers and a layer with material properties similar to concrete. This problem had 39,191,319 degrees of freedom. In addition, $PreCG_{cp}$, $PreCG_c$, and $PreCG$ had 659,544, 5,118,339, and 39,191,319 degrees of freedom, respectively. The target domain was decomposed into four sub-domains, and four MPI processes were used in the computation. We used 10 OpenMP threads per MPI process when using CPUs so that all CPU cores on an ABCI compute node were used. We applied semi-infinite absorbing boundary conditions on the sides and bottom of the domain. We can incorporate any constitutive laws into our proposed solver. Here, we used modified RO model [9] and the Masing rule [16]. Kobe waves observed during the 1995 Southern Hyogo Earthquake [10] were input at the bottom of the model. The time increment was 0.01 seconds, and we computed 25 time steps. Convergence in the conjugate gradient loops was judged using a tolerance value of $\epsilon = 1.0 \times 10^{-8}$. In addition, the tolerances in $PreCG_{cp}$, $PreCG_c$, and $PreCG$ were set to 0.05, 0.7, and 0.25, respectively, according to Ref. [8].

4.1   Performance Evaluation of FP21 Computation

We evaluated the performance of each computation in the solver. The elapsed time was measured using MPI_Wtime. In this section, we compared the original CPU-based implementation, the baseline implementation using OpenACC, and our proposed implementation.

First, we measured the performance of the real Alpha X Plus Y (AXPY) operation. We extracted a computation in the $PreCG$ solver of $x(i) = x(i) + \alpha y(i)$, where the arrays $x(i)$ and $y(i)$ are in FP32 or FP21 and the coefficient α is in FP32. The elapsed times of all the implementations are described in Table 1. This computation was a memory-bound computation. Given that the theoretical memory bandwidths of the CPUs and GPUs per MPI process are 63.9 GB/s and 900 GB/s, the expected performance ratio was (CPU):(baseline OpenACC):(proposed) = 1/(32/63.9):1/(32/900):1/(21/900) = 1:14.1:21.5. Judging from this ratio, our GPU implementation achieved a reasonable speedup. In addition, the measured bandwidth was close to the results of another benchmark [12]: 900 GB/s × 83.3% = 750 GB/s; therefore, we concluded that our performance was reasonable. In addition, using FP21 variables resulted in a 1.5-fold speedup; therefore, we confirmed that the computational cost for the data type conversion was negligible.

Second, we measured the performance of a dot product. The target kernel computes $\alpha = \sum_i ((x(1,i) \times y(1,i) + x(2,i) \times y(2,i) + x(3,i) \times y(3,i)) \times z(i))$, where the arrays $x(,i)$ and $y(,i)$ are in FP32 or FP21 and the array $z(i)$ is in FP32. The expected performance ratio was (CPU):(baseline OpenACC):(proposed) $= 1/((32 \times 7)/63.9):1/((32 \times 7)/900):1/((21 \times 6 + 32)/900) = 1:14.1:20.0$. Compared to the AXPY kernel, the measured memory bandwidth in the baseline OpenACC implementation decreased because OpenACC cannot use the reduction option for arrays and causes stride memory access to the vectors. Conversely, our proposed implementation with CUDA attained nearly the same bandwidth as the AXPY kernel.

Finally, we show the performance of the matrix-vector multiplication kernel in Table 1. The simple implementation and our proposed method obtained 15.0-fold and 14.8-fold speedups for our CPU-based kernel. The performance for these kernels on the GPUs reached 4 TFLOPS. The bottlenecks of this kernel are not memory bandwidth but the atomic addition to the global vector and the element-wise multiplication; therefore, we were unable to observe a significant difference in the performance even when using FP21 data types for the input vectors. Regarding this kernel, the data conversion between FP32 and FP21 in our proposed method was a possible reason for the slight performance gap between these two kernels.

Table 1. Performance of each kernel in the solver.

| | Precision | CPU-based | Baseline OpenACC | Proposed |
		FP32	FP32	FP32/21
AXPY	Elapsed time	9.61 ms	0.605 ms	0.401 ms
	Measured bandwidth	50.2 GB/s	797.1 GB/s	802.2 GB/s
	Speeding up ratio	1	15.8	24.0
Dot product	Elapsed time	6.20 ms	0.456 ms	0.277 ms
	Measured bandwidth	54.0 GB/s	735.1 GB/s	822.9 GB/s
	Speeding up ratio	1	13.6	22.4
Matrix-vector product	Elapsed time	54.61 ms	3.65 ms	3.69 ms
	Measured FLOPS per MPI process	0.27 TFLOPS	4.11 TFLOPS	4.07 TFLOPS
	Speeding up ratio	1	15.0	14.8

4.2   Performance Evaluation of the Entire Solver

In this section, we evaluate the elapsed time for the entire solver. We compare the original CPU-based solver, a solver simply ported using OpenACC, a solver simply ported using CUDA, our proposed solver based on OpenACC, and the SC18GBF solver [8]. The SC18GBF solver improved its performance at the cost of portability. For example, shared memory on the V100 GPU was used to summarize the element-wise computation results and reduce the number of atomic operations in the element-by-element kernel and two-way packed FP16 computations in the V100 GPU were also applied. Moreover, matrix-vector multiplication and point-to-point communication were reordered as described in Ref. [17] so that computationally expensive data transfers could be overlapped. The SC18GBF solver, designed for large-scale computers, conducted further reductions in the data transfer cost by splitting the four time steps into two sets of two vectors and overlapping point-to-point communications with other vector operations. However, we compared the performance of the solver using only one compute node in this paper. Each GPU in the compute node was connected via NVLink; therefore, the data transfer cost was lower. Considering these problem settings, we computed the four time step vectors without splitting. In the GPU computations, we used atomic operations when the element-wise results were added to the global vector; therefore, numerical errors occur due to differences in the computation order. The final results of the analysis are consistent within the tolerance of the conjugate gradient solver; however, the number of iterations in the solver differs every time we run the program. Accordingly, we took the average of 10 trials for each solver.

The elapsed time for each solver is described in Table 2. The test took 781.8 s when using only CPUs on an ABCI compute node. Conversely, we reduced the computation time to 66.71 s via the simple implementation of OpenACC, resulting in a speedup ratio of 11.7. It took 61.02 s using the simple implementation with CUDA. This gap in performance between OpenACC and CUDA is attributed to the following three factors. The first is the performance decline in the dot product kernels. The second is that kernels that conduct complex computations and require many variables cause register spilling, which does not occur in CUDA implementations. The third is that OpenACC has a larger overhead for launching each kernel than CUDA, which resulted in a large gap in $PreCG_{cp}$. Our proposed solver based on OpenACC used the FP21 data types and introduced techniques to circumvent the overhead in the OpenACC kernels. The elapsed time of this solver was 55.84 s; it was 9% faster than the original OpenACC implementation as well as faster than the simple implementation using CUDA. Therefore, we confirmed that the introduction of the FP21 data types was beneficial in accelerating the solver. Our proposed solver attained approximately 86% of the SC18GBF solver performance. Performance gap in $PreCG_{cp}$ between our proposed solver and the SC18GBF solver was larger than those in $PreCG_c$ and $PreCG$. This was because the degrees of freedom in $PreCG_{cp}$ was smaller than other preconditioning solvers and data transfer cost was relatively higher, which was mostly overlapped in the SC18GBF solver. The performance of our proposed solver is very good from a practical point of view considering the portability provided by OpenACC.

Table 2. Elapsed time for the entire solver measured on ABCI. The total elapsed time includes the output of the analysis results. Performance of the preconditioning solvers is summarized in order of their appearance in CG solver. The numbers of iteration in each solver are also shown in parentheses.

Precision in $PreCG_c$, $PreCG_{cp}$, and $PreCG$	CPU-based	Baseline OpenACC	Baseline CUDA	Proposed	SC18GBF
	FP32	FP32	FP32	FP32/21	FP32/21/16
$PreCG_c$	161.4 s	14.89 s	14.21 s	9.79 s	7.47 s
	(6199)	(6300)	(6210)	(4751)	(4308)
$PreCG_{cp}$	69.9 s	15.94 s	12.20 s	13.22 s	8.98 s
	(28830)	(28272)	(28491)	(28861)	(26887)
$PreCG$	372.0 s	22.90 s	22.30 s	18.27 s	16.98 s
	(2674)	(2729)	(2735)	(2575)	(2797)
CG	83.9 s	5.77 s	4.57 s	5.89 s	8.32 s
	(91)	(89)	(89)	(122)	(129)
Other	94.8 s	7.21 s	7.73 s	8.66 s	5.99 s
Total	**781.8 s**	**66.71 s**	**61.02 s**	**55.84 s**	**47.75 s**
Speeding up ratio	1	11.7	12.8	14.0	16.4

When we used lower-precision numbers, e.g., FP16 or FP21, the convergence characteristics in the solver changed. When we replaced a computation in FP21 with a computation in bfloat16 for comparison, the solver failed to converge. These results indicate that more fraction bits than provided by bfloat16 were required for our problem settings. A detailed verification of the convergency when using lower-precision data types will be a future task.

Finally, we solved problems with complicated geometry comprised of the ground and underground structures with 16,291,917,564 degrees of freedom and 3,961,851,160 elements, as demonstrated in Ref. [8]. Here we used 384 compute nodes of the supercomputer Summit [22]. We computed for 2,500-time steps with time increment $dt = 0.001$ s. As shown in Fig. 9, we obtained the displacement distribution reflecting complex geometries; therefore, the importance of our method was demonstrated.

Regarding the developmental cost, the introduction of CUDA required an additional 18,342 lines of code (our original code had 33,527 lines in total). Our OpenACC implementation required the addition of 9,300 lines of code; therefore, maintenance of our codes are expected to become easier when using OpenACC.

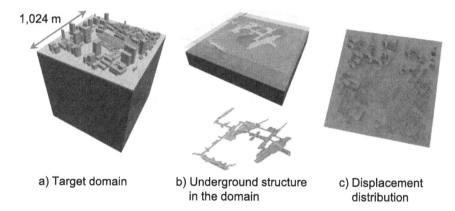

a) Target domain   b) Underground structure   c) Displacement
                          in the domain   distribution

Fig. 9. Application example on Summit. a) 1,024 m × 1,024 m city area with underground and building structures surrounded by two-layered ground modeled; b) underground structures in the domain; c) displacement distribution at $t = 2.50\,\mathrm{s}$.

5   Conclusions

To increase productivity in science and engineering fields, providing performance improvements that are portable and maintainable is a big challenge. In this paper, we target an implicit low-order finite element solver, for which it is considered difficult to attain high performances. The acceleration of this solver is required to enable practical applications in commerce or industry. We have developed fast solvers using supercomputers to reduce computational costs. Our latest solver has a sophisticated algorithm including AI and transprecision computing. Moreover, we thoroughly optimized the performance of each kernel using specialized hardware in our targeted architecture. Accordingly, the developed codes lacked portability and maintainability.

We applied OpenACC to this finite element solver. Via a performance measurement on ABCI, we confirmed that the OpenACC-based implementation achieved a 14.0-fold speedup compared to the original CPU codes. This is approximately 86% the performance of our extremely tuned solver using CUDA. Considering that the number of lines modified for the GPU implementation is much less than the number modified for CUDA and that the developmental cost is smaller, our proposed solver is sufficiently suitable for practical use. Our developed template to use transprecision computing with FP21 data types is available to the public [26]; therefore it can provide an example of how to accelerate other scientific computing applications using lower-precision data types.

Acknowledgement. Our results were obtained using Computational resource of AI Bridging Cloud Infrastructure (ABCI), National Institute of Advanced Industrial Science and Technology (AIST). We acknowledge support from Post K computer project (Priority Issue 3 - Development of integrated simulation systems for hazards and disasters induced by earthquakes and tsunamis), and Japan Society for the Promotion of Science (17K14719, 18H05239, 18K18873). Part of our results were obtained using the Summit at Oak Ridge Leadership Computing Facility, a US Department of Energy, Office of Science User Facility at Oak Ridge National Laboratory.

Data Availability Statement.

Summary of the Experiments Reported

We ran our built-from-scratch implicit solver for unstructured finite elements on AI bridging cloud infrastructure with PGI compiler and OpenMPI.

Artifact Availability

Software Artifact Availability: Some author-created software artifacts are NOT maintained in a public repository or are NOT available under an OSI-approved license.

Hardware Artifact Availability: There are no author-created hardware artifacts.

Data Artifact Availability: Some author-created data artifacts are NOT maintained in a public repository or are NOT available under an OSI-approved license.

Proprietary Artifacts: There are associated proprietary artifacts that are not created by the authors. Some author-created artifacts are proprietary.

List of URLs and/or DOIs where artifacts are available:

http://doi.org/10.6084/m9.figshare.11603382
http://www.data.jma.go.jp/svd/eqev/data/kyoshin/jishin/hyogo_nanbu/dat/ H1171931.csv.

Details regarding baseline experimental setup, and modifications made for the paper are available at [26].

References

1. Bielak, J., Ghattas, O., Kim, E.: Parallel octree-based finite element method for large-scale earthquake ground motion simulation. Comput. Model. Eng. Sci. **10**(2), 99 (2005)
2. Computing Resources of AI bridging Clound Infrastructure. https://abci.ai/en/about_abci/computing_resource.html. Accessed 11 Oct 2019
3. Farber, R.: Parallel programming with OpenACC. Newnes, Oxford (2016)
4. Fujita, K., et al.: Development of element-by-element kernel algorithms in unstructured implicit low-order finite-element earthquake simulation for many-core Wide-SIMD CPUs. In: Rodrigues, J., et al. (eds.) ICCS 2019. LNCS, vol. 11536, pp. 267–280. Springer, Cham (2019). https://doi.org/10.1007/978-3-030-22734-0_20

5. Fujita, K., Yamaguchi, T., Ichimura, T., Hori, M., Maddegedara, L.: Acceleration of element-by-element kernel in unstructured implicit low-order finite-element earthquake simulation using OpenACC on pascal GPUs. In: Proceedings of the Third International Workshop on Accelerator Programming Using Directives, pp. 1–12. IEEE Press (2016)

6. Golub, G.H., Ye, Q.: Inexact preconditioned conjugate gradient method with inner-outer iteration. SIAM J. Sci. Comput. **21**(4), 1305–1320 (1999)

7. Ichimura, T., et al.: A fast scalable implicit solver with concentrated computation for nonlinear time-evolution problems on low-order unstructured finite elements. In: 2018 IEEE International Parallel and Distributed Processing Symposium (IPDPS), pp. 620–629. IEEE (2018)

8. Ichimura, T., et al.: A fast scalable implicit solver for nonlinear time-evolution earthquake city problem on low-ordered unstructured finite elements with artificial intelligence and transprecision computing. In: SC18: International Conference for High Performance Computing, Networking, Storage and Analysis, pp. 627–637. IEEE (2018)

9. Idriss, I.M., Dobry, R., Sing, R.: Nonlinear behavior of soft clays during cyclic loading. J. Geotech. Geoenviron. Eng. **104**(ASCE 14265), 1427–1447 (1978)

10. Japan Meteorological Agency: Strong ground motion of The Southern Hyogo prefecture earthquake in 1995 observed at Kobe JMA observatory. https://www.data.jma.go.jp/svd/eqev/data/kyoshin/jishin/hyogo_nanbu/dat/H1171931.csv. Accessed 11 Oct 2018

11. Jeong, S., Solenthaler, B., Pollefeys, M., Gross, M., et al.: Data-driven fluid simulations using regression forests. ACM Trans. Graph. (TOG) **34**(6), 199 (2015)

12. Jia, Z., Maggioni, M., Staiger, B., Scarpazza, D.P.: Dissecting the NVIDIA volta GPU architecture via microbenchmarking. arXiv preprint arXiv:1804.06826 (2018)

13. Kahan, W.: IEEE standard 754 for binary floating-point arithmetic. Lecture Notes Status IEEE **754**(94720–1776), 11 (1996)

14. Kurth, T., et al.: Exascale deep learning for climate analytics. In: Proceedings of the International Conference for High Performance Computing, Networking, Storage, and Analysis, p. 51. IEEE Press (2018)

15. Malossi, A.C.I., et al.: The transprecision computing paradigm: concept, design, and applications. In: 2018 Design, Automation & Test in Europe Conference & Exhibition (DATE), pp. 1105–1110. IEEE (2018)

16. Massing, G.: Eigenspannungen und verfestigung beinn messing. In: Proceedings of the 2nd International Congress of Applied Mechanics (1926)

17. Micikevicius, P.: 3D finite difference computation on GPUs using CUDA. In: Proceedings of 2nd Workshop on General Purpose Processing on Graphics Processing Units, pp. 79–84. ACM (2009)

18. Miyazaki, H., Kusano, Y., Shinjou, N., Shoji, F., Yokokawa, M., Watanabe, T.: Overview of the K computer system. Fujitsu Sci. Tech. J. **48**(3), 302–309 (2012)

19. NVIDIA Tesla V100 GPU architecture. https://images.nvidia.com/content/volta-architecture/pdf/volta-architecture-whitepaper.pdf. Accessed 11 Oct 2019

20. OpenACC. http://www.openacc.org/. Accessed 11 Oct 2019

21. Saad, Y.: Iterative Methods for Sparse Linear Systems, vol. 82. SIAM, Philadelphia (2003)

22. Summit. https://www.olcf.ornl.gov/olcf-resources/compute-systems/summit/. Accessed 11 Oct 2019

23. Using bfloat16 with tensorflow models. https://cloud.google.com/tpu/docs/bfloat16. Accessed 11 Oct 2019

24. Winget, J.M., Hughes, T.J.: Solution algorithms for nonlinear transient heat conduction analysis employing element-by-element iterative strategies. Comput. Methods Appl. Mech. Eng. **52**(1–3), 711–815 (1985)
25. Yamaguchi, T., Fujita, K., Ichimura, T., Hori, M., Lalith, M., Nakajima, K.: Implicit low-order unstructured finite-element multiple simulation enhanced by dense computation using OpenACC. In: Chandrasekaran, S., Juckeland, G. (eds.) WACCPD 2017. LNCS, vol. 10732, pp. 42–59. Springer, Cham (2018). https://doi.org/10.1007/978-3-319-74896-2_3
26. Yamaguchi, T., Fujita, K., Ichimura, T., Naruse, A., Lalith, M., Hori, M.: FP21AXPY. Figshare (2020). https://doi.org/10.6084/m9.figshare.11603382. Accessed 22 Jan 2020

Acceleration in Acoustic Wave Propagation Modelling Using OpenACC/OpenMP and Its Hybrid for the Global Monitoring System

Noriyuki Kushida[1]([✉]) [iD], Ying-Tsong Lin[2] [iD], Peter Nielsen[1], and Ronan Le Bras[1]

[1] Comprehensive Nuclear-Test Ban Treaty Organization, Vienna, Austria
{noriyuki.kushida,peter.nielsen,ronan.lebras}@ctbto.org
http://www.ctbto.org
[2] Woods Hole Oceanographic Institution, Woods Hole, MA 02543, USA
ytlin@whoi.edu

Abstract. CTBTO is operating and maintaining the international monitoring system of Seismic, Infrasound, Hydroacoustic and Airborne radionuclide facilities to detect a nuclear explosion over the globe. The monitoring network of CTBTO, especially with regard to infrasound and hydroacoustic, is quite unique because the network covers over the globe, and the data is opened to scientific use. CTBTO has been developing and improving the methodologies to analyze observed signals intensively. In this context, hydroacoustic modelling software, especially which that solves the partial differential equation directly, is of interest. As seen in the analysis of the Argentinian submarine accident, the horizontal reflection can play an important role in identifying the location of an underwater event, and as such, accurate modelling software may help analysts find relevant waves efficiently. Thus, CTBTO has been testing a parabolic equation based model (3D-SSFPE) and building a finite difference time domain (FDTD) model. At the same time, using such accurate models require larger computer resources than simplified methods such as ray-tracing. Thus we accelerated them using OpenMP and OpenACC, or the hybrid of those. As a result, in the best case scenarios, (1) 3D-SSFPE was accelerated by approximately 19 times to the original Octave code, employing the GPU-enabled Octfile technology, and (2) FDTD was accelerated by approximately 160 times to the original Fortran code using the OpenMP/OpenACC hybrid technology, on our DGX—Station with V100 GPUs.

Keywords: OpenACC/OpenMP hybrid · OpenACC with Octave/Matlab · Split Step Fourier · FDTD · Hydroacoustic modelling

---

Electronic supplementary material The online version of this chapter (https://doi.org/10.1007/978-3-030-49943-3_2) contains supplementary material, which is available to authorized users.

ⓒ Springer Nature Switzerland AG 2020
S. Wienke and S. Bhalachandra (Eds.): WACCPD 2019, LNCS 12017, pp. 25–46, 2020.
https://doi.org/10.1007/978-3-030-49943-3_2

1   Introduction

The Comprehensive Nuclear-Test-Ban Treaty (CTBT) is the treaty which bans nuclear explosions in any environment over the globe, such as in the atmosphere, in the ocean, and underground. Although the treaty has not entered into force, Preparatory Commission for the CTBT Organization (CTBTO) has been monitoring signs of nuclear explosions using four technologies, namely, seismic, infrasound, hydroacoustic and air-borne radionuclide. The monitoring network of CTBTO, especially with regard to infrasound and hydroacoustic, is quite unique because the network covers over the globe and the data is opened to scientific use. Therefore, CTBTO has been developing and improving the methodologies to analyze observed signals intensively. Because of the complex natures of the oceans and the atmosphere, computer simulation can play an important role in understanding the observed signals. In this regard, methods which depend on partial differential equations, in other words an "*ab-initio*" approach, are preferable in order not to overlook any subtle phenomena. However, there have been only a few groups which perform such computer modelling with the parabolic equation (PE) methods [10,11]. Based on such circumstances, CTBTO has been testing and developing hydroacoustic simulation software packages based on PE called 3D-SSFPE [20], and the finite difference method (FDM) [18] respectively. Lin et al. explained the advantages of 3D-SSFPE over other PE methods in their literature i.e. 3D-SSFPE is designed for long distance modelling.

One of the biggest drawbacks of using such accurate methods is the high demand on computer resources, especially the arithmetic computing performance. Although computer simulation is not considered as a necessary product for the treaty, providing the member states with modelling results promptly may help their decision-making.

At the same time, computing accelerators such as general purpose graphics processing unit (GPGPU), field-programmable gate arrays (FPGA), and so forth are now prevalent in the computer simulation field. Particularly, a GPGPU is available at an affordable price thanks to the active development in deep learning. Thus, we have started evaluating the performance gain with GPGPUs on our simulation programs. Considering the effort we could spare for porting the codes, the directive-based parallel programming is practically the only choice for a non-research organization, even though there is a known gap in the achievable performance between the special languages, such as CUDA and OpenCL, and the directive based parallel programming languages, such as OpenACC. Finally, we have implemented our software on the DGX-station by NVIDIA using OpenACC.

In the following sections, the details of each program and performance evaluation results as well as the computing environment will be described.

2   Computing Environment

In the present study, we have employed the DGX–station produced by NVIDIA [1] as a test–bed of a GPGPU environment. The DGX–station equips four NVIDIA Tesla V100s. In the OpenACC framework, using one GPU per process is the standard. In the present study, we employed OpenMP to launch multiple threads and assigned one GPU to a thread for multi-GPU computation in Sect. 4. The CPU installed is Intel Xeon E5-2698 v4 20 cores. The theoretical peak performance of the CPU is 0.576 tera floating point operations per second (TFLOPS) in double precision (0.0288 TFLOPS/core) and the memory bandwidth is 71.53 giga byte per second (GB/s). At the same time, a V100 performs 7.5 TFLOPS in double precision and 900GB/s. The operating system is Ubuntu 18.04.2 LTS. The CUDA version is 10.0. The compilers employed are (1) GCC version 9.1, which is available through the ubuntu-toolchain-r/test repository [5] and (2) PGI compiler version 19.5. Both compilers have the capability of compiling OpenACC-enabled codes. However, the PGI compiler fails to generate an object file which works together with Octave. Therefore, we employed GCC for 3D-SSFPE, while the PGI compiler provides advanced features of OpenACC such as managed memory. The PGI technical team recognizes this issue. Readers who try to implement OpenACC-enabled codes on Octave with the PGI compiler may check the release notes. The PGI compiler for Fortran 90 (pgf90) was used throughout the FDM simulation development and it's performance evaluation. Octave is installed using `apt-get` and the version is 4.2.2.

3   3D-SSFPE

3.1   Overview

3D-SSFPE is a three-dimensional (3D) underwater sound propagation model based on the parabolic equation (PE) combined with the Split-Step Fourier method (SSF) [20]. In the literature, Lin et al. developed the code in the three dimensional Cartesian coordinate as well as a cylindrical coordinate. In the present study, since the long range wave propagation is of interest, we focus on the Cartesian coordinate. The theoretical background as well as the implementation of 3D-SSFPE are given in the literature, and here, we provide readers with a brief explanation, toward the GPU implementation. The 3D SSF solves a linear wave equation by marching a two-dimensional (2D) grid ($Y - Z$ plane) along the perpendicular direction of the grid (X-axis) from the source term to the point of interest, and each 2D solution grid is computed in spatial and wavenumber domains alternately. The spatial and wavenumber domain transform is performed through Fast Fourier Transform. As an analogy, the computation progresses like a wave-front propagates. However, SSF does not solve the time evolution, instead it solves a boundary value problem. In the implementation point of view, 3D-SSFPE repeats the following steps;

1. Calculate the sound pressure at $x_{n+1/2} = x_n + \Delta x/2$ in the wavenumber domain
2. Correct the amplitude and phase of the sound pressure due to sound speed changes (the index of refraction) at $x_{n+1/2}$ in the spatial domain
3. Proceed to x_{n+1} in the wavenumber domain
4. if necessary, update the environment information

where x_n denotes the nth grid point on the X-axis, and Δx denotes the grid length. The conversion of the pressure between the spatial and wavenumber domains is undertaken using the Fast Fourier Transform (FFT) and the inverse FFT (iFFT). Since there are many well-tuned FFT libraries, the point of the discussion of implementation is how to compute the remaining part efficiently. In the following section, we discuss it for our computing environment.

3.2   Implementation

3D-SSFPE has been developed on Matlab, which is a well known commercial scientific software development environment. 3D-SSFPE solves the state of a wave of a specific frequency, whilst hydroacoustic researchers would like to solve problems of a spatial domain with various wave frequencies. It is worth noting that the problem of each frequency is completely independent and can be solved in parallel. Therefore, launching multiple instances at the same time is beneficial. In other words, avoiding the limitation on the number of licenses increases the total computational speed. Thus we employed Octave, which is an open source clone of Matlab. It should be also noted that pre/post processes are implemented with Matlab's unique file format, and we can avoid the re-implementation of such processes by using Octave. 3D-SSFPE calls FFT and iFFT frequently. In our preliminary experiment, the GPU enabled FFT function on Matlab was also examined. However, probably because of the data transfer between GPU and CPU, the total computational speed remained the same level with the non-GPU version. This fact also motivated us to use OpenACC.

Octave, as well as Matlab, provides users with a functionality to call a routine written in C++. The functionality is called "Octfile" in Octave, or "Mex file" in Matlab. Since the Octfile is written in C++, we can apply OpenMP and OpenACC. Considering the similarity in OpenMP and OpenACC, and the complexity appears only in OpenACC, specifically data transfer, we followed the following three steps, namely;

1. Re-write the target functions in C++
2. Apply the OpenMP directives
3. Apply the OpenACC directives based on 2

FFT and iFFT are performed using FFTW [9](Step 1 and 2) or cuFFT [4](in Step 3).

In the following sections, the details will be given to apply OpenMP and OpenACC to the Octfile. For readers' convenience, a 3D SSF implementation for the Lloyd's Mirror Problem in Matlab/Octave and its GPU version are available on Zenodo (Matlab/Octave version [19] and GPU version [15]). Although 3D-SSFPE deals with more complex geometries and the inhomogeneity of medium which lead to additional complexity into the codes, we believe those samples help readers understand the efforts in the present study.

Accessing Arrays. Octave provides users with the functionality to access a multidimensional array in the Fortran style, specifically in the "array(i,j)" form, in the Octfile. However, this style involves function calls which prevents OpenACC compilers from generating GPU enabled loops. On the other hand, there is a way to handle a raw pointer of an array. In the present study, we construct all loops with raw pointers of multi-dimensional arrays including vectors and matrices so that all the loops can be computed on GPU. In the following program, a matrix Mat is initialized using the raw pointer. In the program, Mat is a matrix defined in Octave and passed to the Octfile, Nc and Nr are the numbers of columns and rows of Mat, and Mat_p is the pointer, which stores the content of Mat. As the name of the method to obtain the raw pointer, fortran_vec(), indicates, the matrix is stored in the column-major manner as Fortran. A vector and higher dimensional arrays can be accessed in the same way.

Example of the initialization of a matrix with the raw pointer

```
double _Complex *Mat_p = reinterpret_cast<double _Complex *>
 (const_cast<Complex *>(Mat.fortran_vec()));
octave_idx_type  Nc = Mat.cols();
octave_idx_type  Nr = Mat.rows();
for (int i=0; i< Nr; i++){
   for (int j=0; j< Nc; j++){
      Mat_p[j*Nr+i] = 0.0;
   }
}
```

Double Complex Data Type. Since 3D-SSFPE uses FFT and iFFT, a complex value data type is necessary. In the Octfile, the Complex data type is the standard. However, with GCC version 9.1, more precisely, g++ version 9.1, the Complex data type prevents the compiler from generating GPU enabled loops. In the present study, we discovered that the double _Complex data type can be used as an alternative of the Complex data type although this is a data type in C. The binary format of the double _Complex data type and the Complex data type is identical, and users can use the double _Complex data type with matrices by casting the data type. The actual usage can be found in Section **Accessing arrays**. With the double _Complex data type, compilers can generate GPU enabled loops, even with mathematical functions such as cexp, which computes the exponential of a complex value.

Memory Mapping for OpenACC. Basically, OpenACC compilers should allocate arrays on GPU automatically using directives, such as #pragma acc data copy. However, in the Octfile, neither GCC nor PGI handles such directives as expected. More precisely, error messages relevant to the memory address were observed such as "Failing in Thread:1 call to cuMemcpyDtoHAsync returned error 700: Illegal address during kernel execution". In the present study, we manually allocate arrays on GPU and associate them with corresponding arrays on the main memory. In the following program, `acc_malloc` allocates arrays on GPU, and `acc_map_data` associates arrays on GPU with corresponding arrays on CPU. Finally, users can generate a GPU enabled loop using directives.

Example of the allocation of matrix on CPU and GPU in the Octfile

```
octave_idx_type  Nc = Mat.cols();
octave_idx_type  Nr = Mat.rows();

double _Complex *Mat_p = reinterpret_cast<double _Complex *>
                         (const_cast<Complex *>(Mat.fortran_vec()));
double _Complex *Mat_d = (double _Complex*)
                         acc_malloc(sizeof(double _Complex)*Nc*Nr);
acc_map_data(Mat_p,Mat_d,sizeof(double _Complex)*Nc*Nr);

#pragma acc parallel loop independent present(Mat_p[0:Nc*Nr])
for (int i=0; i< Nr*Nc; i++){
   Mat_p[i] = 0.0;
}
```

Calling cuFFT with OpenACC. CuFFT is the FFT library which is one of the best for GPUs provided by NVIDIA. NVIDIA also provides another FFT library, called cuFFTW. The main difference in those libraries is that cuFFTW takes arrays on CPU as input, while cuFFT takes arrays on GPU as input. Since we are aiming to confine all the arrays into GPU, cuFFT is the choice in the present study. CuFFT is designed to use together with CUDA, which is the language that handles the pointers of arrays on GPU explicitly, whilst OpenACC handles the pointers on GPU implicitly. To circumvent this issue, we employed `#pragma acc host_data use_device` as inspired by the site [2]. An example of the Octfile which calls cuFFT from OpenACC is shown in the following program. In the program, a matrix `Matrix` is given from Octave, and iFFT is performed on it. The result is stored in `out`, and normalized using the number of matrix elements as Octave's native function does. The working example can be found at Zenodo [17]. It is worth noting that, since both the iFFT part and the normalization part are in the same `#pragma acc data copy` region, only the arrays on GPU are accessed during the computation, which is essential for performance.

Example of calling cuFFT from OpenACC in the Octfile

```
void inv_CUFFT(double _Complex *in_data,
               double _Complex *out_data,
               int nc, int nr, void *stream)
{
    cufftHandle plan;
```

```
        cufftResult ResPlan = cufftPlan2d(&plan, nc,nr, CUFFT_Z2Z);
        cufftSetStream(plan, (cudaStream_t)stream);
        cufftResult ResExec = cufftExecZ2Z(plan,
                                    (cufftDoubleComplex*)in_data,
                                    (cufftDoubleComplex*)out_data,
                                    CUFFT_INVERSE);
        cufftDestroy(plan);
}


DEFUN_DLD(testFFTGPU, args, ,
            "main body;")
{
    ComplexMatrix Matrix(args(0).complex_matrix_value());
    octave_value_list retval;
    ComplexMatrix out(Matrix.dims());

    double _Complex *pmat = reinterpret_cast<double _Complex*>
                    (const_cast<Complex *>(Matrix.fortran_vec()));
    double _Complex *pout = reinterpret_cast<double _Complex*>
                    (const_cast<Complex *>(out.fortran_vec()));
    int Nc = pmat.cols();
    int Nr = pmat.rows();
#pragma acc data copy(pmat[0:Nc*Nr],pout[0:Nc*Nr])
{
    void *stream = acc_get_cuda_stream(acc_async_sync);
#pragma acc host_data use_device(pmat,pout)
{
    inv_CUFFT((double _Complex*)pmat,(double _Complex*)pout,Nc,Nr,stream);
}

#pragma acc parallel
    for(int i=0;i<Nr*Nc;i++){
        pout[i] = pout[i]/double(Nr*Nc);
    }
}
    retval(0) = out;
    return retval;
}
```

Conditional Access. It is well known that loops should be avoided in Matlab and Octave, in terms of computational speed. Instead, users are encouraged to use a technique called vectorization (note that, this vectorization is not equivalent to the one in the context of supercomputing, especially on vector supercomputers). In the vectorization technique, users apply built-in operations and functions which perform over the entire elements of vectors and arrays. In the case that one needs to process only a part of an array, a new array needs to be created, as;

```
smallArray = Array(find(X > 0.0))
```

In the above example, `Array` and `X` are the vectors which have the same number of elements, and if an element of `X` is greater than 0.0, the corresponding element of `Array` is extracted and copied to `smallArray`. Finally, one can apply vectorized operations on `smallArray`. On the other hand, the same operation can be implemented in C++ as follows, where `n` is the size of `Array` and `X`;

```
int idx = 0;
for(int i; i<n; i++){
    if(X[i] > 0.0){
        smallArray[idx] = Array[i];
        idx++;
    }
}
```

This operation cannot be parallelized, because `idx` needs to be incremented sequentially, and therefore, it cannot be implemented on GPU. As a result, `Array` and `smallArray` need to be transferred between CPU and GPU, which should be avoided from the computational performance point of view. In the present study, we avoided creating such small arrays by processing all the elements of `Array` with `if` branch.

3.3   Performance Evaluation and Conclusion

In order to evaluate the performance of the GPU implementation as well as the multi-core implementation with OpenMP, the computation time was measured. Table 1 gives the computation times of each implementation on three sizes of problems, namely $ny \times nz = 1000 \times 2000, 2000 \times 4000, 4000 \times 8000$, where ny and nz are the numbers of grid points along the Y-axis and the Z-axis respectively. In the table, "Octave + FFTW (single)" denotes the computation time of Octave with a single threaded FFTW, "Octave + FFTW (20cores)" denotes the computation time of Octave with multi-threaded FFTW on 20 cores, "OpenMP" denotes the multi-threaded version with OpenMP on 15 cores, and "OpenACC" denotes the GPU version. The numbers listed in the table represent the computation time in seconds. Figure 1 shows the relative acceleration of each implementation to "Octave + FFTW (single)". In all the cases, OpenACC shows the best performance in all implementations. In addition, the larger the problem becomes, the better the acceleration becomes. In the largest case, OpenACC is approximately 19 times faster than Octave + FFTW (single). Regarding OpenMP, the same tendency with OpenACC is observed although the performance is worse than Octave + FFTW (single), in the smallest case. Except in the smallest problem case, OpenMP shows better performance than "Octave + FFTW (20cores)".

At the same time, "Octave + FFTW (20cores)" is always better than "Octave + FFTW (single)". This implies that although FFT is dominant in 3D-SSFPE, the remaining parts are not negligible.

Table 1. Computation time of each implementation on various problem sizes. Computation time in seconds is listed. Problem size indicates the numbers of grid points along the Y-axis and the Z-axis. The marching distance along the X-axis is identical in all cases.

Problem size	Octave + FFTW (single)	Octave + FFTW(20cores)	OpenMP	OpenACC
4000 × 8000	163	103	25.1	8.60
2000 × 4000	36.8	25.3	9.52	2.94
1000 × 2000	5.11	3.68	5.65	1.58

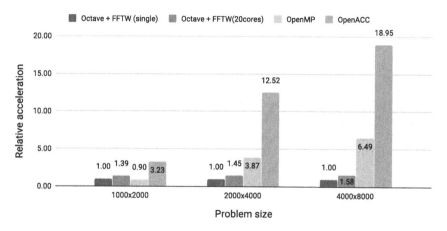

Fig. 1. Relative acceleration of each implementation to Octave + FFTW (single). Problem size indicates the numbers of grid points along the Y-axis and the Z-axis. The marching distance along the X-axis is identical in all cases.

Finally, we can conclude that porting the entire kernel of 3D-SSFPE to GPU is necessary for high performance even though a well-tuned FFT on GPU is provided. This is because (1) the communication between CPU and GPU is expensive as well known and in order to avoid such communication, all the computation should be performed on GPU, and (2) although FFT is dominant, the remaining parts are also perceptible if FFT is sufficiently fast.

4   Global Acoustic Simulation with FDM

4.1   Overview

As discussed, an FDM-based global acoustic model has a favorable nature to analyze CTBTO observation. One of the advantages of employing a FDM model over PE methods is that one can apply a waveform directly to a source term. However, so far, to our best knowledge, such models have not been developed (pp 147–161 of ref [8,23]). The main difficulties in building such simulation codes are: (1) considering the inhomogeneity of medium including background flows, (2) high aspect ratio of computational domain, (3) stability during long time integration. To overcome these difficulties, we employ a 2D FDM scheme on a spherical coordinate with the Yin-Yang overset grid [12] solving the governing equation of acoustic waves introduces by Ostashev et al. [21]. In the following section, we discuss the formulation and the implementation on CPU as well as GPU.

4.2   Formulation

Ostashev et al. give the formulation of the wave propagation over the moving inhomogeneous media as;

$$\left(\frac{\partial}{\partial t} + \mathbf{v} \cdot \nabla\right) p + \rho c^2 \nabla \cdot \mathbf{w} = \rho c^2 Q \tag{1}$$

$$\left(\frac{\partial}{\partial t} + \mathbf{v} \cdot \nabla\right) \mathbf{w} + (\mathbf{w} \cdot \nabla)\mathbf{v} + \frac{\nabla p}{\rho} = \frac{\mathbf{F}}{\rho} \tag{2}$$

where p is the pressure, $\mathbf{w}$ is the velocity vector of the wave, $\mathbf{v}$ is the velocity vector of background media, ρ is the density of the background media, c is the adiabatic sound speed, Q is a mass source, and $\mathbf{F}$ is a force acting on the background media. Since we are interested in solving the wave propagation over the globe, we need to know the explicit form of Eqs. 1 and 2 in a spherical coordinate. We now define the spherical coordinate we use in the present study as;

$$x = r \sin\theta \cos\phi$$
$$y = r \sin\theta \sin\phi \tag{3}$$
$$z = r \cos\theta$$

where the radial distance r, the inclination θ, and the azimuth ϕ. Based on Eq. 3, we have the operator ∇,

$$\nabla = \left(\frac{\partial}{\partial r}, \frac{1}{r}\frac{\partial}{\partial \theta}, \frac{1}{r \sin\theta}\frac{\partial}{\partial \phi}\right). \tag{4}$$

We write down the explicit form of $(\mathbf{v} \cdot \nabla)\mathbf{w}$,

$$(\mathbf{v} \cdot \nabla)\mathbf{w} = \left(v_r\frac{\partial}{\partial r} + \frac{v_\theta}{r}\frac{\partial}{\partial \theta} + \frac{v_\phi}{r \sin\theta}\frac{\partial}{\partial \phi}\right)(w_r\mathbf{e}_r + w_\theta\mathbf{e}_\theta + w_\phi\mathbf{e}_\phi), \tag{5}$$

where $\mathbf{e}_r$, $\mathbf{e}_\theta$ and $\mathbf{e}_\phi$ are the unit vectors of r, θ and ϕ, and v and w with subscripts denote the components of each vector along each direction. Finally,

$$
\begin{aligned}
(\mathbf{v} \cdot \nabla)\, \mathbf{w} = {} & \left(v_r \frac{\partial w_r}{\partial r} + \frac{v_\theta}{r} \frac{\partial w_r}{\partial \theta} + \frac{v_\phi}{r \sin \theta} \frac{\partial w_r}{\partial \phi} - \frac{v_\theta w_\theta + v_\phi w_\phi}{r} \right) \mathbf{e}_r \\
& + \left(v_r \frac{\partial w_\theta}{\partial r} + \frac{v_\theta}{r} \frac{\partial w_\theta}{\partial \theta} + \frac{v_\phi}{r \sin \theta} \frac{\partial w_\theta}{\partial \phi} + \frac{v_\theta w_r}{r} - \frac{v_\phi w_\phi \cot \theta}{r} \right) \mathbf{e}_\theta \\
& + \left(v_r \frac{\partial w_\phi}{\partial r} + \frac{v_\theta}{r} \frac{\partial w_\phi}{\partial \theta} + \frac{v_\phi}{r \sin \theta} \frac{\partial w_\phi}{\partial \phi} + \frac{v_\phi w_r}{r} + \frac{v_\phi w_\theta \cot \theta}{r} \right) \mathbf{e}_\phi.
\end{aligned}
\tag{6}
$$

In the same way, we have,

$$
\begin{aligned}
(\mathbf{w} \cdot \nabla)\, \mathbf{v} = {} & \left(w_r \frac{\partial v_r}{\partial r} + \frac{w_\theta}{r} \frac{\partial v_r}{\partial \theta} + \frac{w_\phi}{r \sin \theta} \frac{\partial v_r}{\partial \phi} - \frac{w_\theta v_\theta + w_\phi v_\phi}{r} \right) \mathbf{e}_r \\
& + \left(w_r \frac{\partial v_\theta}{\partial r} + \frac{w_\theta}{r} \frac{\partial v_\theta}{\partial \theta} + \frac{w_\phi}{r \sin \theta} \frac{\partial v_\theta}{\partial \phi} + \frac{w_\theta v_r}{r} - \frac{w_\phi v_\phi \cot \theta}{r} \right) \mathbf{e}_\theta \\
& + \left(w_r \frac{\partial v_\phi}{\partial r} + \frac{w_\theta}{r} \frac{\partial v_\phi}{\partial \theta} + \frac{w_\phi}{r \sin \theta} \frac{\partial v_\phi}{\partial \phi} + \frac{w_\phi v_r}{r} + \frac{w_\phi v_\theta \cot \theta}{r} \right) \mathbf{e}_\phi.
\end{aligned}
\tag{7}
$$

The divergence of $\mathbf{w}$ is,

$$
\nabla \cdot \mathbf{w} = \frac{1}{r} \frac{\partial}{\partial r} \left(r^2 w_r \right) + \frac{1}{r \sin \theta} \frac{\partial}{\partial \theta} \left(\sin \theta w_\theta \right) + \frac{1}{r \sin \theta} \frac{\partial w_\phi}{\partial \phi}.
\tag{8}
$$

By using Eqs. 6, 7, and 8, we have the explicit form of Eqs. 1 and 2 in the spherical coordinate,

$$
\begin{aligned}
\frac{\partial p}{\partial t} = {} & -\left(v_r \frac{\partial p}{\partial r} + \frac{v_\theta}{r} \frac{\partial p}{\partial \theta} + \frac{v_\phi}{r \sin \theta} \frac{\partial p}{\partial \phi} \right) \\
& - \kappa \left(\frac{1}{r} \frac{\partial}{\partial r} \left(r^2 w_r \right) + \frac{1}{r \sin \theta} \frac{\partial}{\partial \theta} \left(\sin \theta w_\theta \right) + \frac{1}{r \sin \theta} \frac{\partial w_\phi}{\partial \phi} \right) + \kappa Q, \\[4pt]
\frac{\partial w_r}{\partial t} = {} & -\left(v_r \frac{\partial w_r}{\partial r} + \frac{v_\theta}{r} \frac{\partial w_r}{\partial \theta} + \frac{v_\phi}{r \sin \theta} \frac{\partial w_r}{\partial \phi} - \frac{v_\theta w_\theta + v_\phi w_\phi}{r} \right) \\
& - \left(w_r \frac{\partial v_r}{\partial r} + \frac{w_\theta}{r} \frac{\partial v_r}{\partial \theta} + \frac{w_\phi}{r \sin \theta} \frac{\partial v_r}{\partial \phi} - \frac{w_\theta v_\theta + w_\phi v_\phi}{r} \right) - b \frac{\partial p}{\partial r} + b F_r, \\[4pt]
\frac{\partial w_\theta}{\partial t} = {} & -\left(v_r \frac{\partial w_\theta}{\partial r} + \frac{v_\theta}{r} \frac{\partial w_\theta}{\partial \theta} + \frac{v_\phi}{r \sin \theta} \frac{\partial w_\theta}{\partial \phi} + \frac{v_\theta w_r}{r} - \frac{v_\phi w_\phi \cot \theta}{r} \right) \\
& - \left(w_r \frac{\partial v_\theta}{\partial r} + \frac{w_\theta}{r} \frac{\partial v_\theta}{\partial \theta} + \frac{w_\phi}{r \sin \theta} \frac{\partial v_\theta}{\partial \phi} + \frac{w_\theta v_r}{r} - \frac{w_\phi v_\phi \cot \theta}{r} \right) - b \frac{1}{r} \frac{\partial p}{\partial \theta} + b F_\theta, \\[4pt]
\frac{\partial w_\phi}{\partial t} = {} & -\left(v_r \frac{\partial w_\phi}{\partial r} + \frac{v_\theta}{r} \frac{\partial w_\phi}{\partial \theta} + \frac{v_\phi}{r \sin \theta} \frac{\partial w_\phi}{\partial \phi} + \frac{v_\phi w_r}{r} + \frac{v_\phi w_\theta \cot \theta}{r} \right) \\
& - \left(w_r \frac{\partial v_\phi}{\partial r} + \frac{w_\theta}{r} \frac{\partial v_\phi}{\partial \theta} + \frac{w_\phi}{r \sin \theta} \frac{\partial v_\phi}{\partial \phi} + \frac{w_\phi v_r}{r} + \frac{w_\phi v_\theta \cot \theta}{r} \right) - \frac{b}{r \sin \theta} \frac{\partial p}{\partial \phi} + b F_\phi,
\end{aligned}
\tag{9}
$$

where $\kappa = \rho c^2$ and $b = 1/\rho$. By dropping the radial component in Eq. 9, we have the governing equation of the wave propagation in the horizontal direction,

$$
\frac{\partial p}{\partial t} = -\left(\frac{v_\theta}{r} \frac{\partial p}{\partial \theta} + \frac{v_\phi}{r \sin \theta} \frac{\partial p}{\partial \phi} \right) - \kappa \left(\frac{1}{r \sin \theta} \frac{\partial}{\partial \theta} (\sin \theta w_\theta) + \frac{1}{r \sin \theta} \frac{\partial w_\phi}{\partial \phi} \right) + \kappa Q,
$$

$$
\frac{\partial w_\theta}{\partial t} = -\left(\frac{v_\theta}{r} \frac{\partial w_\theta}{\partial \theta} + \frac{v_\phi}{r \sin \theta} \frac{\partial w_\theta}{\partial \phi} - \frac{v_\phi w_\phi \cot \theta}{r} \right) - \left(\frac{w_\theta}{r} \frac{\partial v_\theta}{\partial \theta} + \frac{w_\phi}{r \sin \theta} \frac{\partial v_\theta}{\partial \phi} - \frac{w_\phi v_\phi \cot \theta}{r} \right)
$$
$$
- b \frac{1}{r} \frac{\partial p}{\partial \theta} + b F_\theta,
$$

$$
\frac{\partial w_\phi}{\partial t} = -\left(\frac{v_\theta}{r} \frac{\partial w_\phi}{\partial \theta} + \frac{v_\phi}{r \sin \theta} \frac{\partial w_\phi}{\partial \phi} + \frac{v_\phi w_\theta \cot \theta}{r} \right) - \left(\frac{w_\theta}{r} \frac{\partial v_\phi}{\partial \theta} + \frac{w_\phi}{r \sin \theta} \frac{\partial v_\phi}{\partial \phi} + \frac{w_\phi v_\theta \cot \theta}{r} \right)
$$
$$
- \frac{b}{r \sin \theta} \frac{\partial p}{\partial \phi} + b F_\phi.
$$

$$(10)$$

In the present study, we employ Eq. 10 to solve the global acoustic wave propagation.

4.3   Yin-Yang Grid

Kageyama and Sato developed an overset grid Called the Yin-Yang grid to overcome the issues in FDM in a spherical coordinate. Namely, the Yin-Yang Grid resolves the singularity at poles and provides a near uniform grid over the globe. On the other hand, it leads to an additional complexity which originates in combining two identical grids. The Yin-Yang grid, as the name implies, uses two identical grids. In Fig. 2, we visualized the positional relationship of the Yin and Yang grids. As can be seen in Fig. 2 [a], both are identical and a grid can be projected onto the other grid only with rotation. We also visualised the locations of each grid on the globe (Fig. 2 [b]). Since those two grids are identical, there is no need to distinguish them by applying labels. However, for convenience, we put the label of Yin on the blue grid, and Yang on the red grid. In order to comprehend the geographical location of each grid, we projected them with the plate carree projection as well (Fig. 3). With those figures, we see that the poles are covered by the Yang grid, whilst neither the Yin nor Yang grid has poles which appear in the standard spherical coordinate grid. In addition, we can observe that the grid width, which determines the time step length and therefore the total computation time, is uniform. More precisely, in the standard spherical coordinate grid, the grid lengths close to the poles are smaller than the ones around the equator. Because of the stability in numerical computing, one needs to choose a time step length based on the smallest grid length, which results in a larger number of time steps. In this context, a uniform grid length reduces the total computation time.

In the Yin-Yang grid, the computation proceeds by exchanging the physical values on the boundaries of each grid. Kageyama and Sato pointed out that there are regions which are computed twice, around the corners of each grid. Ideally, such wasteful computations should be avoided, and Kageyama and Sato also proposed a grid for this purpose. However, because of the following reasons, we employed the one which is visualized in the figures; (1) The optimized grid requires additional "if" statement, which may impact on the computational speed, especially on GPU, (2) The number of such doubly computed grids is negligible in practice.

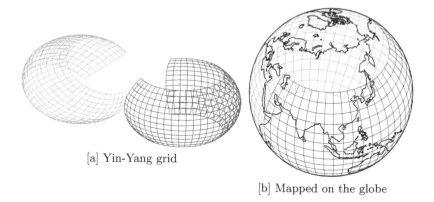

[a] Yin-Yang grid

[b] Mapped on the globe

Fig. 2. Visualization of Yin-Yang grid. [a] Yin and Yang grids are identical and can be projected only with rotation [b] Yin-Yang grid mapped on the globe (Color figure online)

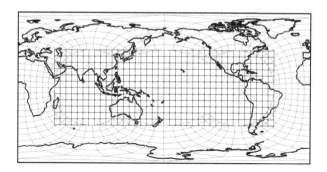

Fig. 3. Yin-Yang grid projected on the globe with the plate carree projection (Color figure online)

4.4 Computational Schemes

In the present study, we followed the computational schemes which Ostashev had employed, namely, the first order staggered grid for spatial discretization, and the fourth order Runge-Kutta explicit time integration. Figure 4 shows the schematic figure of the configuration of grid points. In the figure, the black dots represent p and other scalar values, and the triangles represent the θ and ϕ components of $\mathbf{w}$ and other vector values. A set of numbers in brackets indicates the addresses of arrays in the Fortran notation. The dashed line indicates the region which need to be computed, and values on the grid points outside the region need to be imported from the other Yin-Yang grid. Equation 11 shows the time integration with the Runge–Kutta method, where n denotes the time step number, ψ_n denotes the physical value at the time step "n", t_n denotes the time at the time step, and f represents a function. ψ^* and ψ^{**} are physical values at intermediate steps which are only for computation. If we assume that the time derivative can be derived using the first order differential, we can introduce the explicit form of f using Eq. 10 without any difficulty.

$$
\begin{aligned}
\psi^*_{n+\frac{1}{2}} &= \psi_n + \frac{\Delta t}{2} f\left(t_n, \psi_n\right) \\
\psi^{**}_{n+\frac{1}{2}} &= \psi_n + \frac{\Delta t}{2} f\left(t_{n+\frac{1}{2}}, \psi^*_{n+\frac{1}{2}}\right) \\
\psi^*_{n+1} &= \psi_n + \Delta t f\left(t_{n+\frac{1}{2}}, \psi^{**}_{n+\frac{1}{2}}\right) \\
\psi_{n+1} &= \psi_n + \frac{\Delta t}{6}\left[f\left(t_n, \psi_n\right) + 2f\left(t_{n+\frac{1}{2}}, \psi^*_{n+\frac{1}{2}}\right) + 2f\left(t_{n+\frac{1}{2}}, \psi^{**}_{n+\frac{1}{2}}\right) + f\left(t_{n+1}, \psi^*_{n+1}\right)\right]
\end{aligned}
\tag{11}
$$

4.5   Performance Optimization

Merging Function Evaluations. Equation 10 gives the functions that should be evaluated in Eq. 11. In a naive implementation, those three functions are implemented into three individual functions. However, at the same time, one can point out that most variables appear in all three equations. For instance, variables loaded to evaluate the first equation can be used in the remaining equations. As well known, modern computers including GPUs, have high arithmetic intensity (the number of floating point operations per word). In other words, reducing the number of memory instructions is the key technique to achieve high performance. Thus, we evaluate those three equations within the same loop so that a variable is reused as many times as possible. In Table 2, the computation times of the naive implementation and the merged function implementation are listed, as well as the speedup from the naive implementation to the merged implementation. The computational time is measured on Intel Xeon CPU E5-1620 v3 one core, only with the Yin grid. The grid sizes used are $n\phi \times n\theta = 1000 \times 3000$ (10 km/grid on the equator), and 3000×9000 (3.3 km/grid) where $n\phi$ and $n\theta$ are the numbers of grid points along ϕ and θ directions, respectively. In the smaller problem case, we obtained 4.85 times acceleration while we obtained 3.31 times acceleration in the larger problem case. The reason why the larger case shows smaller improvement can be attributed to the data cache memory working more effectively in the smaller problem. Since the number of floating point operations required stays the same in both implementations, we believe

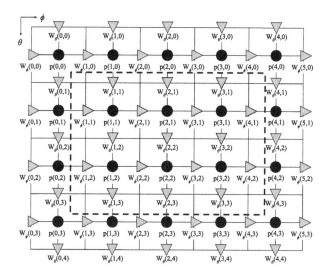

Fig. 4. Configuration of the staggered grid.

that the improvement originates in the reduction of memory access. Therefore, we can expect that this optimization is also effective on GPU, although we are not able to perform this test on GPU because the optimization was applied at an early stage of the development.

Table 2. Computational times of the naive implementation and the merged functions implementation. Times in seconds are listed.

	Naive	Merged	Speedup
1000×3000	0.80	0.17	4.85
3000×9000	7.25	2.19	3.31

Memory Management. The structure data type is efficient in building software. However, currently, handling the allocatable array in a structure is cumbersome, namely, users need to allocate arrays on GPU manually, and transfer the data. In the present study, we employed the managed memory (the unified memory in CUDA is equivalent technology), although this is only supported by the PGI compiler currently. Using the managed memory, all the arrays used on GPU are automatically uploaded. Once an array is uploaded onto GPU, no communication between CPU and GPU is necessary except the case that output files are created.

Double GPU. In the implementation point of view, we need to launch an identical function twice, namely once with the Yin grid and also with the Yang grid. In other words, those two grids can be evaluated independently, if the boundary values are exchanged correctly. Thus, using the two GPUs and assigning a grid to a GPU is quite natural. However, at the same time, one needs to implement a way to import and export the boundary values to the other. Thanks to the managed memory technology which we employed in the present study, communication among GPUs and CPU is carried out automatically. On the other hand, as we will discuss later, the communication cost among GPUs with the managed memory technology is high and the total computational speed is worse than the single GPU configuration. Thus, we implemented a communication functionality with a lower level function "cudaMemcpyPeer". cudaMemcpyPeer enables us to send and receive data directly bypassing the CPU, whilst the data path with the management memory technology is not visible for users. On the other hand, cudaMemcpyPeer requires us to manage the memory space of GPU manually. In the present study, we employ the device array and !$acc deviceptr directive to use cudaMemcpyPeer.

Because of the prevalence of the GPU-cluster (multi-node) type supercomputers, there have been many reports of success in MPI–OpenACC hybridization [7] and even training [3]. Here, MPI stands for Message Passing Interface. Nevertheless, since the DGX–station we employed in the present study as well as DGX–1 and DGX–2 by NVIDIA, which have a similar architecture with DGX–station whilst more powerful, are single-node-multi-GPU computers, discussing the hybridization of OpenMP and OpenACC may draw attention from researchers. One of the biggest advantages of using the OpenMP/OpenACC hybridization is that users can progressively implement their codes based on their sequential version, especially users who can use the managed memory technology. As well known, MPI requires users to reconstruct the data structure which may lead to the major code rewrite.

In the following program, we show the structure of the hybridization with a pseudo code resembling Fortran. In the program, rungeKutta is the function which computes the physical values of the next step using the Runge–Kutta algorithm on the Yin or Yang grid. Since the Yin grid and the Yang grid are identical, we call the same function twice but with separate arrays (yin and yang) in each iteration. In our hybrid program, each grid is assigned on each OpenMP thread, so that two GPUs are used in parallel. The function acc_set_device_num is a function provided within the OpenACC framework, and this specifies the device that is used by a thread. The arrays, yin2yangSend, yin2yangRecv, yang2yinSend and yang2yinRecv are device arrays which are to exchange the boundary values. Since device arrays should be allocated on target devices, they are allocated after acc_set_device_num is called. calcEdge is the function which computes the boundary values on the other grid, and stores such values on yin2yangSend and yang2yinSend. Those arrays are copied to `yang2yinRecv` and `yin2yangRecv` directly using `cudaMemcpyPeer`. Finally the boundary values are copied to the Yin and Yang grids using the function `recoverBoundary` so that we can move on to the next time step. Since we should avoid the communication between CPU and GPUs, the computation in the functions `rungeKutta`, `calcEdge` and `recoverBoundary` are all written in OpenACC. Thus the hybridization of OpenMP/OpenACC is achieved on our FDM code.

Hybridization of OpenMP/OpenACC on the Yin-Yang grid FDM

```
program acousticFDM

! Structure that stores each grid values
type(yinYangGrid) :: yin, yang
! Device array to exchange boundary values
real(8),dimension(:),allocatable, device :: yin2yangSend, yin2yangRecv
real(8),dimension(:),allocatable, device :: yang2yinSend, yang2yinRecv
! GPU number 1 and 2 are used
integer,parameter, dimension(0:1) :: iDev = (/1,2/)

nPhi = 100      ! Number of grid points along Phi-axis
nTheta = nPhi*3 ! Number of grid points along Theta-axis
integer :: nEdge = 2*nPhi + 2*nTheta !Number of grid points on the all edges

!$omp parallel num_threads(2)
do ITER = 1, MAX_ITERATION ! Time integration loop
   if(ITER==1)then
      call acc_set_device_num(iDev(omp_get_thread_num() ) , &
          acc_device_nvidia)
      if(omp_get_thread_num()==0)then
         allocate(yin2yangSend(nEdge))
         allocate(yang2yinRecv(nEdge))
      else
         allocate(yang2yinSend(nEdge))
         allocate(yin2yangRecv(nEdge))
      endif
   endif

   if(omp_get_thread_num()==0)then
! Compute the Yin grid
      call rungeKutta(yin)
! Compute the values of grid point on the edged in the Yang grid
! and store in yin2yangSend
      call calcEdge(yin,yin2yangSend)
! Copy yin2yangSend to yin2yangRecv which is on the other device
      istat = cudaMemcpyPeer(yin2yangRecv,iDev(1), &
                    yin2yangSend,iDev(0),nEdge)
      call recoverBoundary(yang2yinRecv,yin)
   else
      call rungeKutta(yang)
      call calcEdge(yang,yang2yinSend)
      istat = cudaMemcpyPeer(yang2yinRecv,iDev(0), &
                    yang2yinSend,iDev(1),nEdge)
```

```
        call recoverBoundary(yin2yangRecv,yang)
      endif
enddo
!$omp end parallel
end program acousticFDM
```

4.6   Software Evaluation

Accuracy Evaluation with a Live Experiment. Since this software has been developed from scratch, we first would like to check the validity of our code from the modelling point of view. In the present study, we refer to the experiment performed in 1960 [22]. In this experiment, a chemical explosive (amatol) was used as a source of the hydroacoustic wave, and it was detonated by the research vessel Vema offshore Perth, Australia. A hydrophone was set in the Bermuda area to catch the hydroacoustic wave. In the literature, authors identified the propagation path and the effective sound speed was estimated. In the present study, we employed the parameters given in the literature to perform the modelling, namely,

- sound speed: 1485 m/s
- location of hydrophone: 32.10 N and 64.35 W
- location of detonation: 33.36 S and 113.29 E in the SOFAR channel
- travel time: 3 h 41 min 18 s to 3 h 42 min 24 s.

Since our FDM code does not take into account the radial direction, we assume that the wave propagates at 1,000 m depth, close to where the SOFAR channel is situated. ETOPO1 [6] is employed as the bathymetry data. The solid earth is treated as the rigid body, in other words, the velocity of wave becomes zero at the boundary.

As a result, the wave travels from Vema to Bermuda in 3 h 43 min 0 s, which is slightly longer than the experiment. Although further evaluation and development are necessary, we believe the implementation so far is successful. A visualization animation of the wave propagation of this experiment is uploaded to Zenodo [16].

Computational Speed. In order to evaluate the improvements in computational speed, we measured the computation time per iteration of each implementation with various problem sizes (Table 3. Figures in the table are in seconds). In the present study, we used the following grids: $n\phi \times n\theta = 1000 \times 3000 (10\,\text{km/grid}$ on the equator$), 3000 \times 9000 (3.33\,\text{km/grid})$, $6000 \times 18000 (1.67\,\text{km/grid}), 8000 \times 24000 (1.25\,\text{km/grid})$ and 9000×27000 $(1.11\,\text{km/grid})$, where $n\phi$ and $n\theta$ are the numbers of grid points along the ϕ-axis and the θ-axis. In the table, "CPU" denotes FDM implementation with one core CPU, "OpenMP" denotes 20 cores parallel with OpenMP, "Multicore" denotes 20 cores parallel with OpenACC with the -ta=multicore option,

"Single GPU" denotes one GPU implementation with OpenACC, "managed memory" denotes the dual-GPU implementation with the managed memory technology, and "cudaMemcpyPeer" denotes the dual-GPU implementation with the cudaMemcpyPeer function (please note that single GPU also relies on the managed memory technology). In all the cases, CPU shows the slowest. The multicore parallel implementations (OpenMP and Multicore) are the second slowest. Managed memory is faster than CPU, but slower than Single GPU although two GPUs are involved in. Finally, cudaMemcpyPeer shows the best performance. We observed that Single GPU with the 8000×24000 and 9000×27000 grids took over 5 min for one time step computation. Thus we aborted the computation and "Not Available (NA)" is indicated in the table. Thanks to the managed memory technology, although the required memory size is larger than the actual device memory size, the processes continued working. However, because many communication instructions were issued between CPU and GPU, the performance became worse than CPU.

We listed the acceleration of each implementation to CPU (Table 4). In most cases cudaMemcpyPeer and Single GPU show over 100 times acceleration to one core CPU. In the best case scenario, we obtained approximated 160 times acceleration with two GPUs. In this case, cudaMemcpyPeer shows 1.4 better performance than Single GPU, although it is still lower than the ideal acceleration. We observed that the ideal acceleration can be obtained by ignoring cudaMemcpyPeer and recoverBoundary in our preliminary test. This implies that there is a space for further optimization in the boundary exchange phase. Finally, managed memory shows worse performance than Single GPU while the problem size is sufficiently small. At the same time, managed memory allows us to solve larger problem than Single GPU, and it runs faster than CPU. The multicore implementations show approximately 10 times acceleration to CPU, whilst Multicore is slightly faster than OpenMP.

For readers' evaluation, we provide the CPU version [14], and the cudaMemcpyPeer version [13] on Zenodo.

Table 3. Computational times at one time step of each implementation with various problem sizes. Figures are in second. NA denotes "Not Available"

	CPU	OpenMP	Multicore	Single GPU	Managed memory	cuda Memcpy Peer
1000×3000	6.10E–01	7.28E–02	6.76E–02	7.65E–03	1.07E–01	1.42E–02
3000×9000	6.76E+00	7.40E–01	6.51E–01	5.91E–02	6.48E–01	5.26E–02
6000×18000	2.72E+01	3.00E+00	2.69E+00	2.45E–01	2.02E+00	1.71E–01
8000×24000	4.95E+01	5.52E+00	5.12E+00	NA	8.93E+00	3.87E–01
9000×27000	6.04E+01	7.12E+00	6.73E+00	NA	9.44E+00	4.43E–01

Table 4. Acceleration of each implementation to CPU with various problem sizes. NA denotes "Not Available"

	CPU	OpenMP	Multicore	Single GPU	Managed memory	cudaMemcpyPeer
1000 × 3000	x1.00	x8.38	x9.03	x79.82	x5.71	x43.00
3000 × 9000	x1.00	x9.13	x10.39	x114.32	x10.43	x128.36
6000 × 18000	x1.00	x9.08	x10.12	x111.30	x13.50	x158.71
8000 × 24000	x1.00	x8.97	x9.67	NA	x5.54	x127.76
9000 × 27000	x1.00	x8.49	x8.99	NA	x6.40	x136.35

5 Conclusion

In the present study, we have implemented two hydroacoustic modelling codes on GPU with OpenACC and gained better performance than on CPU. Since those two modelling codes will be used to understand the observed signals in the international monitoring system of CTBTO, the larger the number of hypothetical events we can solve, the better we can understand the observed signals. In this context, the acceleration obtained in this study contributes to the mission of the organization. The summaries of the achievements are: (1) In 3D-SSFPE, we succeeded in implementing GPU enabled code which works together with Octave, which is a high-level computer language. As a result, we gained approximately 19 times acceleration to the original Octave code, in the best case scenario. Although the obtained acceleration is lower than that can be observed in our sample codes (50 times acceleration), which are relatively simpler than 3D-SSFPE, we are proud of achieving high performance in a realistic problem. In addition, we may gain further acceleration with updates on compilers. (2) In the in-house FDM code, we succeeded in implementing an OpenMP/OpenACC hybrid code to use two GPUs. As a result, we gained approximately 160 times speedup to one core CPU in the best case scenario. Although there have been many research projects which successfully implemented OpenACC codes on supercomputers, our experience might be of interest to researchers, especially those who are not familiar with supercomputing.

Disclaimer. The views expressed on this article are those of the authors' and do not necessarily reflect the view of the CTBTO.

Acknowledgement. One of the authors, Noriyuki Kushida, would like to express his gratitude to Dr Tammy Taylor, the director of the International Data Centre of CTBTO, on her encouragement on the work. And also he would like to express his gratitude to CEA in France as well as PRACE, on their support for the development of FDM by awarding the machine times on Irena Skylake. Finally, he would like to thank Dr Yuka Kushida for her English correction. She has pointed out errors which had been overlooked even by a native speaker.

References

1. DGX Station web page. https://www.nvidia.com/en-us/data-center/dgx-station/. Accessed 12 July 2019
2. Interoperability between OpenACC and cuFFT. https://www.olcf.ornl.gov/tutorials/mixing-openacc-with-gpu-libraries/. Accessed 16 July 2019
3. MULTI GPU PROGRAMMING WITH MPI AND OPENACC. https://gputechconf2017.smarteventscloud.com/connect/sessionDetail.ww?SESSION_ID=110507&tclass=popup. Accessed 22 July 2019
4. The API reference guide for cuFFT. https://docs.nvidia.com/cuda/cufft/index.html. Accessed 13 July 2019
5. ubuntu-toolchain-r/test web page. https://launchpad.net/~ubuntu-toolchain-r/+archive/ubuntu/test. Accessed 13 July 2019
6. Amante, C.: Etopo1 1 arc-minute global relief model: procedures, data sources and analysis (2009). https://doi.org/10.7289/v5c8276m, https://data.nodc.noaa.gov/cgi-bin/iso?id=gov.noaa.ngdc.mgg.dem:316
7. Calore, E., Gabbana, A., Kraus, J., Schifano, S.F., Tripiccione, R.: Performance and portability of accelerated lattice Boltzmann applications with OpenACC. Concurr. Comput.: Pract. Exper. **28**(12), 3485–3502 (2016). https://doi.org/10.1002/cpe.3862
8. Etter, P.: Underwater Acoustic Modeling and Simulation, 4th edn. Taylor & Francis (2013)
9. Frigo, M., Johnson, S.G.: The design and implementation of FFTW3. Proc. IEEE **93**(2), 216–231 (2005). Special issue on "Program Generation, Optimization, and Platform Adaptation"
10. Heaney, K.D., Campbell, R.L.: Three-dimensional parabolic equation modeling of mesoscale eddy deflection. J. Acoust. Soc. Am. **139**(2), 918–926 (2016). https://doi.org/10.1121/1.4942112
11. Heaney, K.D., Prior, M., Campbell, R.L.: Bathymetric diffraction of basin-scale hydroacoustic signals. J. Acoust. Soc. Am. **141**(2), 878–885 (2017). https://doi.org/10.1121/1.4976052
12. Kageyama, A., Sato, T.: "Yin-Yang grid": an overset grid in spherical geometry. Geochem. Geophys. Geosyst. **5**(9) (2004). https://doi.org/10.1029/2004GC000734
13. Kushida, N.: Globalacoustic2D dual GPU (2019). https://doi.org/10.5281/zenodo.3351369
14. Kushida, N.: Globalacoustic2D OpenMP (2019). https://doi.org/10.5281/zenodo.3351284
15. Kushida, N.: GPU version of "Split Step Fourier PE method to solve the Lloyd's Mirror Problem", August 2019. https://doi.org/10.5281/zenodo.3359888
16. Kushida, N.: Hydroacoustic wave propagation from Vema to Bermuda using FDM, July 2019. https://doi.org/10.5281/zenodo.3349551
17. Kushida, N.: OpenACC enabled oct file (2019). https://doi.org/10.5281/zenodo.3345905
18. Kushida, N., Le Bras, R.: Acoustic wave simulation using an overset grid for the global monitoring system. In: AGU Fall Meeting. Oral Presentation: AGU Fall Meeting 2017, New Orleans, USA, 11–15 December 2017 (2017)
19. Lin, Y.T.: Split Step Fourier PE method to solve the Lloyd's Mirror Problem, August 2019. https://doi.org/10.5281/zenodo.3359581

20. Lin, Y.T., Duda, T.F., Newhall, A.E.: Three-dimensional sound propagation models using the parabolic-equation approximation and the split-step Fourier method. J. Comput. Acoust. **21**(01), 1250018 (2013). https://doi.org/10.1142/s0218396x1250018x
21. Ostashev, V.E., Wilson, D.K., Liu, L., Aldridge, D.F., Symons, N.P., Marlin, D.: Equations for finite-difference, time-domain simulation of sound propagation in moving inhomogeneous media and numerical implementation. J. Acoust. Soc. Am. **117**(2), 503–517 (2005). https://doi.org/10.1121/1.1841531
22. Shockley, R.C., Northrop, J., Hansen, P.G., Hartdegen, C.: Sofar propagation paths from Australia to Bermuda: comparison of signal speed algorithms and experiments. J. Acoust, Soc. Am. **71**(1), 51–60 (1982). https://doi.org/10.1121/1.387250
23. Wang, L.S., Heaney, K., Pangerc, T., Theobald, P., Robinson, S.P., Ainslie, M.: Review of underwater acoustic propagation models. NPL report, October 2014. http://eprintspublications.npl.co.uk/6340/

Accelerating the Performance of Modal Aerosol Module of E3SM Using OpenACC

Hongzhang Shan[1], Zhengji Zhao[2(✉)], and Marcus Wagner[3]

[1] CRD, Lawrence Berkeley National Laboratory,
Berkeley, CA 94720, USA
hshan@lbl.gov

[2] NERSC, Lawrence Berkeley National Laboratory,
Berkeley, CA 94720, USA
zzhao@lbl.gov

[3] Cray, a Hewlett Packard Enterprise company, Seattle, WA 98164, USA
marcus.wagner@hpe.com

Abstract. Using GPUs to accelerate the performance of HPC applications has recently gained great momentum. Energy Exascale Earth System Model (E3SM) is a state-of-the-science earth system model development and simulation project and has gained national recognition. It has a large code base with over a million lines of code. How to make effective use of GPUs, however, remains a challenge. In this paper, we use the modal aerosol module (MAM) of E3SM as a driving example to investigate how to effectively offload computational tasks to GPUs using the OpenACC directives. In particular, we are interested in the performance advantage of using GPUs and in understanding performance-limiting factors from both application characteristics and the GPU or OpenACC.

1 Introduction

E3SM is an Energy Exascale Earth System Model to investigate energy-relevant science using the code optimized for the U.S. DOE's advanced computers [4]. Its mission is to project critical changes that will impact the U.S. energy sector, including water availability, extreme temperature, energy resource potentials, sea level rise, etc. It combines the atmosphere, ocean, land ice, river, sea ice, and land component models together to advance the DOE's understanding of and ability to predict the earth system. Among those components, atmosphere and ocean are the two critical components that consume most of the run time.

As a more energy efficient approach, GPUs have been widely accepted in the HPC community. As a result, developers of HPC applications have needed to port their applications to various GPU accelerated platforms. Due to the rapid

Electronic supplementary material The online version of this chapter (https://doi.org/10.1007/978-3-030-49943-3_3) contains supplementary material, which is available to authorized users.

This is a U.S. government work and not under copyright protection in the U.S.; foreign copyright protection may apply 2020

S. Wienke and S. Bhalachandra (Eds.): WACCPD 2019, LNCS 12017, pp. 47–65, 2020.
https://doi.org/10.1007/978-3-030-49943-3_3

evolution of GPU and CPU technology, it is critical for application developers to adopt a program model or framework that can deliver both performance and portability while allowing minimal code development and maintenance efforts. Some frameworks or ecosystems, such as Kokkos, have been developed to help programmers write portable applications by hiding the complexity of low level architectures, and have been successfully adopted by many applications [13]. However, Kokkos targets C++ only, leaving a large number of scientific codes written in Fortran untouched, including the entirety of the E3SM code. As a matter of fact, some E3SM code teams have rewritten the atmospheric dynamical core (High-Order Methods Modeling Environment, HOMME) of E3SM in C++ to employ Kokkos with success [1]. Their effort produced 13,000 new lines of C++ and 2000 new lines of Fortran, required significant programming effort. Directive-based programming models, such as OpenMP and OpenACC with their offload features, are preferred options, especially when porting Fortran applications to GPUs. OpenMP has a clear path forward in delivering performance and portability with relatively little development effort, as its language standards have been widely accepted among many compiler vendors and developers. As of right now, however, not many compilers support OpenMP offload yet, meaning developers may find themselves spending more time dealing with compiler bugs. On the other hand, OpenACC is well supported in PGI compilers (GCC is catching up with the OpenACC support as well), and offers performance and portability across GPUs and CPUs with a single source, which can largely reduce the code maintenance effort. Additionally, with the support of CUDA unified memory, data management becomes an easier task and efficient development can be ensured. Due to its efficiency, OpenACC has been widely adopted in HPC applications; as of GTC19, there have been 194 application codes ported to GPUs with OpenACC, including the top three HPC applications, VASP, Gaussian, and MAS [7]. OpenACC has been previously explored by the E3SM multi-scale modeling framework project [8], but not for current production run codes. Notice that there is a consensus [3] in the HPC community that after filling important gaps in ISO standards the directive-based parallel programming models as well as the tools like Kokkos will eventually diminish when the parallel constructs emerge in the native programming languages, such as C/C++ and Fortran. This further assures the choice of OpenACC, which is capable of delivering performance with relatively little programming effort and minimal code changes.

In this work, we focus on accelerating the aerosol module (MAM) of the atmosphere component of E3SM by offloading the work to GPUs using OpenACC directives. The relevant MAM part includes tens of thousands of lines of code written in Fortran 2003 while the whole atmosphere component includes a few hundred thousand lines. Since the run time is dispersed among many functions, we cannot focus our attention on a couple of kernels only, instead working on many kernels with different performance characteristics. By exploring the performance of different kernels and optimizing them for effective execution on GPUs, our goal is to infer guidelines for future GPU porting. We found that to offload the work efficiently to GPUs, we had to refactor the code significantly, including breaking big irregular kernels to smaller ones, moving expensive I/O operations out of the loops, reorganizing the code to expose more parallelism, and also minimizing data movement wherever possible by using unstructured data regions. Ultimately, we were able to improve performance more than 5X using GPU accelerators compared with using CPUs only. We have also observed that for some kernels, significant overhead incurred when offloading to GPUs, neutralizing the benefit of GPU usage.

The rest of the paper is organized as follows: we describe the OpenACC programming model in Sect. 2, focusing on the language features used in this work, and describe our experimental platform and approach in Sect. 3. After introducing the MAM algorithms and the four selected kernels in Sect. 4, we describe how we offload the MAM kernels to GPUs using the OpenACC directives and discuss their performance in Sect. 5. Then in Sect. 6, we discuss how to tune the performance by launching multiple processes on a single GPU, and provide further performance analysis. We will conclude the paper by summarizing our observations and future work in Sect. 7.

2   OpenACC Programming Model

OpenACC is a directive-based programming approach to parallel computing. It is designed for simplicity and performance portability. A single source code can be run on different accelerator devices. Figure 1 shows a high level diagram of generic OpenACC programming. Applications run on the host, and data and computational kernels can be offloaded to accelerator devices through OpenACC directives. However, offloading details are hidden; programmers do not need to understand exactly how data is transferred between the host and device memories, or how computational kernels are executed on the devices. OpenACC is thus easy to learn and easy to use, and the developers remain in familiar with C, C++, or Fortran. This simplicity greatly speeds up the development process, though extensive tuning may be required to achieve the best possible performance.

OpenACC provides plenty of directives and clauses for parallelizing loops, transferring and synchronizing data between hosts and GPUs. In this section, we introduce only the concepts and directives we used in the MAM porting work. For further information, please refer to [9,10].

2.1   Parallelizing Loops

Two OpenACC directives, *kernels and parallel*, to parallelize the loops are shown in Code 2.1. Lines 1–3 are for a *kernels* loop while lines 5–7 are for a *parallel* loop. The main difference between these two directives is that a *kernels* loop allows more freedom for compilers to optimize the loop, especially in the case of a nested loop. In our experience, we always use a *kernels* loop first, examine the compiler report, then switch to a *parallel* loop to explicitly define the parallelization and data movement.

In concept, OpenACC exposes three levels of parallelism via gang, worker, and vector parallelism. A number of gangs will be launched on the accelerator,

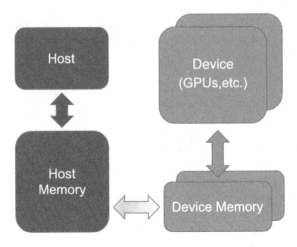

Fig. 1. OpenACC's abstract programming model

2.1 Directives for Parallelizing Loops in Fortran

```
1: !$acc kernels loop [clause-list]
2:      do loop
3: !$acc end kernels loop
4:
5: !$acc parallel loop [clause-list]
6:      do loop
7: !$acc end parallel loop
```

---

each gang having one or more workers. Vector parallelism is for SIMD or vector operations within a worker. How these three levels of parallelism will be mapped to accelerators will be implementation dependent.

2.2 Data Transfer

OpenACC supports a couple of ways to control data transfer between the host and device memories. Code 2.2 shows three ways to transfer data using the vector add operation as an example. The main difference between these three approaches is the lifetime of the device variables.

The first approach (lines 2–7) defines a structured data region. Arrays used within the data region will remain on the device until the region's end. The *copyin* clause will allocate memory for variables *a* and *b* on device memory and copy values from the host to the device. The *copyout* clause will allocate memory for variable *c* and copy the value back from the device to the host when computation has finished.

The second approach (lines 10–17) uses an unstructured data region. This approach uses *enter data* to define the start of the lifetime of the device variables and *exit data* to define the end of their lifetime. This approach is used when the

2.2 Directives for Data Transfer in Fortran

```
 1: 1. Structured:
 2: !$acc data copyin(a,b) copyout(c)
 3: !$acc parallel loop
 4: do i = 1, n
 5:     c(i) = a(i) + b(i)
 6: enddo
 7: !$acc end data
 8:
 9: 2. Unstructured:
10: !$acc enter data copyin(a,b) create(c)
11: ...                                          ▷ Do something else
12: !$acc parallel loop
13: do i = 1, n
14:     c(i) = a(i) + b(i)
15: enddo
16: ...
17: !$acc exit data copyout(c) delete(a,b)
18:
19: 3. Using Declare:
20: double precision, allocatable, dimension(:) :: a,b,c    ▷ a,b,c are module variables
21: !$acc declare create(a,b,c)
22: ...
23: allocate(a(n), b(n), c(n))        ▷ a,b,c will be allocated both on host and device
24: ...
25: !$acc update device(a,b)          ▷ a,b have been initialized on host, update device
26: !$acc parallel loop
27: do i = 1, n
28:     c(i) = a(i) + b(i)
29: enddo
30: !$acc update host(c)                                      ▷ update host c
```

structured data regions are not convenient to use, such as when using constructors and destructors.

The third approach (lines 20–30) is to use the *declare* directive. This is used in the declaration section of a Fortran subroutine, function, or module to specify that a variable needs to be allocated on the device memory, and that its lifetime is the duration of the implicit data region of a function, subroutine or program. The *update* directive is used to synchronize variable values between the host and the device.

3 Experimental Platforms and Approach

The platform we worked on is called Summit [12], located at Oak Ridge National Laboratory. It has a theoretical peak double-precision performance of approximately 200 PF, capable of running a wide range of scientific applications. Its node architecture is illustrated in Fig. 2.

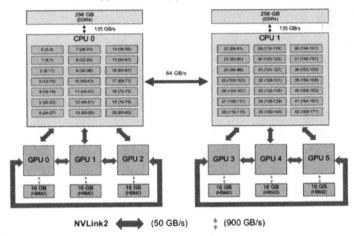

Fig. 2. The node architecture of Summit.

Each node contains two IBM Power9 processors (CPU0, CPU1) and six Nvidia V100 GPUs. Each Power9 processor has 21 IBM SIMD Multi-Cores (SMC) with separate 32 KB L1 data and instruction caches. Each pair of SMCs shares a 512 KB L2 cache and a 10 MB L3 cache. Each SMC supports four hardware threads. The Power9 CPUs are connected with GPUs through dual NVLINK bricks, each capable of a 25 GB/s data transfer rate in each direction. Each node contains 512 GB of DDR4 memory for Power9 CPUs and 96 GB of high bandwidth memory (HBM) for GPUs. Each Nvidia V100 contains 80 streaming multiprocessors (SMs), 16 GB of HBM, and a 6 MB L2 cache. Each SM contains 64 FP32 cores, 64 INT32 cores, 32 FP64 cores. Table 1 lists the key features of Nvidia V100 GPUs. The V100 SM is partitioned into four processing blocks, each with a new L0 instruction cache, a warp scheduler, a dispatch unit, and a 64 KB register file.

Table 1. Summary of the key features of Nvidia V100 GPU.

SMs	80	FP32 cores/SM	64
FP64 Cores/SM	32	GPU Boost Clock	1530 MHz
Memory Interface	4096-bit HBM2	Memory Size	16 GB
L2 Cache Size	6144 KB	Shared Memory Size/SM	96 KB
Register File Size/SM	256 KB	TDP	300 W
Threads/Warp	32	Max Warps/SM	64
Max Thread Blocks/SM	32	Max Thread Block Size	1024

We used the PGI compiler version 19.4, spectrum-mpi version 10.3.0.1, and CUDA 10.1.168. Other libraries used in the E3SM code included NETCDF 4.6.1, NETCDF-FORTRAN 4.4.4, ESSL 6.1.0, Parallel NETCDF 1.8.1, and HDF5 1.10.3. The data set for E3SM is SMS_PS_Ld5.ne16_ne16.FC5AV1C-L, which stresses the atmosphere physics. Here, ne16_ne16 defines the cubed sphere grid resolution (more details in the next section).

4   MAM Algorithms and Kernels

E3SM was developed to reliably project decade-to-century scale changes that could critically impact the U.S. energy sector. It combined the atmosphere, ocean, land, river, ice, and other components. The computation of the atmosphere component is based upon the Spectral Element (SE) numerical discretization of underlying PDEs for stratified, hydrostatic fluid dynamics on rotating spheres. MAM is a submodule from the atmosphere component that plays an important role in the climate system by influencing the Earth's radiation budgets and modifying cloud properties [5,6]. It predicts the mass and mixing ratios of cloud liquid and cloud ice, diagnoses the mass and mixing ratios of rain and snow, and handles complicated conversions between cloud hydrometeors.

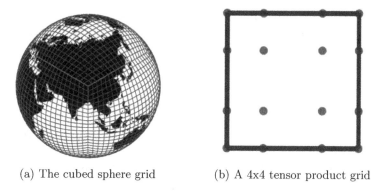

(a) The cubed sphere grid   (b) A 4x4 tensor product grid

Fig. 3. The cubed sphere grid for elements and the 4×4 tensor product grid of GLL nodes used within each element. Copied from https://www.earthsystemcog.org/projects/dcmip-2012/cam-se

E3SM models the Earth with a cubed-sphere grid as illustrated in Fig. 3a. The sphere is divided into six panels (or faces) with no gaps or overlaps. These panels are further divided into grid meshes. The resolution of the meshes is defined as the number of spectral elements ne along the edge of each cube face. There are therefore $6ne^2$ elements total in the mesh. For any spectral element grid with ne elements, the number of unique points (or physics columns) is $(np-1)^2 * ne + 2$, where each element contains a $np*np$ tensor product of Gauss-Lobatto-Legendre

4.1 The Loop Structure for Computations

```
1: do j = 1, nchunks                                    ▷ number of chunks
2:     do k = 1, nlev            ▷ vertical levels, may exist data dependency
3:         do i = 1, ncols(j)                  ▷ number of columns in chunk j
4:                                ▷ sum(ncols(j) = total physical columns
5:                 computation kernels()            ▷ many different kernels
6:         enddo
7:     enddo
8: enddo
```

(GLL) points depicted in Fig. 3b [2]. With the exception of the sphere faces, there exists another dimension, namely the vertical direction.

To compute the physical parameterizations for atmosphere including aerosol subcomponents, we refer to all grid points by a given horizontal location. Therefore, computations between physical columns are independent, and dependencies only exist in the vertical direction. We used 72 as the maximum number of vertical levels in the tests.

In the parallel implementation as described in [11], physical columns are distributed among the processes based on a set of load balancing strategies. To get better caching effects, all the columns assigned to a process will be grouped in a data structure called a chunk. In each chunk, a maximum number of columns $PCOL$ is specified at compilation time. We used $PCOL = 16$ in the tests when not specified explicitly. Grid points in a chunk can be referenced with a local column index and a vertical index.

The loop structure is shown in Code 4.1.

5   Offloading Computations to GPUs

Our initial thought was to copy all the data needed by MAM to GPUs when beginning the computation of atmosphere physics, then to copy the data back to the host when exiting. However, this is unfeasible because 1) MAM has a large code base with tens of thousands of lines of source code, 2) MAM does checkpointing with various I/O operations scattered all over the code, and 3) an excessive number of temporary subroutines or function variables need to be promoted and explicitly allocated on the GPU memory as well.

Therefore, we profiled the code first and identified particularly expensive loops. Unfortunately, profiling results showed that the run time distributed across many functions, meaning we could not focus on just a couple of loops; instead, we had to work on many loops at the same time. The programming effort needed to optimize different kernels also varies significantly by kernel. In this section, we will show four representative kernels in increasing order of code refactoring effort.

5.1   Kernel: subgrid_mean_updraft

The first kernel is called *subgrid_mean_updraft* shown in Algorithm 5.1, which calculates the mean updraft velocity inside a general circulation model grid. Later in the code, the mean velocity is used as the characteristic updraft velocity to calculate the ice nucleation rate. The loop body has been modified from its original implementation to remove some temporary variables and get slightly better performance.

By examining the loops, we can find that there is no data dependence across loops k and i. Therefore, we can collapse these two loops and create $pver *
ncol$ independent threads on GPUs. As we mentioned before, the number of maximum vertical levels $pver$ is defined as 72, and each block can hold at most $PCOL$ (=16) number of columns ($ncol <= PCOL$). These two collapsed loops can thus create at most 1152 threads on GPUs. For each thread, variables zz and wa can be treated as private variables, while variables $wsig$ and $w0$ need to be copied from host to GPU memory. The amount of data is small (only $2 * PCOL * pver * sizeof(real(r8))$ bytes, roughly 18 KB). Variable ww needs to be created on GPUs and copied back to the host. The OpenACC directive in line 1 is used to offload to GPUs. The PGI compiler can automatically figure out the parallelism for loop $ibin$ in line 7 and sum computation in line 17, creating the corresponding threads. There is therefore no need to add explicit OpenACC directives.

For initial simplicity, we measured the performance using six MPI processes on a Summit node so that each MPI rank can offload its work to one exclusive GPU, as there are six Nvidia Volta GPUs on a node. The performance is shown in Fig. 4 labeled as *subgrid*. The run times of six MPI ranks on IBM Power9 only are labeled as *CPU*. The run times of using IBM Power9 with Nvidia GPUs are labeled as *CPU+GPU*. For kernel *subgrid_mean_updraft*, using GPUs can improve the performance by roughly 20X compared with running on CPU only. The OpenACC directive maps threads to the GPU with $num\_gangs = 1152$, $num\_worker = 1$, and $num\_vectors = 128$. We can limit the length of vector threads to 64 instead of 128 to reduce memory usage on GPUs by defining $vector\_length(64)$. However, we did not observe a noticeable performance difference.

As we only needed to look into the kernel itself, the kernel is only about 20 lines, and only a small amount of data needs to be transferred between the host and the device, the first kernel was overall relatively simple to offload.

Notice that the performance comparison between $GPUs + CPUs$ and $CPUs$ in Fig. 4 was to see the role of GPU offloading, not for fair performance comparisons between GPUs and CPUs (See Section VI for fair comparisons). In addition, we compared the OpenACC ports to the original CPU implementations as our main focus was on offloading from the original CPU version. OpenACC offers portability across GPUs and CPUs with a single source. We ran our OpenACC code on CPUs as well to verify the performance portability, and observed a slightly better performance when compared to the original CPU implementation of the code. We didn't include the portability discussion across GPUs and CPUs in this paper again to focus on the offloading discussion.

5.1 Kernel: subgrid_mean_updraft (subgrid)

```
1: !$acc parallel loop collapse(2) copyin(wsig,w0) copyout(ww) private(zz,wa)
2: do k = 1, pver
3: do i = 1, ncol
4:    sigma = max(0.001_r8, wsig(i,k))
5:    wlarge = w0(i,k)
6:    xx = 6._r8 * sigma / nbin
7:    do ibin = 1, nbin                              ▷ constant nbin=50
8:       yy = wlarge - 3._r8*sigma + 0.5*xx
9:       yy = yy + (ibin-1)*xx
10:      zz(ibin) = yy * exp(-1.*(yy-wlarge)**2/(2*sigma**2))/(sigma*sqrt(2*pi))*xx
11:      if (zz(ibin) .gt. 0._r8) then
12:         wa(ibin) = zz(ibin)
13:      else
14:         wa(ibin) = 0._r8
15:      endif
16:   end do
17:   sum_wa = sum( wa(:))
18:   if (sum_wa .gt. 0._r8) then
19:      ww(i,k) = sum_wa
20:   else
21:      ww(i,k) = 0.001_r8
22:   end if
23: end do
24: end do
```

5.2 Kernel: hetfrz_classnuc_cam_calc

The next kernel is called *hetfrz_classnuc_cam_calc*, which calculates the heterogeneous freezing rates from classical nucleation theory. The code is shown in Algorithm 5.2. First, we reordered the indices of three-dimensional variables, *awcam*, *awfacm*, etc., from (*pcols, pver, 3*) to (*3, pcols, pver*) to get better data locality. This change improved the kernel performance about 3% on CPUs.

One big difference from Algorithm 5.1 is that this kernel calls the subroutines *hetfrz_classnuc_calc*, *svp_water*, and *svp_ice*, which are developed in other source files. These subroutines then further call other subroutines. We needed to go over all the subroutines and functions in the caller-callee tree to add *routine* directives. Another major difference is that this kernel uses many more variables defined either in modules or subroutines. For module variables, we use the *declare* directive to create the variable on the GPU device and the *update* directive to transfer the data between host and device memory. For other variables, we use unstructured data regions to explicitly control data movement so that these variables can be reused by several offloaded kernels together. The *default(present)* directive indicates that data used in the kernel but not defined in the *parallel* loop directive are treated as present in the device memory. No data transfer is needed.

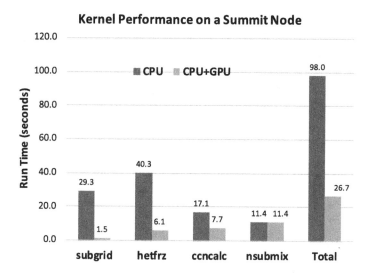

Fig. 4. The CPU and CPU+GPU performance for different kernels when running six MPI ranks on a Summit node.

The performance of the second kernel is shown in Fig. 4 labled as *hetfrz*. Compared with the CPU results, we observed about a 6X speedup with GPUs, much less than the 20X speedup for the previous kernel *subgrid_mean_updraft*. This is reasonable, as this kernel is much more complicated. The inside subroutine *hetfrz_classnuc_calc* itself has over 500 lines of code, with many *if* statements. Although the Nvidia Volta GPU handles *if* statements much more efficiently than earlier generations, many nested *if* statements could still slow down the performance significantly. In addition, this subroutine uses 15,304 bytes of stack frame, producing 420 bytes of spill stores and 420 bytes of spill loads. This kernel also does not have an additional nested loop to be parallelized like the first kernel does; the parallelism is limited to the k and i loops, which is mapped to the GPUs with $num\_gangs = ncol$, $num\_workers = 1$, and $vector\_length = 128$. As *ncol* is at most 16, the 80 SMs on a GPU could not be fully utilized.

5.3   Kernel: ccncalc

The third kernel is called *ccncalc*, and is used to calculate the number of concentrations of aerosols activated when cloud condensation nuclei are at supersaturation. The code is shown in Algorithm 5.3. The *loadaer* subroutine called in line 8 is used to extract data from *pbuf* to the three variables *naerosol, vaerosol,* and *hygro*. E3SM adopts a very complicated buffer management strategy. Extracting data through the buffer (pointed by the top level pointer *pbuf*) not only involves pointer tracing and type casting but also needs to access a lot of auxiliary data structures. To avoid such complexity, we separated this subroutine from other codes as shown in Algorithm 5.4. At the same time, we augmented variables

5.2 Kernel: hetfrz_classnuc_cam_calc (hetfrz)

```
 1: !$acc declare create(ncnst, nmodes, ...)          ▷ create module variables on device
 2: !$acc update device(ncnst, nmodes, ...)
 3: ...
 4: !$acc enter data create(total_aer_num, ...)
 5: ...
 6: !$acc parallel loop collapse(2) private(fn), copyin(t,pmid) &
 7: !$acc& copyout(frzbccnt,...) default(present)
 8: do k = top_lev, pver
 9: do i = 1, ncol
10:    if (t(i,k) .gt. 235.15_r8 .and. t(i,k) .lt. 269.15_r8) then
11:       qcic = min(qc(i,k)/lcldm(i,k), 5.e-3_r8)
12:       ncic = max(nc(i,k)/lcldm(i,k), 0._r8)
13:       con1 = 1._r8/(1.333_r8*pi)**0.333_r8
14:       r3lx = con1*(rho(i,k)*qcic/(rhoh2o*max(ncic*rho(i,k), 1.0e6_r8)))**0.333_r8
15:       r3lx = max(4.e-6_r8, r3lx)
16:       supersatice = svp_water(t(i,k))/svp_ice(t(i,k))
17:                                         ▷ svp_water and svp_ice are two functions
18:       fn(1) = factnum(i,k,mode_accum_idx)
19:       if (nmodes == MAM3_nmodes .or. nmodes == MAM4_nmodes) then
20:          fn(2) = factnum(i,k,mode_accum_idx)
21:          fn(3) = factnum(i,k,mode_coarse_idx)
22:       else if (nmodes == MAM7_nmodes) then
23:          fn(2) = factnum(i,k,mode_finedust_idx)
24:          fn(3) = factnum(i,k,mode_coardust_idx)
25:       end if
26:       call hetfrz_classnuc_calc( &
27:          deltatin, t(i,k), pmid(i,k), supersatice, &
28:          fn, r3lx, ncic*rho(i,k)*1.0e-6_r8, frzbcimm(i,k), frzduimm(i,k), &
29:          frzbccnt(i,k), frzducnt(i,k), frzbcdep(i,k), frzdudep(i,k), hetraer(:,i,k), &
30:          awcam(:,i,k), awfacm(:,i,k), dstcoat(:,i,k), total_aer_num(:,i,k), &
31:          coated_aer_num(:,i,k), uncoated_aer_num(:,i,k), &
32:          total_interstitial_aer_num(:,i,k), &
33:          total_cloudborne_aer_num(:,i,k), errstring)
34:                        ▷ hetfrz_classnuc_calc is a sequential routine with hundreds of lines
35:    end if
36: end do
37: end do
38: ...
39: !$acc exit data delete(total_aer_num, ...)
```

naerosol, vaerosol, and hygro from one dimension (pcols) to three dimensions (pcols, ntot_amode, pver) to save their values for the next loop.

We created a data region to transfer data between the host and device memories so that they can be used by other kernels as well. The *parallel* loop directive at line 11 can map the kernel to the GPU with $num\_gangs = pver - top\_lev + 1$, $num\_workers = 1$ and $vector\_length = 128$. The compilers can automatically

5.3 Kernel: ccncalc

```
 1: do k=top_lev,pver
 2:     do i=1,ncol
 3:         a(i)=surften_coef/tair(i,k)
 4:         smcoef(i)=smcoefcoef*a(i)*sqrt(a(i))
 5:     end do
 6:     do m=1,ntot_amode
 7:         phase=3
 8:         call loadaer(state, pbuf, 1, ncol, k, &
 9:             m, cs, phase, naerosol, vaerosol, hygro)
10:                              ▷ get data from pbuf to naerosol, vaerosol, and hygro
11:         where(naerosol(:ncol) .gt. 1.e-3_r8)
12:             amcube(:ncol)=amcubecoef(m)*vaerosol(:ncol)/naerosol(:ncol)
13:             sm(:ncol)=smcoef(:ncol)/sqrt(hygro(:ncol)*amcube(:ncol))
14:         elsewhere
15:             sm(:ncol)=1._r8
16:         endwhere
17:         do l=1,psat
18:             do i=1,ncol
19:                 arg(i)=argfactor(m)*log(sm(i)/super(l))
20:                 ccn(i,k,l)=ccn(i,k,l)+naerosol(i)*0.5_r8*(1._r8-erf(arg(i)))
21:             enddo
22:         enddo
23:     enddo
24: enddo
```

parallelize lines 13, 19, and 26. Performance results are shown in Fig. 4. For this kernel, we only achieved a 2.2X speedup. This was because the *loadaer* loop consumes about one quarter of the total run time. This part cannot be accelerated. If we exclude the *loadaer* effect, the actual speedup is about 5X. Also, profiling results indicate that transferring the data consumes more time than the actual kernel computation.

5.4 Kernel: nsubmix

The last kernel is called *nsubmix* and computes the vertical diffusion and nucleation of cloud droplets. The source code is outlined in Algorithm 5.5. Line 1 is the outermost loop. There are more than four hundred lines of code between line 1 and line 3 consisting of many small loops. At first, we tried to parallelize the outermost loop, but the code complexity and the amount of data needing to be transferred meant the overhead ultimately neutralized the benefits. Next, we shifted our focus to line 3, which consumes about 40% of the run time. From line 5, we deduced that variables *srcn, raercol*, and *raercol_cw* depend on their previous iteration values. As such, the loop at line 3 must be executed sequentially. Finally, we focused on the loop at line 17. The variable *ntot_amode* is a small number unimportant to parallelize. By carefully examining the code, we found an approach to combine the loops at lines 17 and 28 by creating a new variable

5.4 Kernel: ccncalc gpu

```
1: do k=top_lev,pver
2: do m = 1, ntot_amode
3:    call loadaer(state, pbuf, 1, ncol, k, &
4:        m, cs, phase, naerosol(:,m,k), vaerosol(:,m,k), hygro(:,m,k))
5:                              ▷ define naerosol, vaeroosol, hygro as 3D instead of 1D
6: end do
7: end do
8:
9: !$acc data copy(ccn) copyin(vaerosol, naerosol, hydro) &
10: !$acc& copyin(super,amcubecoef,argfactor,tair,smccoefcoef,surften_coef)
11: !$acc parallel loop private(a,smcoef,arg,sm,amcube,m,i,l) default(present)
12: do k=top_lev,pver
13:    do i=1,ncol
14:      a(i)=surften_coef/tair(i,k)
15:      smcoef(i)=smcoefcoef*a(i)*sqrt(a(i))
16:    end do
17:    do m=1,ntot_amode
18:      phase=3
19:      where(naerosol(:ncol) .gt. 1.e-3_r8)
20:        amcube(:ncol)=amcubecoef(m)*vaerosol(:ncol.m.k)/naerosol(:ncol,m,k)
21:        sm(:ncol)=smcoef(:ncol)/sqrt(hygro(:ncol,m,k)*amcube(:ncol))
22:      elsewhere
23:        sm(:ncol)=1._r8
24:      endwhere
25:      do l=1,psat
26:        do i=1,ncol
27:          arg(i)=argfactor(m)*log(sm(i)/super(l))
28:          ccn(i,k,l)=ccn(i,k,l)+naerosol(i,m,k)*0.5_r8*(1._r8-erf(arg(i)))
29:        enddo
30:      enddo
31:    enddo
32:  enddo
33: ...
34: !$acc end data
```

mam_idx_1d. The new code structure for lines 17–36 is shown in Algorithm 5.6. We could then achieve parallelism of $ncnst\_tot \times (pver - top\_lev + 1)$ and offload it to GPUs. Although the computation itself was accelerated greatly, the total run time was still slightly longer than that without offloading; the performance suffers from the high cost of data movement and the high overhead of kernel launching. We will leave this kernel on CPUs and pursue other approaches, such as async operation, to accelerate the computation.

5.5 Kernel: nsubmix outline

```
1:  do i = 1, ncol
2:  ...                                              ▷ more than 400 lines of code
3:    do n = 1, nsubmix
4:    qncld(:) = qcld(:)
5:    nnew ⟷ nsav                                    ▷ nnew = 1, nnsav=0
6:    srcn(:) = 0
7:    do m = 1, ntot_amode
8:      mm = mam_idx(m,0)
9:      srcn(top_lev:pver-1) = srcn(top_lev:pver-1) + &
10:         nact(top_lev:pver-1,m)*raercol(top_lev+1:pver,mm,nsav)
11:      tmpa = raercol(pver,mm,nsav)*nact(pver,m) + &
12:         raercol_cw(pver, mm, nsav) * (...)
13:      srcn(pver) = srcn(pver) + max(0.0_r8, tmpa)
14:    enddo
15:    call explmix(qcld, srcn, ..., qncld)          ▷ compute qcld from qncld
16:
17:    do m = 1, ntot_amode
18:      mm = mam_idx(m,0)
19:      source(top_lev:pver-1) = &
20:         nact(top_lev:pver-1,m)*(raercol(top_lev+1:pver,mm,nsav))
21:      tmpa = ...                                   ▷ same as line 9
22:      source(pver) = max(0.0_r8, tmpa)
23:      call explmix(raercol_cw(:, mm, nnew), source, ..., raercol_cw(:, mm, nsav), ...)
24:                          ▷ compute raercol_cw(,,nnew) from raercol_cw(,,nsav)
25:      call explmix(raercol(:, mm, nnew), source, ..., raercol(:, mm, nsav), &
26:         raercol_cw(:, mm, nsav))
27:                ▷ compute raercol(,,nnew) from raercol(,,nsav) and raercol_cw(,,nsav)
28:      do l = 1, nspec_amode(m)
29:        mm = mam_idx(m, l)
30:        source(top_lev:pver-1) = ▷ same as line 17 except using mact instead nact
31:        tmpa =          ▷ same as line 19 except using mact instead nact variable
32:        source(pver) = max(0.0_r8, tmpa)
33:        call explmix                              ▷ same as line 23
34:        call explmix                              ▷ same as line 25
35:      enddo
36:    enddo
37:    enddo
38:  ...
39: end do
```

6   MAM Kernel Performance Discussion

By analyzing these four kernels, we first realized that our kernels are light, as the average run time for each is within milliseconds. Table 2 shows the average run times on CPUs and GPUs.

Secondly, the parallelism mainly comes from the vertical level ($pver$) and the number of columns in a block ($pcol$). Considering that the Nvidia GPUs use

5.6 Kernel: nsubmix restructure

```
1: do mm = 1, ncnst_tot
2:     do k = top_lev, pver
3:         m = mam_idx_1d(1, mm)
4:         l = mam_idx_1d(2, mm)
5:         kp1 = min(k+1,pver)
6:         km1 = max(k-1,top_lev)
7:         if (l == 0) then
8:             tmpa = nact(k,m)*raercol(kp1,mm,nsav)
9:             if (k == pver) then
10:                tmpa = tmpa + raercol_cw(pver,mm,nsav)*(nact(pver,m) - taumix)
11:                tmpa = max(0.0_r8, tmpa)
12:            endif
13:         else
14:             tmpa = mact(k,m)*raercol(kp1,mm,nsav)
15:             if (k == pver) then
16:                tmpa = tmpa + raercol_cw(pver,mm,nsav)*(mact(pver,m) - taumix)
17:                tmpa = max(0.0_r8, tmpa)
18:            endif
19:         endif
20:         call explmix(raercol_cw(k, mm, nnew), source, ...)
21:         call explmix(raercol(k, mm, nnew), source, ...)
22:     end do
23: end do
```

Table 2. The average run times on CPUs and GPUs.

	Total CPU time (s)	Total GPU time (s)	Number of calls	Avg on CPU (ms)	Avg on GPU (ms)
subgrid	29.3	1.5	5520	5.3	0.3
hetfrz	40.3	6.1	5520	7.3	1.1
ccncalc	17.1	2.8 [3]	5520	3.1	1.4
nsubmix	11.4	11.4	88740	0.1	

a warp size of 32 as the scheduling unit, neither $pver(= 72)$ nor $ncol(<= 16)$ is a perfect fit, resulting in thread resource waste. This waste exceeds half the resource total when $ncol$ threads are scheduled together as vector threads.

To improve the performance from an application perspective, the size of $pcol$ and $pver$ can therefore be aligned to multiples of warp size. Figure 5 shows the performance of increasing the $pcol$ from 16 to 32, then to 64 on GPUs. Increasing the $pcol$ size can improve the CPU performance only slightly (<5%). But for GPUs, increasing the $pcol$ value from 16 to 64 can improve the performance 6.9X, 6.5X, and 4.0X for *subgrid, hetfrz,* and *ccncalc*, respectively, leaving the unparallelized kernel *nsubmix* as the major performance bottleneck. While only consuming about 12% of the total time initially, *nsubmix* takes up more than 80% of the total time when *pcol* = 64.

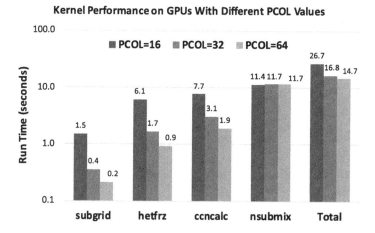

Fig. 5. The GPU performance for different kernels when running six MPI ranks on a Summit node using different *PCOL* values.

6.1 Multi-Process Service (MPS)

For simplicity, we ran only six MPI ranks on a node so that each process can offload its work to one exclusive GPU. The Nvidia Volta GPUs support multi-process services. When mapping one, two, and four MPI processes to a Nvidia Volta GPU, we can see that all kernels scale almost linearly as shown in Fig. 6. The performance results also reflect the fact that our application does not provide enough parallelism. Therefore, mapping one MPI rank to a Volta GPU cannot saturate the thread resources. Unfortunately, assigning more than four MPI ranks to a GPU causes an out of memory error.

6.2 Scaling Results

Figure 7 shows the parallel scaling results when running across multiple nodes. For the CPU results, we used 42 MPI ranks per node while for the CPU+GPU results, we used 24 MPI ranks per node (full node !) so that four MPI ranks were launched on each GPU. As shown earlier, running more than four MPI ranks per GPU node causes an out of memory error. The results show that both CPU and CPU+GPU versions scale well across different numbers of nodes. However, when using GPUs the performance improves about 5X. Currently, the GPU performance is limited by the *nsubmix* kernel.

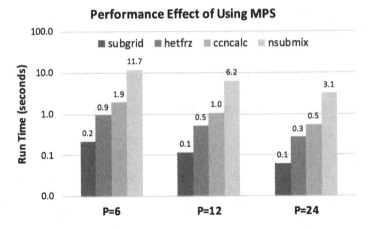

Fig. 6. The MPS performance effect on a Summit node. Doubling the number of MPI ranks doubles the performance.

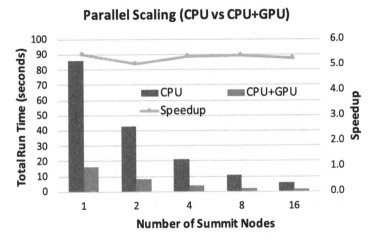

Fig. 7. The scaling performance of MAM kernels for both CPU and CPU+GPU and their relative speedups.

7   Summary and Conclusion

In this work, we investigated how to use GPUs to accelerate the performance of MAM, a module of E3SM on Summit through OpenACC. We have achieved over a 5X performance speedup by offloading some of the kernels to Nvidia Volta GPUs. The results revealed that under the current E3SM configuration for product runs, some parameter settings do not suit offloading, such as the number of columns per block and the number of vertical levels. These settings not only severely limit the degree of parallelism but also fail to make effective use of GPU thread resources, becoming a performance bottleneck.

Moreover, run times scatter across many kernels, and each computational kernel is relatively light, with average run times in milliseconds or less per call. Such light computational kernels particularly require OpenACC implementation to further reduce overhead from kernel launching, data transfer, etc. The results also showed that performance was primarily limited by the kernel *nsubmix*, which did not benefit from GPU offloading; we plan to work on this in the future. We are currently looking into different approaches to improve MAM's performance, such as overlapping computations and data transfer using async OpenACC directives and possibly merging kernel computations.

Acknowledgements. All authors from Lawrence Berkeley National Laboratory were supported by the Office of Advanced Scientific Computing Research in the Department of Energy Office of Science under contract number DE-AC02-05CH11231. This research used resources of the Oak Ridge Leadership Computing Facility at the Oak Ridge National Laboratory, which is supported by the Office of Science of the U.S. Department of Energy under Contract No. DE-AC05-00OR22725.

References

1. Bertagna, L., et al.: HOMMEXX 1.0: a performance portable atmospheric dynamical core for the energy exascale earth eystem model. Geosci. Model Dev. **12**, 1423–1441 (2019)
2. Dennis, J.M., et al.: CAM-SE: a scalable spectral element dynamical core for the Community Atmosphere Model. Int. J. High Perform. Comput. **26**, 74–89 (2012)
3. https://doep3meeting2019.lbl.gov
4. Energy Exascale System Scale. https://e3sm.org
5. Gettelman, A., Morrison, H.: Advanced two-moment bulk microphysics for global models. Part I: off-line tests and comparison with other schemes. J. Clim. **28**, 1268–1287 (2015)
6. Gettelman, A., Morrison, H.: Advanced two-moment bulk microphysics for global models. Part II: global model solutions and aerosol-cloud interactions. J. Clim. **28**, 1288–1307 (2015)
7. Larkin, J.: OpenACC, Performance Portability Delivered? https://drive.google.com/drive/folders/1f5Txw6hnlp5YhcJUfa_bX7uBYDfQqwf0
8. Norman, C., et al.: The OpenACC port of the Cloud Resolving Model (CRM) in the E3SM-Multi-scale Modeling Framework. https://www2.cisl.ucar.edu/sites/default/files/Norman-multicore_2018.pdf
9. OpenACC: More science, less programming. https://www.openacc.org
10. The OpenACC Application Programming Interface, version 2.7. https://www.openacc.org/sites/default/files/inline-files/OpenACC.2.7.pdf
11. Worley, P.H., Drake, J.B.: Performance portability in the physical parameterizations of the community atmospheric model. Int. J. High Perform. Comput. Appl. **19**, 187–201 (2005)
12. Summit: Summit User Guide. https://www.olcf.ornl.gov/for-users/system-user-guides/summit/summit-user-guide/
13. Trott, C.: The Kokkos C++ Performance Portability EcoSystem. https://drive.google.com/drive/folders/1f5Txw6hnlp5YhcJUfa_bX7uBYDfQqwf0

Evaluation of Directive-Based GPU Programming Models on a Block Eigensolver with Consideration of Large Sparse Matrices

Fazlay Rabbi[1]([⊠]), Christopher S. Daley[2], Hasan Metin Aktulga[1], and Nicholas J. Wright[2]

[1] Michigan State University, East Lansing, MI 48823, USA
{rabbimd,hma}@msu.edu
[2] Lawrence Berkeley National Laboratory, Berkeley, CA 94720, USA
{csdaley,njwright}@lbl.gov

Abstract. Achieving high performance and performance portability for large-scale scientific applications is a major challenge on heterogeneous computing systems such as many-core CPUs and accelerators like GPUs. In this work, we implement a widely used block eigensolver, Locally Optimal Block Preconditioned Conjugate Gradient (LOBPCG), using two popular directive based programming models (OpenMP and OpenACC) for GPU-accelerated systems. Our work differs from existing work in that it adopts a holistic approach that optimizes the full solver performance rather than narrowing the problem into small kernels (*e.g.*, SpMM, SpMV). Our LOPBCG GPU implementation achieves a $2.8\times$–$4.3\times$ speedup over an optimized CPU implementation when tested with four different input matrices. The evaluated configuration compared one Skylake CPU to one Skylake CPU and one NVIDIA V100 GPU. Our OpenMP and OpenACC LOBPCG GPU implementations gave nearly identical performance. We also consider how to create an efficient LOBPCG solver that can solve problems larger than GPU memory capacity. To this end, we create microbenchmarks representing the two dominant kernels (inner product and SpMM kernel) in LOBPCG and then evaluate performance when using two different programming approaches: tiling the kernels, and using Unified Memory with the original kernels. Our tiled SpMM implementation achieves a $2.9\times$ and $48.2\times$ speedup over the Unified Memory implementation on supercomputers with PCIe Gen3 and NVLink 2.0 CPU to GPU interconnects, respectively.

Keywords: Sparse solvers · Performance optimization · Performance portability · Directive based programming models · OpenMP 4.5 · OpenACC

Electronic supplementary material The online version of this chapter (https://doi.org/10.1007/978-3-030-49943-3_4) contains supplementary material, which is available to authorized users.

© Springer Nature Switzerland AG 2020
S. Wienke and S. Bhalachandra (Eds.): WACCPD 2019, LNCS 12017, pp. 66–88, 2020.
https://doi.org/10.1007/978-3-030-49943-3_4

1   Introduction

There is a pressing need to migrate and optimize applications for execution on GPUs and other accelerators. Future planned systems for the Department of Energy Office of Advanced Scientific Computing Research (DOE ASCR) include Perlmutter at NERSC (AMD CPU + NVIDIA GPU nodes), Aurora at ALCF (Intel CPU + Intel Xe accelerator nodes), and Frontier at OLCF (AMD CPU + AMD GPU nodes). The full capability of these systems can only be realized by making efficient use of the accelerators on the compute nodes. Most efforts to use accelerators to date have involved scientists using the CUDA programming language to target NVIDIA GPUs. The success of these efforts, the expected marginal gains in general-purpose CPU performance, and the understanding that special purpose accelerators are the best way to obtain significant performance gains within a fixed financial and power budget convinced DOE ASCR to invest in accelerator-based systems. However, CUDA alone is not an appropriate method to target accelerators produced by different vendors, e.g. NVIDIA, AMD, Intel, Xilinx, although there are efforts by AMD to use the HIP framework to convert CUDA to a more portable style of C++ [4].

In recent years, OpenACC and OpenMP have emerged as portable, base-language independent, and an increasingly robust and performant way to target accelerators. These directive-based methods have lowered the barrier of entry for application developers to target accelerators and are anticipated to be a key enabler for DOE users to efficiently use forthcoming supercomputers. However, there needs to be wider testing of OpenMP and OpenACC in scientific applications to address any shortcomings in the language specifications, improve the robustness and performance of vendor compilers, and continue to refine our understanding of best practices to migrate applications to accelerators. At the same time, the most efficient way to use accelerators is often achieved using optimized math and scientific libraries, e.g. cuBLAS and Tensorflow. Therefore, it will frequently be the case that non-trivial applications will increasingly need to mix optimized library calls with directives to obtain highest performance for the full application.

In this paper, we port and optimize a block eigensolver for GPUs using a combination of directives and optimized library calls. Sparse matrix computations (in the form of eigensolvers and linear solvers) are central to several applications in scientific computing and data analytics, from quantum many-body problems to graph analytics to machine learning. In the context of eigensolvers, performance of traditional sparse matrix-vector multiplication (SpMV) based methods are essentially limited by the memory system performance [33]. As such, block solver alternatives that rely on higher intensity operations such as sparse matrix-matrix multiplication (SpMM) and multiplication of vector blocks (*i.e.*, tall skinny matrices) have garnered the attention of several groups [7,29]. We adopt the Locally Optimal Block Preconditioned Conjugate Gradient (LOBPCG) [19,20] algorithm to represent block eigensolvers. Given that LOBPCG is a relatively popular method and requires a fairly complex implementation, it represents a suitable choice for our purposes.

An important issue in large scientific computing and data analysis work-loads is that applications' data usage often exceeds the available device memory space. For instance, Many Fermion Dynamics - nuclei (MFDn), which is a quantum many-body code based on the configuration interaction model, is a "total memory-bound" application, *i.e.*, scientific studies using this code typically utilize all memory (DRAM) space available, thus easily exceeding the total device memory available [5,24]. As such, our evaluation extends into such scenarios and we present remedies for the significant performance degradations observed due to large data transfers between host and device memories.

Our contributions in this study can be summarized as follows:

- We demonstrate that a complex block eigensolver can be implemented efficiently using a mix of accelerator directives (in both OpenMP and OpenACC frameworks) and optimized library functions. We obtain up to a 4.3× speedup over a well optimized CPU implementation.
- We show that the performance of the Unified Memory version of SpMM, the dominant kernel in LOBPCG, depends on the supercomputer used and apparently the underlying CPU to GPU interconnect, when application working set exceeds GPU memory capacity. We measure a 13.4× performance loss when migrating from a supercomputer with a PCIe Gen3 CPU to GPU interconnect to one with NVLink 2.0.
- We address the Unified Memory performance portability issue by tiling the dominant kernels in LOBPCG. This obtains the highest performance on both supercomputers which have different CPU to GPU interconnects.

The paper is organized as follows. In Sect. 2, we describe the related work on efforts to port LOBPCG solvers to GPUs, application experience using OpenMP and OpenACC directives, and the use of Unified Memory to simplify porting applications to GPUs. In Sect. 3, we describe the kernel steps in the LOBPCG solver, the baseline OpenMP version of the LOBPCG solver including the library dependencies, and the steps we took to port the LOBPCG solver to GPUs. It also describes our tiling method for expensive kernels in the LOBPCG algorithm when a problem exceeds the GPU memory capacity. Finally, it describes the Cori-GPU and Summit platforms used to evaluate the performance of our directive based LOBPCG implementation and tiled microbenchmarks. In Sect. 4, we present performance results obtained on the Cori-GPU and Summit supercomputers. Section 5 discusses the key lessons and aims to provide advice for application developers based on our observations. Finally, Sect. 6 summarizes our conclusions and plans for future work.

2   Background and Related Work

Sparse Matrix Operations (SpMV/SpMM) on GPUs: Sparse matrix-vector multiplication (SpMV) and sparse matrix-matrix multiplication (SpMM) are the main kernels of many iterative solvers [19,22], machine learning techniques and other scientific applications. Several optimization techniques have been proposed for SpMV on GPUs [8,9,15,35]. However, performance of SpMV is bounded by memory bandwidth [33]. The main appeal of block eigensolvers (i.e. LOBPCG algorithm) is their high arithmetic intensity which is especially important to reap the full benefits of GPUs. The main computational kernels involved in block iterative solvers are the multiplication of a sparse matrix with multiple vectors and level-3 BLAS operations on dense vector blocks. Optimizing the SpMM kernel on GPUs has been studied in several research works. Yang et al. [34] propose two novel algorithms for SpMM operation on GPUs that take the sparse matrix input in compressed-sparse-row (CSR) format and focus on latency hiding with instruction-level parallelism and load-balancing. They find out a memory access pattern that allows efficient access into both input and output matrices which is the main enabler for their excellent performance on SpMM. A common optimization strategy of SpMM is to rely on a special sparse matrix representation to exploit the nonzeros efficiently. Most commonly used sparse matrix storage variants other than CSR format are ELLPACK called ELLPACK-R [27] and a variant of Sliced ELLPACK called SELL-P [7]. Hong et al. [16] separates the sparse matrix into heavy and light rows in order to perform dynamic load-balancing. They process the heavy rows by CSR and the light rows by doubly compressed sparse row (DCSR) in order to take advantage of tiling. However, these special matrix storage formats incur some additional computational and format conversion cost in the full computational pipeline.

Anzt et al. [7] optimize the performance of SpMM using ELLPACK format [6] and compare the performance of their CPU-GPU implementation with the multithreaded CPU implementation of LOBPCG provided in the BLOPEX [21] package. All of their kernels were written in CUDA 5.5 and they evaluated the performance experiment on two Intel Sandy Bridge CPUs and one NVIDIA K40 GPU. Dziekonski et al. [13] implement LOBPCG method with an inexact nullspace filtering approach to find eigenvalues in electromagnetics analysis.

Most of the prior work focused on optimizing either the SpMV or the SpMM operation on GPUs with the ultimate goal of accelerating the iterative solver used in a scientific application. A distinguishing aspect of this paper is that we adopt a holistic approach that includes all computational kernels required for the LOBPCG solver. We use directive based programming models to achieve portability. We also investigate the scenario where the total memory footprint exceeds the device memory capacity and propose a solution that addresses performance degradations seen with NVIDIA's generic "Unified Memory" approach (see below).

OpenMP/OpenACC: OpenMP and OpenACC are two directive-based methods to parallelize serial applications. Both languages enable a programmer to run application kernels on a GPU. Multiple compilers support these directives and can generate GPU code. The quality of GPU support in OpenMP and OpenACC compilers is evaluated in [23] on a suite of 4 mini applications. Here, the authors find issues with all compilers as well as challenges in creating a single portable code which compiles and executes efficiently for all compilers. The interoperability of CUDA and OpenACC is evaluated in [32]. The author successfully combines hand-written CUDA with OpenACC when using the PGI compiler. Our work evaluates the performance of OpenMP and OpenACC implementations of a block eigensolver, as well the interoperability of these runtime systems with optimized CUDA libraries for 3 different compilers.

Unified Memory: Unified Memory (UM) is a programming feature which provides a single memory address space accessible by all processors in a compute node. It greatly simplifies GPU programming because the same single pointer to data can be used on both CPU and GPU. The NVIDIA Volta V100 GPU provides a page migration engine to move memory pages between CPU and GPU when the page is not in the memory of the processor accessing the data. NVIDIA evaluated UM performance using the PGI OpenACC compiler in [12]. The authors created UM versions of the OpenACC applications in the SPEC ACCEL 1.2 benchmark suite. They ran the applications on the Piz-Daint supercomputer and found that the UM versions ran at 95% of the performance of the original explicit data management versions. In [28], the NVIDIA presenter shows that the Gyrokinetic Toroidal Code (GTC) has almost identical performance on a x86+V100 system whether OpenACC data directives are used or not. Our work also compares UM against explicit data management, but additionally considers problems whose memory requirements are significantly over the device memory capacity. The performance of oversubscribing UM is evaluated in [18]. The authors find that UM can be up to 2× slower than explicit data management in several applications on an x86+V100 system. Our work considers performance on both x86 and Power GPU-accelerated systems.

3   Methodology

In this section, we provide an overview of the LOBPCG algorithm, our baseline CPU implementation, and the steps we took to port and optimize the CPU implementation to run efficiently on GPU-accelerated systems using OpenMP and OpenACC. We then describe our pathfinding activities for creating an efficient LOBPCG algorithm which can operate on matrices exceeding the device memory capacity. In particular, we discuss how we tiled the two most expensive kernels in LOBPCG and created microbenchmarks that enable performance comparison of programmer-controlled and system-controlled (i.e. Unified Memory) data movement schemes between the CPU and GPU. Finally, we describe the experimental platforms used for evaluating the performance of our LOBPCG and microbenchmark implementations on GPU-accelerated systems.

3.1   The LOBPCG Algorithm

LOBPCG is a commonly used block eigensolver based on the sparse matrix multiple vector multiplication kernel [19]. It is designed to find a prescribed number of the largest (or smallest) eigenvalues and the corresponding eigenvectors of a

---

Algorithm 1: LOBPCG Algorithm (for simplicity, without a preconditioner) used to solve $\hat{H}\Psi = E\Psi$

Input: $\hat{H}$, matrix of dimensions $N \times N$
Input: Ψ_0, a block of randomly initialized vectors of dimensions of $N \times m$
Output: Ψ and E such that $\|\hat{H}\Psi - \Psi E\|_F$ is small, and $\Psi^T\Psi = I_m$
1 Orthonormalize the columns of Ψ_0
2 $P_0 \leftarrow 0$
3 **for** $i = 0, 1, \ldots,$ *until convergence* **do**
4 $\quad E_i = \Psi_i^T \hat{H} \Psi_i$
5 $\quad R_i \leftarrow \hat{H}\Psi_i - \Psi_i E_i$
6 $\quad$ Apply the Rayleigh–Ritz procedure on span$\{\Psi_i, R_i, P_i\}$
7 $\quad \Psi_{i+1} \leftarrow \underset{S\in\text{span}\{\Psi_i.R_i,P_i\},\ S^TS=I_m}{\text{argmin}} \text{trace}(S^T\hat{H}S)$
8 $\quad P_{i+1} \leftarrow \Psi_{i+1} - \Psi_i$
9 $\quad$ Check convergence
10 **end**
11 $\Psi \leftarrow \Psi_{i+1}$

---

symmetric positive definite generalized eigenvalue problem $H\Psi = EB\Psi$ for a
given pair (H, B) of complex Hermitian or real symmetric matrices, where the
matrix B is also assumed positive-definite. Here, E is a diagonal matrix of the
sought eigenvalues and Ψ is the corresponding block of eigenvectors. Algorithm 1
shows the pseudocode of the LOBPCG algorithm for the standard eigenvalue
problem $H\Psi = E\Psi$. LOBPCG comprises high arithmetic intensity operations
(SpMM and Level-3 BLAS). In terms of memory, while the $\hat{H}$ matrix takes
up considerable space, when a large number of eigenpairs are needed (e.g., in
dimensionality reduction, spectral clustering or quantum many-body problems),
memory needed for the block vector Ψ can be comparable to or even greater than
that of $\hat{H}$. In addition, other block vectors (residual R, preconditioned residual
W, previous direction P), block vectors from the previous iteration and the preconditioning matrix T must be stored (not shown in Algorithm 1 for simplicity),
and accessed at each iteration.

3.2 Baseline CPU Implementation

We implemented the baseline CPU version of LOBPCG using OpenMP and
OpenACC directives in C/C++. We adopted the Compress Sparse Row (CSR)
format to store the sparse matrix and used the `mkl_dcsrmm` routine from Intel
MKL library for the SpMM kernel. We also implemented a custom SpMM kernel
in both OpenMP and OpenACC, again based on the CSR format, and used it
with the PGI and IBM compilers. For all LAPACK and BLAS routines needed,
we used Intel MKL, the PGI-packaged LAPACK and BLAS libraries, and IBM
ESSL for Intel, PGI and IBM compilers, respectively.

3.3   A GPU Implementation of LOBPCG

The most expensive kernels in the baseline CPU version are the SpMM operation and the inner product of vector blocks $(X^T Y)$. The cuSPARSE [26] and cuBLAS CUDA libraries provide tuned versions of these kernels. We used `cusparseDcsrmm` for the SpMM operation and replaced `cblas_dgemm` routine with `cublasDgemm` for the vector block operations. We allocated the device data for these routines using `cudaMalloc`. We ported the remaining application kernels using OpenMP and OpenACC offloading pragmas. The application kernels are grouped together inside device data regions to avoid data movement between successive application kernels. However, the performance of this implementation was still poor because significant time was spent moving data between CPU and GPU. This happened because the application and library kernels were operating on distinct data on the GPU.

OpenMP and OpenACC provide a clause to enable the application kernels to operate on data already resident on the device. The clause is named `is_device_ptr` in OpenMP and `deviceptr` in OpenACC. We used the pointer returned by `cudaMalloc` in our OpenACC implementation. This approach caused a run time error in our OpenMP implementation compiled with LLVM/-Clang. We therefore replaced `cudaMalloc` with `omp_target_alloc` in our OpenMP implementation because the OpenMP 5.0 specification [2] states that "Support for device pointers created outside of OpenMP, specifically outside of the `omp_target_alloc` routine and the `use_device_ptr` clause, is implementation defined.". Figure 1 shows an example of the structure of most of our application kernels after using this clause. It enabled us to remove multiple Open-MP/OpenACC data regions and thus considerable data movement between the CPU and GPU[1].

All kernels run on the GPU except for some LAPACK routines, i.e., `LAPACKE-_dpotrf` and `LAPACKE_dsygv` which are not available in the CUDA toolkit math libraries. This causes 10 small matrices to move between CPU and GPU in each iteration of the LOBPCG method. As the sizes of those matrices are very small, we find that the overhead associated with these data movements are insignificant compared to the total execution time.

3.4   Tiling LOBPCG Kernels to Fit in GPU Memory Capacity

The LOBPCG GPU implementation described in Sect. 3.3 allocated the tall skinny matrices and the sparse matrix in GPU memory. This approach is limited to cases where the aggregated matrix memory footprint is less than the GPU memory capacity. However, a major challenge in many scientific domains [5,25, 30] (such as configuration interaction in MFDn) is the massive size of the sparse

---

[1] Alternatively, we could have copied the data to the device using OpenMP/OpenACC and then passed the device pointer to the CUDA library functions using OpenMP's `use_device_ptr` clause or OpenACC's `use_device` clause. We did not use this approach because we wanted the option to use `cudaMallocManaged` to allocate data in managed memory.

Before using `is_device_ptr`

```
// d_R and other device arrays allocated with omp_target_alloc
cublasDgemm(handle, CUBLAS_OP_N, CUBLAS_OP_N, b, numrows, b,
    &cudaAlpha, d_lambda, b, d_X, b, &cudaBeta, d_R, b);

// Copy output array d_R to the host array R
omp_target_memcpy(R, d_R, R_size * sizeof(double), 0, 0, h, t);

// Copy host array R to the device in OpenMP target data region
#pragma omp target data map(tofrom: newX[0 : X_size])\
    map(to: X[0 : X_size], R[0 : R_size])
{
    mat_mult(X, R, newX, numrows, b);
}

void mat_mult(double *src1, double *src2, double *dst,
              int row, int col)
{
#pragma omp target teams distribute parallel for collapse(2)
    for(int i = 0; i < row ; i++)
        for(int j = 0 ; j < col ; j++)
            dst[i * col + j] = src1[i * col + j] * src2[i * col + j];
}
```

After using `is_device_ptr`

```
// d_R and other device arrays allocated with omp_target_alloc
cublasDgemm(handle, CUBLAS_OP_N, CUBLAS_OP_N, b, numrows, b,
    &cudaAlpha, d_lambda, b, d_X, b, &cudaBeta, d_R, b);

// Pointers to device arrays passed into mat_mult function
mat_mult(d_X, d_R, d_newX, numrows, b);

void mat_mult(double *src1, double *src2, double *dst,
              int row, int col)
{
    // Use is_device_ptr because data is already on the device
#pragma omp target is_device_ptr(src1, src2, dst)
#pragma omp teams distribute parallel for collapse(2)
    for(int i = 0; i < row ; i++)
        for(int j = 0 ; j < col ; j++)
            dst[i * col + j] = src1[i * col + j] * src2[i * col + j];
}
```

Fig. 1. The use of `is_device_ptr` to avoid memory copies. Error checking is omitted for brevity.

matrix, which can have several billions of rows and columns and the total number of nonzeros can easily exceed trillions. In this subsection, we explain how we tiled the SpMM and inner product kernels ($X^T Y$) to operate on problems larger than the GPU memory capacity. We extracted each kernel into a standalone microbenchmark to check for correctness and enable performance evaluation. Although not described in this paper, we have also implemented and evaluated the linear combination kernel (XY) which has similar characteristics to the inner product kernel ($X^T Y$), but involves the multiplication of a tall-skinny vector block (X) with a small square matrix (Y).

SpMM Kernel: The SpMM kernel is typically the most expensive operation in LOBPCG. Figure 2 shows the tiling idea for the SpMM kernel for cases when the LOBPCG data is too large to fit into the GPU memory. For a given tile size β, we divide the sparse matrix into block of rows. Algorithm 2 describes the steps in our tiled SpMM kernel. In short, we copy the Y matrix to the GPU at the beginning and it resides there until all sparse matrix tiles are processed. Then, we extract the CSR format of each of the tiles and copy that to GPU memory. Then we apply the `cusparseDcsrmm` routine on the sparse matrix block and Y.

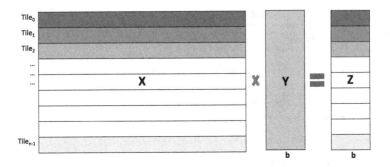

Fig. 2. Overview of tiling SpMM operation.

Algorithm 2: Tiled SpMM (`cusparseDcsrmm`) kernel

Input: X($m \times m$) sprase matrix in CSR format (val, rowPtr, colIndex),
  Y($m \times b$), β(tile size)
Output: Z($m \times b$)

1 $nrowblk = \lceil \frac{m}{\beta} \rceil$
2 **for** $i = 0$ to $nrowblk$ - 1 **do**
     // extract_CSR_tile() method extracts the CSR format of the i-th
     tile from the given sparse matrix
3   [rowPtrTile, colIndxTile, valTile, nnz_Tile] = extract_CSR_tile(val, rowPtr, colIndex, i)
4   cusparseDcsrmm(β, b, m, nnz_tile, 1.0, valTile, rowPtrTile, colIndxTile, R, m, 0.0, AR, β)
5   cudaDeviceSynchronize()
6   cudaMemcpy(Z[i-th tile], AR, cudaMemcpyDeviceToHost)
7   cudaDeviceSynchronize()
8 **end**

This produces the corresponding row blocks of the final output matrix Z. After processing each tile, we copy back the partial output to the corresponding tile of the Z matrix.

Inner Product Kernel: One of the most frequently invoked and expensive kernels in LOBPCG is the inner product operation ($Z = X^T Y$) between two tall skinny matrices. Hence, a well performing tiled inner product kernel is crucial for large problem sizes. Figure 3 shows the overview of the matrix tiling idea for the inner product kernel. X and Y are of size $m \times b$ where $m \gg b$. Both matrices are partitioned into $n = \lceil \frac{m}{\beta} \rceil$ tiles. In our custom inner product kernel, we transfer each tile of X and Y from CPU to GPU and apply `cublasDgemm` routine on each tile. We keep accumulating the partial output to a $b \times b$ matrix on the GPU. After processing all tiles, we copy back the final result to Z. Algorithm 3 gives an overview of our custom inner product kernel.

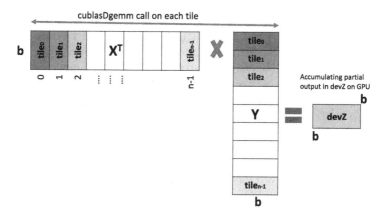

Fig. 3. Overview of tiling Inner Product kernel

Algorithm 3: Tiled Inner Product (`cublasDgemm`) Kernel

Input: X($m \times b$), Y($m \times b$), β(tile size)
Output: Z($b \times b$)
1 $nrowblk = \lceil \frac{m}{\beta} \rceil$
2 cudaMemset(devZ, 0.0, b*b*sizeof(b))
3 **for** $i = 0$ to $nrowblk$ - 1 **do**
4 $\quad$ cudaMemcpy(devX, X[i-th block], β * b, cudaMemcpyHostToDevice);
5 $\quad$ cudaMemcpy(devY, Y[i-th block], β * b, cudaMemcpyHostToDevice);
6 $\quad$ cudaDeviceSynchronize();
7 $\quad$ cublasDgemm(b, b, β, 1.0, devY, β, devX, β, 1.0, devZ, β);
8 $\quad$ cudaDeviceSynchronize()
9 **end**
10 cudaMemcpy(Z, devZ, b * b, cudaMemcpyDeviceToHost);

3.5 Hardware and Software Environment

We conducted all of our experiments on the Cori-GPU testbed at the National Energy Research Scientific Computing Center (NERSC) [1] and the Summit supercomputer at the Oak Ridge Leadership Computing Facility (OLCF) [3]. Cori-GPU is a Cray CS-Storm 500NX consisting of 18 compute nodes. Each compute node has two 20-core Skylake processors clocked at 2.4 GHz and 8 NVIDIA Tesla V100 "Volta" GPUs with 16 GBs of HBM per GPU. The V100 GPU model has a peak double precision performance of 7.0 TFLOP/s. There is a total of 384 GB DDR4 DRAM space on each node. The CPUs are connected to the GPUs via four PCIe 3.0 switches and the GPUs are connected to each other via NVIDIA's NVLink 2.0 interconnect. The Summit supercomputer is an IBM AC922 system consisting of 4608 compute nodes [31]. Each compute node has two 22-core IBM Power9 processors clocked at 3.1 GHz and 6 NVIDIA Tesla V100 "Volta" GPUs with 16 GBs of HBM per GPU. The V100 GPU model is based on the SXM2 form factor and has a peak double precision performance of 7.8

TFLOP/s. There is a total of 512 GB DDR4 DRAM space per node. Unlike Cori-GPU, the CPUs and GPUs in a Summit compute node are all connected with the high bandwidth NVLink 2.0 interconnect. This also provides cache coherence between CPUs and GPUs and enables system-wide atomics. The theoretical peak uni-directional bandwidth between 1 CPU and 1 GPU is 16 GB/s on Cori-GPU and 50 GB/s on Summit. However, the highest pageable bandwidth we measured from CPU to GPU was 5.2 GB/s on Cori-GPU and 25.0 GB/s on Summit.

The Cori-GPU and Summit supercomputers provide extensive software environments to compile OpenMP and OpenACC programs. Here, we list the software environment used in this paper. The software used on the Cori-GPU system were Intel Compiler v19.0.3 (OpenMP for CPU), LLVM/Clang compiler v9.0.0-git (OpenMP for GPU), and PGI compiler v19.5 (OpenACC for CPU and GPU). We used Intel MKL with the Intel and LLVM/Clang compilers and PGI's version of LAPACK with the PGI compiler. The GPU accelerated libraries were cuSPARSE and cuBLAS provided with CUDA v10.1.168. The software used on Summit were IBM XLC Compiler v16.1.1-3 (OpenMP for CPU and GPU) and PGI compiler v19.5 (OpenACC for CPU and GPU). We used IBM ESSL with the IBM XLC Compiler and PGI's version of LAPACK with the PGI compiler. Once again, the GPU accelerated libraries were cuSPARSE and cuBLAS provided with CUDA v10.1.168.

3.6   Experiments

In this section we explain the experiments conducted. The first set of experiments are used to evaluate the LOBPCG GPU implementation. The second set of experiments are used to evaluate our microbenchmarks on problems exceeding the GPU memory capacity.

Performance of the LOBPCG Solver: The CPU and GPU implementations of LOBPCG are evaluated using a series of real-world matrices with different sizes, sparsity patterns and application domains as shown in Table 1. The first 2 matrices are from the SuitSparse Matrix Collection [11] and the **Nm7** and **Nm8** matrices are extracted from two very large Hamiltonian matrices that arise in nuclear structure calculations with MFDn. Note that the test matrices have millions of rows and hundreds of millions of nonzeros. The memory footprint of these matrices vary from 2 GB to 7.8 GB using the CSR matrix format.

Table 1. Test matrices.

Matrix	Rows	Columns	Nonzeros	Size (GB)	Domain
Queen_4147	4,147,110	4,147,110	166,823,197	2.018	3D strctural problem
HV15R	2,017,169	2,017,169	283,073,458	3.405	Computational fluid dynamics
Nm7	4,985,422	4,985,422	647,663,919	7.792	MFDn
Nm8	7,579,303	7,579,303	592,099,416	7.136	MFDn

We measured the runtime of the LOBPCG CPU implementation on a single CPU socket on Cori-GPU and Summit nodes. The configurations used 1 thread per core and used the appropriate slurm, jsrun and OpenMP/OpenACC environment variables to bind the process and child threads. We did not use hyperthreading/SMT because our kernels are memory bandwidth bound. We measured the runtime of the LOBPCG GPU implementation on a single CPU socket and one GPU on Cori-GPU and Summit nodes. Our configurations only ever used a single CPU socket to avoid potential performance issues associated with non-uniform memory access time. We evaluated the compiler combinations described in Sect. 3.5 and measured runtime with application timers.

Performance of $X^T Y$ and SpMM Kernels for Large Matrices: Our next experiment evaluated the $X^T Y$ microbenchmark and SpMM microbenchmark on input problems exceeding GPU memory capacity on Cori-GPU and Summit. This experiment is designed to inform our future sparse solver implementations. We tested the tiled versions of the microbenchmarks so that we could easily separate how much time is spent in computation versus data movement between the CPU and GPU. If more time is spent in computation then data movement costs can potentially be hidden. In the $X^T Y$ microbenchmark, we chose to multiply two matrices of size $67,108,864 \times 48$ leading to a memory footprint of 51.54 GB. We set the tile size (β) to $131,072$ for the $X^T Y$ microbenchmark and $2,597,152$ for the SpMM microbenchmark as this gives us the best performance. The tile size (β) is an optimization parameter and one can vary it as long as the memory footprint required to process a single tile is less than GPU memory capacity. In the SpMM microbenchmark, we used a synthetic input matrix of 24 GB, leading to a memory footprint of 35.1 GB. The dimension of the synthetic sparse matrix is $14,957,833 \times 14,957,833$ with $1,946,671,770$ nonzeros. We multiplied this sparse matrix with a dense matrix of dimension $14,957,833 \times 48$. We used a multi-threaded RMAT graph generator [17] to generate our synthetic sparse matrix. We measured compute and data movement time using the nvprof profiler.

Performance of Tiled and Unified Memory Versions of SpMM: Our final experiment evaluated the Unified Memory version of the SpMM microbenchmark. The Unified Memory version was written in OpenACC and compiled with the PGI compiler and the compiler option -ta:tesla:managed to replace regular system memory allocations with managed memory allocations. We compared runtime against the tiled version of SpMM on Cori-GPU and Summit for two input matrices. The first input matrix is Nm7 (see Table 1) and leads to a microbenchmark memory footprint of 11.7 GB. The second input matrix is the synthetic sparse matrix ($14,957,833 \times 14,957,833$ with $1,946,671,770$ nonzeros) and leads to a microbenchmark memory footprint of 35.1 GB. The matrices are chosen to create problems less than GPU memory capacity and greater than GPU memory capacity. In both cases, we multiplied these sparse matrices with a dense matrix of 48 vector blocks. We set the tile size (β) to $2,597,152$ for both of matrices as it is the highest tile size that we can use without overflowing the

GPU memory and it gives the best performance. The `nvprof` profiler is used to collect compute time, data movement time, and Unified Memory data movement and page fault time.

4 Results

In this section we show performance results on the Cori-GPU and Summit supercomputers. Section 4.1 shows the performance of the CPU and GPU versions of LOBPCG when parallelized with either OpenMP or OpenACC. We then consider how we could use the LOBPCG solver on matrices larger than GPU memory capacity. Section 4.2 shows performance results when tiling the dominant $X^T Y$ and SpMM kernels so that each tile fits within GPU memory capacity. Finally, Sect. 4.3 compares the performance of the tiled implementation of the SpMM kernel against a naive Unified Memory implementation.

4.1 Performance of the LOBPCG Solver

We compared the performance of the LOBPCG solver when using a suite of different compilers. The compilers can all generate code for the host CPU and sometimes also for the GPU. In the following sentences, we place CPU or GPU in parenthesis to indicate whether we used the compiler to generate code for the CPU or GPU. The OpenMP compilers were Intel (CPU) and Clang (GPU) on Cori-GPU and IBM (CPU and GPU) on Summit. The OpenACC compiler was always PGI (CPU and GPU). In all cases we used a hand-written portable SpMM kernel except for our Intel compiler experiment which used `mkl_dcsrmm` from Intel MKL. We did this to obtain the best possible CPU time to more transparently show the value of our GPU implementation. The performance results for the Nm7 matrix are shown in Fig. 4. The execution time of the LOBPCG solver is averaged over 10 iterations.

The results show that the execution time of our GPU implementation is almost independent of directive based programming model and evaluation platform. Our reasoning is that the OpenMP and OpenACC configurations use the same GPU math libraries, the GPUs are nearly identical in Cori-GPU and Summit (different V100 models), and that our LOBPCG implementation has been highly tuned to minimize data movement between CPU and GPU. The best GPU performance is 3.05x faster than the best CPU performance for Nm7 matrix. The CPU versions show more variable performance for different combinations of compilers and math libraries used on Cori-GPU and Summit. The highest performance is obtained with the OpenMP version when compiled with Intel compiler on Cori-GPU. The performance differences can mostly be attributed to the host CPU and SpMM performance: `mkl_dcsrmm` is 1.4× faster than our hand-written SpMM kernel in OpenMP and the hand-written SpMM kernel is 1.5–3.0× faster when using OpenMP rather than OpenACC. We did not investigate the host CPU performance in any more detail because it is not the focus of our work.

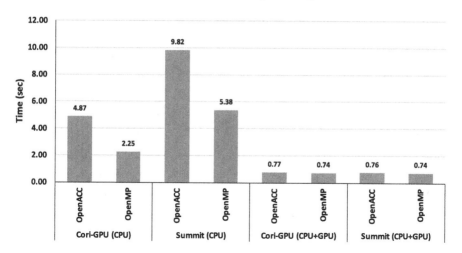

Fig. 4. The time spent in LOBPCG on Cori-GPU and Summit when using various compilers with either OpenMP or OpenACC

Figure 5 shows how time is spent in the best configurations on CPU and GPU when using the Nm7 matrix. Execution time is divided into library time, application kernel time, and unaccounted CUDA API time. The library time is spent in cuBLAS and cuSPARSE in the GPU implementation and Intel MKL in the CPU implementation. The application kernel time is spent in user defined functions in both the CPU and GPU implementations. The CUDA API time includes GPU data allocation and data movement between CPU and GPU and is calculated by subtracting time spent in application and library kernels from the total run time. The library and application kernels speedup by $3.7\times$ and $5.0\times$, respectively, when using GPUs. Application kernel time is a relatively small fraction of total run time on GPU. However, the offload is a key optimization step needed to keep total run time low. Total run time would be significantly slower if we decided to use host application kernels because of unnecessary data movement between CPU and GPU.

Figure 6 shows GPU speedup over the best LOBPCG CPU implementation for all the test matrices in Table 1. The LOBPCG GPU implementation achieves $2.8\times$–$4.3\times$ speedup over the best CPU implementation. The GPU implementation therefore performs well over a range of matrices from different domains with different sparsity patterns.

4.2 Performance of $X^T Y$ and SpMM Kernels for Large Matrices

Figure 7 shows the time spent in the inner product ($X^T Y$) kernel on Cori-GPU and Summit when total memory footprint is 51.54 GB. The tile size is 131,072. The total time is divided into host-to-device (HtoD) data transfer time and computation time in the inner product kernel (device-to-host (DtoH) data transfer times are negligible for this kernel). We measured data transfer and computa-

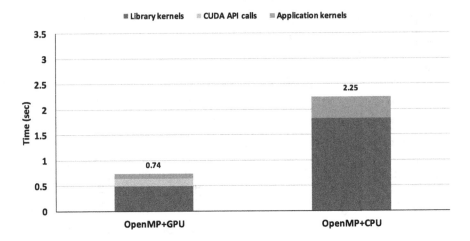

Fig. 5. The time spent in LOBPCG on Cori-GPU when using matrix Nm7

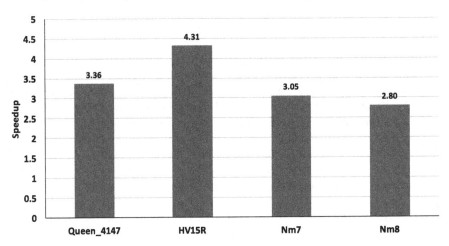

Fig. 6. LOBPCG GPU speedup on Cori-GPU for each test matrix

tion time using `nvprof`. The results show that total run time is dominated by data transfers. Run time is lower on Summit because of the high bandwidth NVLink 2.0 interconnect. We obtained data transfers of 4 GB/s on Cori-GPU and 13 GB/s on Summit in this kernel. Results indicate that data transfer time cannot be hidden behind computation when the matrix exceeds the GPU memory capacity.

Figure 8 shows the time spent in the SpMM kernel. The input sparse matrix is 24 GB and the total memory footprint is 35.1 GB. This time, results show that computation time is greater than the data movement time. This indicates that data movement time could be completely hidden behind computation. It would therefore be possible to obtain nearly the same computational throughput as one

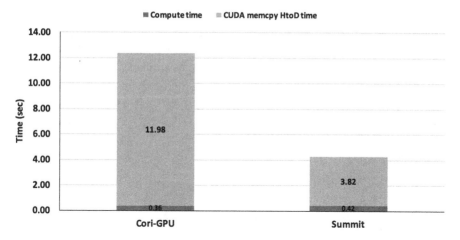

Fig. 7. Time spent in $X^T Y$ kernel on Cori-GPU and Summit when the memory footprint exceeds GPU memory capacity.

would get using matrices completely resident in the GPU memory. However, an actual block eigensolver alternates between SpMM and vector block operations, so this may not be easy to realize in practice.

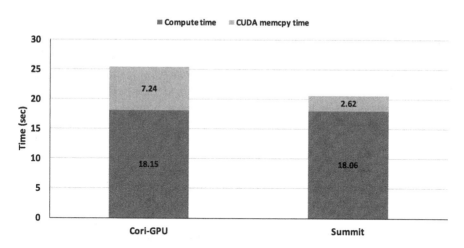

Fig. 8. Time spent in SpMM kernel on Cori-GPU and Summit when the memory footprint exceeds GPU memory capacity

4.3   Performance of Tiled and Unified Memory Versions of SpMM

Figure 9 shows the performance of the tiled SpMM kernel compared to the Unified Memory version of the SpMM kernel when the memory footprint is less than GPU memory capacity. The total memory footprint of this experiment is 11.7 GB. The tiled version is fastest on both platforms. nvprof shows that the tiled version is faster on Summit because of less time in CUDA memcpy. Interestingly, the Unified Memory version performs similarly on both platforms.

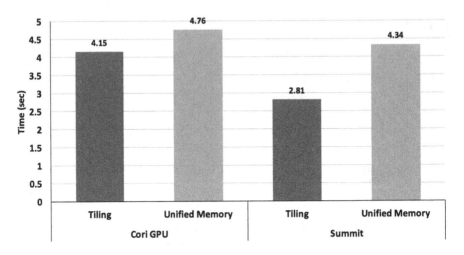

Fig. 9. Time spent in tiled and Unified Memory versions of the SpMM kernel on Cori-GPU and Summit. The memory footprint is less than GPU memory capacity.

Figure 10 shows the performance of the two SpMM kernels when the memory footprint exceeds GPU memory capacity. We used the same tile size (β) for the tiled experiments in Figs. 9 and 10. There are now significant differences between the performance of the tiled and Unified Memory versions. The most surprising result is the 48.2× performance difference between tiled and Unified Memory versions on Summit. This is a performance difference of 13.4× between Cori-GPU and Summit when using Unified Memory on different machines. This is unexpected given the high bandwidth NVLink 2.0 interconnect and hardware managed cache coherency on the Summit IBM system. Although not shown, there is a similar performance difference on Summit for the $X^T Y$ and XY kernels. Unified Memory performance is therefore poor and depends on the machine used.

Figure 11 shows nvprof output for the Unified Memory version of the XY kernel on Cori-GPU and Summit. The results show that the total count of page faults and the total data moved is the same on both systems. As expected, the data transfer is 3× faster on Summit according to the bandwidth of the CPU to GPU interconnect. However, the metric named "Gpu page fault groups" takes 30× more time on Summit compared to Cori-GPU for unknown reasons. This explains the poor performance on Summit. We observed similar performance difference without nvprof (nvprof added a performance overhead of about 10% on both machines). We are currently in contact with OLCF and NVIDIA staff to understand our performance observations.

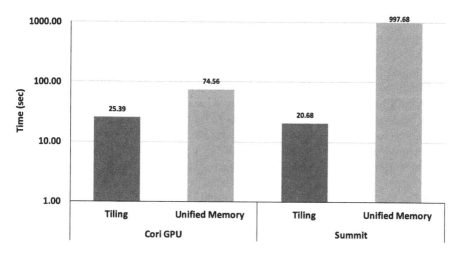

Fig. 10. Time spent in tiled and Unified Memory versions of the SpMM kernel on Cori-GPU and Summit. The memory footprint exceeds GPU memory capacity. We use a logarithmic scale on the *Time (sec)* axis to capture the slow run time for the Unified Memory configuration on Summit.

Cori-GPU

```
Device 'Tesla V100-SXM2-16GB (0)'
   Count   Avg Size   Min Size   Max Size   Total Size   Total Time   Name
  196608   170.67KB   4.0000KB   0.9961MB   32.00000GB    3.326868s   Host To Device
    8526   1.9993MB   4.0000KB   2.0000MB   16.64655GB    1.368811s   Device To Host
   98304        -          -          -           -      10.668444s   Gpu page fault groups
Total CPU Page faults: 98305
```

Summit

```
Device 'Tesla V100-SXM2-16GB (0)'
   Count   Avg Size   Min Size   Max Size   Total Size   Total Time    Name
  163840   204.80KB   64.000KB   960.00KB   32.00000GB    1.078612s    Host To Device
    8525   1.9998MB   64.000KB   2.0000MB   16.64850GB   396.9533ms    Device To Host
   98304        -          -          -           -      313.43688s    Gpu page fault groups
    8524   2.0000MB   2.0000MB   2.0000MB   16.64844GB        -
Remote mapping from device
Total CPU Page faults: 98305
Total remote mappings to CPU: 8524
```

Fig. 11. Unified Memory nvprof profile of the *XY* microbenchmark on Cori-GPU (top) and Summit (bottom).

5   Discussion

In this section we discuss the key learnings from the results in Sect. 4.

The results show that we have successfully ported the LOBPCG solver to NVIDIA GPUs using directives and optimized CUDA library calls. We obtained similar performance for the OpenMP implementation using Clang and XLC compiler as we did for the OpenACC implementation using the PGI compiler. The quality of OpenMP compilers for GPUs have often been criticized over the past few years [23], however, our experience provides evidence that OpenMP compilers are becoming more robust and are capable of generating high performance code.

We found that the key enabler of performance was to keep data resident on the GPU between calls to optimized CUDA math functions. We were able to do this trivially by adding OpenMP/OpenACC accelerator directives to the large number of kernels in the LOBPCG solver. In the past, this would have been much more challenging and time-consuming because the remaining application kernels would need to be ported to CUDA. Our related work section shows that earlier attempts to port a LOBPCG solver to GPUs by other scientists was generally focused on optimizing the SpMM kernel only on GPU whereas we focus on optimizing the full solver on GPU. This highlights the productivity gains from using directives and the importance of interoperability between the code generated by the OpenMP/OpenACC compilers and CUDA. This interoperability is not required in the OpenMP specification and is only recommended as a note to implementors in the OpenACC specification. However, we have highlighted the importance of interoperability, and believe that the HPC community should strongly request this support from compilers as we have done for LLVM/Clang (https://bugs.llvm.org/show_bug.cgi?id=42643).

We have shown that our LOBPCG microbenchmarks can be tiled to solve problems larger than GPU memory capacity. We found that the time spent in `cublasDgemm` for the inner product ($X^T Y$) microbenchmark is shorter than the time spent moving data to and from the GPU. This indicates that it is not possible to write a tiled `cublasDgemm` for larger problems which achieves the same computational throughput as a problem which fits in GPU memory capacity. The tiled `cublasDgemm` performance was mostly determined by the bandwidth of the CPU to GPU interconnect. This will remain a challenge in many CPU+GPU systems in the coming years because PCIe Gen4 has lower bandwidth than NVLink 2.0. The SpMM microbenchmark showed the opposite to $X^T Y$ in that more time was spent in computation than data movement. This indicates that data movement costs could be hidden, i.e., computation on one tile could occur concurrently with the data movement for the next tile. The full LOBPCG solver includes $X^T Y$ and SpMM operations. Therefore, the amount of computation on the GPU relative to data movement between CPU and GPU is more than what is shown in our microbenchmarks. This indicates that it should be possible to write an efficient LOBPCG solver for GPUs which can solve problems larger than the GPU memory capacity.

We had mixed success when using a Unified Memory implementation of the SpMM kernel. The performance was a little worse than the tiled implementation when the memory footprint was less than GPU memory capacity. This could be acceptable to many application programmers because we obtained this performance with much simpler code. This would be a huge productivity win for the application programmer because there is no need to manage separate host and device copies of data; there is just a single pointer to the data which can be used on both host and device. We found that the performance of the Unified Memory implementation was much worse than the tiled implementation when the memory footprint exceeded GPU memory capacity. It was so bad on Summit that it would have been more efficient to use a CPU implementation and leave the GPUs idle. We are still working to understand why Unified Memory performance was so poor on Summit. However, our early experience serves as a warning to application programmers that they should not rely on Unified Memory when application memory footprint is larger than GPU memory capacity. It is also useful information to HPC system providers that the success of their users strongly depends on purchasing GPUs with sufficient memory capacity.

We recommend that tiling be used in large memory footprint applications on CPU+GPU systems. This can deliver both high performance and predictable performance across different CPU+GPU systems. However, it can be a significant amount of work to tile and overlap data transfers with computation in an application. This may become easier in future with enhancements to the OpenMP standard providing directive-based partitioning and pipelining [10]. Alternatively, middleware for sparse solvers on GPUs could abstract away these programming challenges.

6   Conclusions

In this paper, we have described our approaches to mix CUDA library calls with OpenMP/OpenACC offloading pragmas in order to implement and optimize the full LOBPCG eigensolver on GPU-accelerated systems. We successfully used both OpenMP and OpenACC and achieved a speedup of $2.8\times - 4.3\times$ over a baseline CPU implementation. Our experiments with SpMM and inner product microbenchmarks showed that tiling is the preferred approach for larger problem sizes. We found that a naive Unified Memory implementation had worse performance than a tiled implementation by up to an order of magnitude depending on the target supercomputing platform. Our future work will go in the direction of tiling the full LOBPCG solver and attempting to overlap computation with data movement.

Acknowledgments. This work was supported in part by the US Department of Energy, Office of Science under the award DE-SC0018083 (NUCLEI SciDAC-4 collaboration) and the National Science Foundation under the award OAC-1845208. This research used resources of the National Energy Research Scientific Computing Center (NERSC), a U.S. Department of Energy Office of Science User Facility operated under Contract No. DE-AC02-05CH11231. This research also used resources of the

Oak Ridge Leadership Computing Facility, which is a DOE Office of Science User Facility supported under Contract DE-AC05-00OR22725. The authors would like to thank Brandon Cook for helpful discussion about MFDn application requirements and useful research directions for this project.

Data Availability Statement.

Summary of the Experiments Reported

We conducted all of our experiments on the Cori-GPU testbed at the National Energy Research Scientific Computing Center (NERSC) and the Summit supercomputer at the Oak Ridge Leadership Computing Facility (OLCF) using Intel Compiler v19.0.3 (OpenMP for CPU), LLVM/Clang compiler v9.0.0-git (OpenMP for GPU), and PGI compiler v19.5 (OpenACC for CPU and GPU), CUDA v10.1.168, IBM XLC Compiler v16.1.1-3 (OpenMP for CPU and GPU) as described in the paper. Our software and dataset are publicly available at `10.6084/m9.figshare.11636067` [14]. The repository includes necessary instructions and scripts to run our software. Interested individuals can contact the authors if they need they help to run the codebase.

Artifact Availability

Software Artifact Availability. All author-created software artifacts are maintained in a public repository under an OSI-approved license.

Hardware Artifact Availability. All author-created hardware artifacts are maintained in a public repository under an OSI-approved license.

Data Artifact Availability. All author-created data artifacts are maintained in a public repository under an OSI-approved license.

Proprietary Artifacts. None of the associated artifacts, author-created or otherwise, are proprietary.

List of URLs and/or DOIs Where Artifacts are Available. `10.6084/m9. figshare. 11636067.`

The details of the baseline experimental setup, and modifications made for the paper are also available at https://github.com/fazlay-rabbi/WACCPD_2019_Artifact [14].

References

1. Cori-GPU system configuration. https://docs-dev.nersc.gov/cgpu/
2. Openmp specification. https://www.openmp.org/wp-content/uploads/OpenMP-API-Specification-5.0.pdf
3. Summit system configuration. https://www.olcf.ornl.gov/summit/
4. HIP : Convert CUDA to Portable C++ Code (2019). https://github.com/ROCm-Developer-Tools/HIP. Accessed 4 Sept 2019
5. Aktulga, H.M., Buluç, A., Williams, S., Yang, C.: Optimizing sparse matrix-multiple vectors multiplication for nuclear configuration interaction calculations. In: 2014 IEEE 28th International Parallel and Distributed Processing Symposium, pp. 1213–1222. IEEE (2014)

6. Anzt, H., Tomov, S., Dongarra, J.: Implementing a sparse matrix vector product for the SELL-C/SELL-C-σ formats on nvidia gpus. University of Tennessee, Technical report. ut-eecs-14-727 (2014)

7. Anzt, H., Tomov, S., Dongarra, J.: Accelerating the LOBPCG method on GPUs using a blocked sparse matrix vector product. In: Proceedings of the Symposium on High Performance Computing, pp. 75–82. Society for Computer Simulation International (2015)

8. Bell, N., Garland, M.: Implementing sparse matrix-vector multiplication on throughput-oriented processors. In: Proceedings of the Conference on High Performance Computing Networking, Storage and Analysis. p. 18. ACM (2009)

9. Choi, J.W., Singh, A., Vuduc, R.W.: Model-driven autotuning of sparse matrix-vector multiply on GPUs. ACM SIGPLAN Not. **45**, 115–126 (2010)

10. Cui, X., Scogland, T.R.W., de Supinski, B.R., Feng, W.: Directive-based partitioning and pipelining for graphics processing units. In: 2017 IEEE International Parallel and Distributed Processing Symposium (IPDPS), pp. 575–584, May 2017. https://doi.org/10.1109/IPDPS.2017.96

11. Davis, T., Hu, Y., Kolodziej, S.: The suitesparse matrix collection (2018). http://faculty.cse.tamu.edu/davis/suitesparse.html

12. Deldon, S., Beyer, J., Miles, D.: OpenACC and CUDA unified memory. Cray User Group (CUG), May 2018

13. Dziekonski, A., Rewienski, M., Sypek, P., Lamecki, A., Mrozowski, M.: GPU-accelerated LOBPCG method with inexact null-space filtering for solving generalized eigenvalue problems in computational electromagnetics analysis with higher-order fem. Commun. Comput. Phys. **22**(4), 997–1014 (2017)

14. Rabbi, F., Daley, C.S., Aktulga, H.M., Wright, N.J.: Evaluation of directive-based GPU programming models on a block eigensolver with consideration of large sparse matrices (waccpd 2019 paper's artifact). https://doi.org/10.6084/m9.figshare.11636067, https://github.com/fazlay-rabbi/WACCPD_2019_Artifact

15. Garland, M.: Sparse matrix computations on manycore GPU's. In: Proceedings of the 45th annual Design Automation Conference, pp. 2–6. ACM (2008)

16. Hong, C., et al.: Efficient sparse-matrix multi-vector product on GPUs. In: Proceedings of the 27th International Symposium on High-Performance Parallel and Distributed Computing, pp. 66–79. ACM (2018)

17. Khorasani, F., Gupta, R., Bhuyan, L.N.: Scalable SIMD-efficient graph processing on GPUs. In: 2015 International Conference on Parallel Architecture and Compilation (PACT), pp. 39–50. IEEE (2015)

18. Knap, M., Czarnul, P.: Performance evaluation of unified memory with prefetching and oversubscription for selected parallel CUDA applications on NVIDIA Pascal and Volta GPUs. J. Supercomput. **75**, 1–21 (2019)

19. Knyazev, A.V.: Toward the optimal preconditioned eigensolver: locally optimal block preconditioned conjugate gradient method. SIAM J. Sci. Comput. **23**(2), 517–541 (2001)

20. Knyazev, A.V., Argentati, M.E.: Implementation of a preconditioned eigensolver using hypre (2005)

21. Knyazev, A.V., Argentati, M.E., Lashuk, I., Ovtchinnikov, E.E.: Block locally optimal preconditioned eigenvalue xolvers (BLOPEX) in HYPRE and PETSc. SIAM J. Sci. Comput. **29**(5), 2224–2239 (2007)

22. Lanczos, C.: An Iteration Method for the Solution of the Eigenvalue Problem of Linear Differential and Integral Operators. United States Government Press Office, Los Angeles (1950)

23. Larrea, V.G.V., Budiardja, R., Gayatri, R., Daley, C., Hernandez, O., Joubert, W.: Experiences porting mini-applications to OpenACC and OpenMP on heterogeneous systems. In: Cray User Group (CUG), May 2019
24. Maris, P., et al.: Large-scale ab initio configuration interaction calculations for light nuclei. J. Phys.: Conf. Ser. **403**, 012019 (2012)
25. Maris, P., Sosonkina, M., Vary, J.P., Ng, E., Yang, C.: Scaling of ab-initio nuclear physics calculations on multicore computer architectures. Procedia Comput. Sci. **1**(1), 97–106 (2010)
26. Naumov, M., Chien, L., Vandermersch, P., Kapasi, U.: cuSPARSE library. In: GPU Technology Conference (2010)
27. Ortega, G., Vázquez, F., García, I., Garzón, E.M.: FastSpMM: an efficient library for sparse matrix matrix product on GPUs. Comput. J. **57**(7), 968–979 (2014)
28. Sakharnykh, N.: Everything You Need To Know About Unified Memory. Presented at GPU Technology Conference (GTC) (2018). http://on-demand.gputechconf.com/gtc/2018/presentation/s8430-everything-you-need-to-know-about-unified-memory.pdf. Accessed Mar 2018
29. Shao, M., Aktulga, H.M., Yang, C., Ng, E.G., Maris, P., Vary, J.P.: Accelerating nuclear configuration interaction calculations through a preconditioned block iterative eigensolver. Comput. Phys. Commun. **222**, 1–13 (2018)
30. Sternberg, P., et al.: Accelerating configuration interaction calculations for nuclear structure. In: Proceedings of the 2008 ACM/IEEE Conference on Supercomputing, p. 15. IEEE Press (2008)
31. Vazhkudai, S.S., et al.: The design, deployment, and evaluation of the coral pre-exascale systems. In: Proceedings of the International Conference for High Performance Computing, Networking, Storage, and Analysis, p. 52. IEEE Press (2018)
32. Wang, Y.: Research on matrix multiplication based on the combination of OpenACC and CUDA. In: Xie, Y., Zhang, A., Liu, H., Feng, L. (eds.) GSES 2018. CCIS, vol. 980, pp. 100–108. Springer, Singapore (2019). https://doi.org/10.1007/978-981-13-7025-0_10
33. Williams, S., Waterman, A., Patterson, D.: Roofline: an insightful visual performance model for floating-point programs and multicore architectures. Technical report, Lawrence Berkeley National Lab (LBNL), Berkeley, CA, USA (2009)
34. Yang, C., Buluç, A., Owens, J.D.: Design principles for sparse matrix multiplication on the GPU. In: Aldinucci, M., Padovani, L., Torquati, M. (eds.) Euro-Par 2018. LNCS, vol. 11014, pp. 672–687. Springer, Cham (2018). https://doi.org/10.1007/978-3-319-96983-1_48
35. Yang, X., Parthasarathy, S., Sadayappan, P.: Fast sparse matrix-vector multiplication on GPUs: implications for graph mining. Proc. VLDB Endow. **4**(4), 231–242 (2011)

Directive-Based Programming for Math Libraries

Performance of the RI-MP2 Fortran Kernel of GAMESS on GPUs via Directive-Based Offloading with Math Libraries

JaeHyuk Kwack[1]($^{\boxtimes}$) , Colleen Bertoni[1], Buu Pham[2], and Jeff Larkin[3]

[1] Argonne National Laboratory, Lemont, IL 60439, USA
{jkwack,bertoni}@anl.gov
[2] Iowa State University, Ames, IA 50011, USA
buupq@iastate.edu
[3] NVIDIA, Santa Clara, USA
jlarkin@nvidia.com

Abstract. The US Department of Energy (DOE) started operating two GPU-based pre-exascale supercomputers in 2018 and plans to deploy another pre-exascale in 2020, and three exascale supercomputers in 2021/2022. All of the systems are GPU-enabled systems, and they plan to provide optimized vendor-promoted programming models for their GPUs such as CUDA, HIP and SYCL. However, due to their limited functional portability, it is challenging for HPC application developers to maintain their applications in an efficient and effective way with good productivity across all US DOE pre-exascale/exascale systems. Directive-based programming models for accelerators can be one of the solutions for HPC applications on the DOE supercomputers. In this study, we employ OpenMP and OpenACC offloading models to port and re-implement the RI-MP2 Fortran kernel of the GAMESS application on a pre-exascale GPU system, Summit. We compare and evaluate the performance of the re-structured offloading kernels with the original OpenMP threading kernel. We also evaluate the performance of multiple math libraries on the NVIDIA V100 GPU in the RI-MP2 kernel. Using the optimized directive-based offloading implementations, the RI-MP2 kernel on a single V100 GPU becomes more than 7 times faster than on dual-socket Power9 processors, which is near the theoretical speed-up based on peak performance ratios. MPI+directive-based offloading implementations of the RI-MP2 kernel perform more than 40 times faster than a MPI+OpenMP threading implementation on the same number of Summit nodes. This study demonstrates how directive-based offloading implementations can perform near what we expect based on machine peak ratios.

Keywords: GAMESS · RI-MP2 · OpenMP offloading · OpenACC offloading · GPU math libraries

Electronic supplementary material The online version of this chapter (https://doi.org/10.1007/978-3-030-49943-3_5) contains supplementary material, which is available to authorized users.

1   Introduction

Two US Department of Energy (DOE) GPU-based pre-exascale supercomputers (i.e., Summit and Sierra) have been listed as the first and second ranks of the TOP500 list [15] since November 2018. The US DOE also plans to deploy one more pre-exascale supercomputer (i.e., Permultter at NERSC - National Energy Research Scientific Computing Center) in 2020, and three exascale supercomputers (i.e., Aurora at ALCF - Argonne Leadership Computing Facility, El Capitan at LLNL - Lawrence Livermore National Laboratory, and Frontier at OLCF - Oak Ridge Leadership Computing Facility) in 2021/2022, all of which are also GPU-enabled systems. All the systems plan to provide optimized vendor-promoted programming models for their GPUs such as CUDA [6], HIP [7] and SYCL [14]. However, due to the potential limited functional portability, it is very challenging for HPC application developers to maintain their applications in an efficient and effective way with good productivity across all US DOE pre-exascale and exascale systems. For the problem of portability across all systems, directive-based programming models for accelerators can be one of the best solutions for HPC applications on the forthcoming exascale regime.

General Atomic and Molecular Electronic Structure System (GAMESS) [20,27], is a popular quantum chemistry software package which has been around since the 1980s. It can calculate a wide variety of molecular properties using electronic structure methods. GAMESS is written in Fortran 77/90 with an additional GPU-accelerated library [16,17]. It is parallelized with MPI, OpenMP for CPU threads, and CUDA for GPU. In this study, we employ OpenMP and OpenACC offloading models for a kernel of the GAMESS application on the state-of-the-art GPU system, Summit at OLCF. We compare performance of the offloading kernels with the original OpenMP threading kernel, and evaluate it with respect to the theoretical peak. We also evaluate and discuss the performance of multiple math libraries on the NVIDIA V100 GPU compared to multiple CPU-based math libraries on IBM Power9 processors and Intel Skylake processors. Additionally, we consider multi-GPU nodes, and assess the performance of MPI + directive-based offloading kernels on multiple GPUs from multiple Summit nodes is presented compared to MPI + OpenMP threading kernel on the same number of Summit nodes.

This paper is organized as follows: Sect. 2 presents detailed descriptions about the RI-MP2 kernel of GAMESS. In Sect. 3, we provide technical information about the employed systems. The programming environments (i.e., compilers and libraries) are discussed in Sect. 4. Section 5 provides OpenMP and OpenACC offloading implementations for the RI-MP2 kernel and their limited performance on a V100 GPU. In Sect. 6, we present optimal offloading implementations and their performance on the GPU. The performance of the MPI + directive-based offloading implementations on multiple Summit node is discussed in Sect. 7. In Sect. 8, we summarize our work in this study.

2   RI-MP2 Kernel of GAMESS

2.1   RI-MP2 Kernel

One of the methods implemented in GAMESS is resolution of identity Moller-Plesset perturbation (RI-MP2) theory [18,19]. RI-MP2 is an electron correlation method, which is a class of methods that include instantaneous electron-electron interactions, and are required to perform accurate energy and property calculations for certain classes of molecular systems. Of the electron correlation methods, RI-MP2 tends to be one of the more computationally inexpensive methods, but the formal computational complexity is still $O(N^5)$, where N is a measure of system size. Because of the large computational complexity, and because the RI-MP2 algorithm lends itself to being written in terms of many matrix multiplies, RI-MP2 is a good candidate for GPU offloading. We note that there are several RI-MP2 GPU codes in existence currently [21,23,28,29]. However, here the focus is as a case study on the issues involved in converting a CPU MPI/OpenMP Fortran implementation to offload with OpenMP/OpenACC with minimal changes to the code. Figure 1 presents a code structure of the RI-MP2 mini app employed in this study.

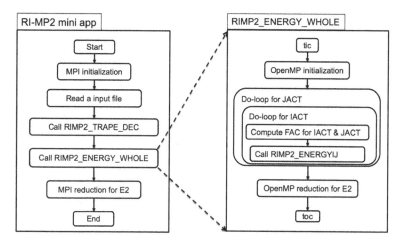

Fig. 1. Code structure of the RI-MP2 mini app

RI-MP2 Equations. After computing the Hartree-Fock energy [26] and wavefunction, the RI-MP2 method computes the correlation energy,

$$E^{(2)} = \sum_{i \leq j}^{occ}(2 - \delta_{ij}) \sum_{ab}^{vir} \frac{(ia|jb)[2(ja|jb) - (ib|ja)]}{\epsilon_i + \epsilon_j - (\epsilon_a + \epsilon_b)} \tag{1}$$

where occ is set of the occupied orbitals, vir is the set of virtual orbitals, and ϵ_x is the orbital energy for orbital x. In the RI-MP2 method, the 4-center 2-electron orbitals $(ia|jb)$ are computed as

$$(ia|jb) = \sum_n^{aux} B_{an}^i B_{bn}^j \tag{2}$$

Where aux is the auxiliary basis set, and B_{an}^i are three-center integrals used to form the 2-electron orbitals.

2.2   Inputs for the RI-MP2 Kernel from GAMESS

The kernel inputs are generated by running regular RI-MP2 calculations, in which fundamental information needed by the kernel is written into a binary file. The inputs include several fundamental parameters (e.g., the number of atomic orbital (N) and auxiliary (X) basis functions, the number of correlated occupied (O) and virtual (V) molecular orbitals), the molecular orbital coefficients, the molecular orbital energies, and 3-index integral matrix $B(X, V, O)$), and the calculated MP2 correlation energy for validation. In this paper, the kernel input for fullerene (c60.kern, see Fig. 2(a)), water clusters of 30 (w30.kern) and 60 (w60.kern, see Fig. 2(b)) water molecules are generated using the atomic and auxiliary bases 6-31G(d) and cc-pVDZ-RI, respectively.

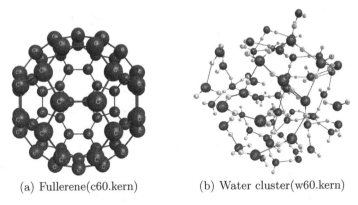

(a) Fullerene(c60.kern)   (b) Water cluster(w60.kern)

Fig. 2. Structure of the inputs for the RI-MP2 kernel

The essential part of the input is the 3-index integral matrix $B(X, V, O)$, whose dimensions depend on the basis sets, and the molecular system size. The size of the integral matrix B for kernel inputs (i.e., c60.kern, w30.kern and w60.kern) are presented in Table 1.

Table 1. Size of the integral matrix B for kernel inputs

	X	V	O	Total size (GB)
c60	3960	360	120	1.37
w30	2520	570	120	1.38
w60	5040	1140	240	11.03

3 Employed Systems

3.1 Summit System at Oak Ridge Leadership Computing Facility

Summit is a 200 petaflop system composed of IBM Power9 processors and NVIDIA Volta V100 GPUs [4]. Summit contains 4,608 nodes, each with 2 IBM Power9s and 6 NVIDIA Volta V100 GPUs, as shown in Fig. 3. The node structure has two sockets, where each socket has one Power9 and three V100s. Each Power9 is connected to three V100s with an NVlink interconnect consisting of two 25 GB/s bidirectional links, for a total bandwidth of 50 GB/s. The three V100s are connected to each other with a 50 GB/s NVlink interconnect, and the two Power9s are connected to each other by a 64 GB/s link.

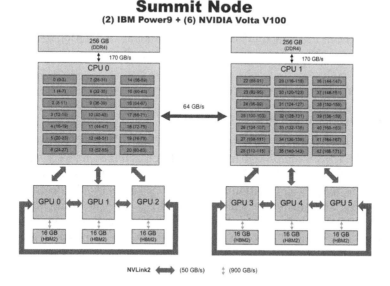

Fig. 3. Summit node (credit: OLCF)

The two IBM Power9 processor per node each have 256 GB DDR4 memory with a 135 GB/s bandwidth. Each Power9 contains 22 SIMD Multi-Cores (SMCs) with 4 hardware threads, where each SMC has a private 32 KB L1 data cache, and a 512 KB L2 and 10 MB L3 cache, which are shared by pairs of SMCs. With a clock rate of 3.10 GHz, the peak performance is 3.1 Ghz * 4 (64-bit operations per cycle per SMC) * 2 (FMA factor) * 21 (SMCs per processor), for a peak flop rate of 540 GFlop/s per processor, and 1.1 TFlop/s per node (note that only 21 SMCs per processor are active, and there are two processors per node).

The 6 NVIDIA V100s per node each have 16 GB of HBM memory with a 900 GB/s bandwidth. Each V100 contains 80 streaming multiprocessors (SMs), each with 32 64-bit CUDA cores, and 128 KB of combined L1 cache and shared memory private to the SM. In addition, all SMs share a 6 MB L2 cache. With a peak clock rate of 1.53 GHz, the peak performance per V100 is 1.53 Ghz * 32 (64-bit operations per SM per cycle) * 2 (FMA factor) * 80 (SMs per V100) = 7.8 TFlop/s per V100, for 46.8 TFlop/s per node [22].

3.2   JLSE System at Argonne Leadership Computing Facility

The Joint Laboratory for System Evaluation (JLSE) is computing cluster at Argonne National Lab meant as a testbed system [3]. Among other hardware architectures, it contains 12 compute nodes with dual-socket Intel Xeon Platinum 8180M Skylake processors [1]. Each Xeon contains 1.5 TB RAM, 32 KB L1 data cache, 1 MB L2 cache, and 39 MB L3 cache per socket. Each socket has 28 cores, with two hardware threads, and each core has two 512-bit vector registers. The two sockets are connected with 3 UPI links, with an unidirectional speed of 20.8 GB/s per UPI link. With a peak clock of 2.3 GHz for AVX512 instructions, each Xeon node has a peak performance of 2.3 GHz * 16 (64-bit operations per core per cycle) * 2 (FMA factor) * 56 (cores per Xeon) = 4.1 TFlops/s theoretical peak performance [2].

4   Programming Environments

4.1   Employed Compilers

IBM XLF for OpenMP Threading/Offloading. IBM XL Fortran compiler [9] version 16.1.1-3 is employed in this study on Summit nodes , and it fully supports the OpenMP API V4.5 specification [25], Via the OpenMP 4.5 implementation, the major computation in the RI-MP2 kernel is offloaded to NVIDIA V100 GPUs on Summit nodes. The OpenMP CPU-only threading implementation for the RI-MP2 kernel is used as a reference of the kernel performance on dual Power9 processors. The following FFLAGS is used during the compilation:

FFLAGS=-qsmp=omp -qoffload -qsuffix=cpp=f90 -g

PGI Fortran for OpenACC Offloading. PGI Fortran compiler [13] version 19.4 is used for the OpenACC 2.6 [24] implementation on Summit nodes. The following FFLAGS is used for the compilation of the kernel:

FFLAGS=-mp -ta=tesla -Minfo=accel -Mpreprocess

Intel Fortran for OpenMP Threading. On Intel Xeon processors, Intel Fortran compiler [10] version 19.0.4.243 is used for OpenMP threading implementation of the RI-MP2 kernel. The compiler flag is set as follows:

FFLAGS=-Ofast -qopenmp -cpp -g

4.2 Math Libraries

The RI-MP2 kernel requires to solve DGEMM (i.e., Double-pprecisionn GEneral Matrix Matrix multiplication) call to compute the whole energy. In this study, we employ ESSL [8] for IBM Power9 processors, MKL [11] for Intel Xeon processors, and NVBLAS [12], cuBLAS [5], and cuBLASXT [5] for NVIDIA V100 GPUs.

IBM ESSL. IBM ESSL [8] (i.e., Engineering and Scientific Subroutine Library) provides mathematical subroutines in nine computational areas such as Linear Algebra Subprograms, Matrix Operations, Linear Algebraic Equations, Eigensystem Analysis, Fourier Transforms, Sorting/Searching, Interpolation, Numerical Quadrature, and Random Number Generation. They are tuned for performance on Power9 processors on Summit, and they can be used with Fortran, C and C++ programs. In this study, ESSL/6.2.0-20190419 is used for DGEMM on Power9 processors of Summit nodes. The following LDFLAGS is used during the linking step:

LDFLAGS=-L$(OLCF_ESSL_ROOT)/lib64 -lessl

Intel MKL. Intel MKL [11] (i.e., Math Kernel Library) provides highly optimized, threaded, and vectorized math functions that maximize performance on Intel Xeon processors. It uses C and Fortran APIs for compatibility with popular BLAS, LAPACK, and FFTW functions, and it dispatches optimized code for each processor automatically without the need to branch code. For the RI-MP2 kernel on Intel Xeon processors, MKL/19.0.4.243 is employed for DGEMM via the standard BLAS symbol. The following LDFLAGS is used for building a binary executable on Intel Xeon processors:

LDFLAGS=-L${MKLPATH} -I${MKLINCLUDE} -lmkl_intel_lp64
-lmkl_sequential -lmkl_core -lpthread -lm

NVBLAS. The NVBLAS [12] Library is a GPU-accelerated Library that implements BLAS (Basic Linear Algebra Subprograms). It can accelerate most BLAS Level-3 routines by dynamically routing BLAS calls to one or more NVIDIA GPUs present in the system, when the characteristics of the call make it likely to obtain a speedup on a GPU over a CPU. It is built on top of the cuBLAS Library using only the cuBLASXT API. NVBLAS also requires the presence of a CPU BLAS library on the system. Depending on the characteristics of BLAS calls, NVBLAS redirects the calls to the GPUs present in the system or to the

CPU. That decision is based on a simple heuristic that estimates whether the BLAS call executes for long enough to amortize the transfers of the input and output data to the GPU. NVBLAS is a host-side library that intercepts calls to the host BLAS library, but will also accept GPU memory, a fact that will be exploited later. It is intended as a drop-in replacement for a traditional CPU BLAS library. NVBLAS is a thin layer above the cuBLASXT library, discussed later.

In this study, NVBLAS of CUDA Toolkit [6] version 10.1.168 is used for DGEMM via the standard BLAS symbol. IBM ESSL library is configured as a fallback option for the CPU math library on Summit nodes. Table 2 shows the configuration file for NVBLAS on Summit nodes. The following LDFLAGS is used for the linking step:

$$LDFLAGS=-L\$(CUDA\_DIR)/lib64/ \text{ -lnvblas}$$
$$-L\$(OLCF\_ESSL\_ROOT)/lib64 \text{ -lessl}$$

Table 2. NVBLAS configuration file on Summit nodes (nvblas.conf)

NVBLAS_LOGFILE nvblas.log
NVBLAS_TRACE_LOG_ENABLED
NVBLAS_CPU_BLAS_LIB $(OLCF_ESSL_ROOT)/lib64/libessl.so
NVBLAS_GPU_LIST ALL0
NVBLAS_TILE_DIM 2048
NVBLAS_AUTOPIN_MEM_ENABLED

CUBLAS. The cuBLAS library [5] is an implementation of BLAS (Basic Linear Algebra Subprograms) on top of the NVIDIA CUDA [6] runtime. To use the cuBLAS API from the cuBLAS library, the application must allocate the required matrices and vectors in the GPU memory space, fill them with data, call the sequence of desired cuBLAS functions, and then upload the results from the GPU memory space back to the host. The cuBLAS library is asynchronous with the CPU, so it is necessary to synchronize appropriately before using results from a cuBLAS routine on the CPU or GPU.

Since the RI-MP2 kernel is written in Fortran, Fortran wrappers for cuBLAS library are used as a form of Fortran module, as presented in Table 12 in Appendix I. The following LDFLAGS is used for the linking step on Summit nodes:

$$LDFLAGS=-L\$(CUDA\_DIR)/lib64/ \text{ -lcublas}$$

CUBLASXT. To use the cuBLASXT API from the cuBLAS library [5], the application may keep the data in CPU memory and the library takes care of dispatching the operation to one or multiple GPUs present in the system. To be able to share the workload between multiple GPUs, the cuBLASXT API uses a tiling strategy as presented in Fig. 4. When one or more matrices are located on some GPU devices, the same tiling approach and workload sharing is applied. The memory transfers are in this case done between devices. However, when the computation of a tile and some data are located on the same GPU device, the memory transfer to/from the local data into tiles is bypassed and the GPU operates directly on the local data. This can lead to a significant performance increase, especially when only one GPU is used for the computation.

In this study, the same LDFLAGS as cuBLAS is used for cuBLASXT, and the Fortran wrapper module in Table 12 in Appendix I is used to call cuBLASXT functions.

5   Offloading the RI-MP2 Kernel

5.1   The RI-MP2 Kernel with OpenMP Threading

As presented in Sect. 2.1, the RI-MP2 kernel computes correlation energy in Eq. 1 for given inputs. Table 3 shows an OpenMP threading implementation of the RI-MP2 kernel. It employs OpenMP threads for multiple occupied orbitals (i.e., do-loops for IACT and JACT in RIMP2_ENERGY_WHOLE). Each thread independently computes the RIMP2_ENERGYIJ kernel. The computation for 4-center 2-electron orbitals in Eq. 2 uses the standard BLAS DGEMM in the kernel. The kernel accumulates energy contribution in E2, and then passes E2 to the RIMP2_ENERGY_WHOLE kernel. In this study, this OpenMP threading implementation is tested with IBM ESSL for IBM Power9 processors on Summit and Intel MKL for Intel Xeon Platinum 8180M Skylake processors on JLSE.

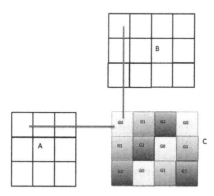

Fig. 4. Example of cublasXtdgemm() tiling (Credit NVIDIA)

Table 3. The RI-MP2 kernels with OpneMP threading

```
subroutine RIMP2_ENERGY_WHOLE ( ... )
...
  !$omp threadprivate(E2_omp)
  call OMP_SET_DYNAMIC(.FALSE.)
  nthreads=omp_get_max_threads()
...
  !$omp parallel NUM_THREADS(nthreads) default(none) shared(...) private(...)
  !$omp do schedule(DYNAMIC)
  do-loop for JACT        ! From 1 to NACT
    do-loop for IACT      ! From 1 to JACT
      Set FAC
        call RIMP2_ENERGYIJ (B32(:,:,IACT), B32(:,:,JACT), FAC, E2, ...)
    enddo
  enddo
  !$omp end do

  !$omp atomic
  E2 = E2 + E2_omp
  !$omp end parallel
end !subroutine RIMP2_ENERGY_WHOLE ( ... )


subroutine RIMP2_ENERGYIJ( ... )
...
  call DGEMM for BI(:,:), BJ(:,:), QVV(:,:)
  do-loop for IB        ! From 1 to NVIR
    do-loop for IA    ! From 1 to NVIR
      compute E2_t with QVV(:,:), eij(:,:), eab(:,:)
    enddo
  enddo
  E2 = E2 + FAC*E2_t
end !subroutine RIMP2_ENERGYIJ( ... )
```

5.2 Offloading the RI-MP2 Kernels to GPUs via OpenMP 4.5 and OpenACC 2.6

Using OpenMP 4.5 from the IBM XLF compiler and OpenACC from the PGI Fortran compiler, the RI-MP2 kernel is re-written for offloading computations to GPUs. In Table 4, directives with blue color represent the OpenMP offloading implementation, while directives in red color show the OpenACC offloading implementation. Before starting dual do-loops for JACT and IACT in the subroutine RIMP2_ENERGY_WHOLE, array QVV is created on the device, and arrays eij, eab and B32 are created and copied from the host to the device. After completing the dual do-loop, all arrays on the device (i.e., QVV, eij, eab, B32) are freed.

In the subroutine RIMP2_ENERGYIJ, the DGEMM from NVBLAS, cuBLAS and cuBLASXT is called on the host, and the device pointers of the

Table 4. The RI-MP2 kernels with OpneMP/OpenACC offloading

```
subroutine RIMP2_ENERGY_WHOLE ( ... )
...
    !$omp target enter data map(alloc: QVV) map(to: eij,eab,B32)
    !$acc enter data create(QVV) copyin(eij,eab,b32)
    do-loop for JACT      ! From 1 to NACT
      do-loop for IACT    ! From 1 to JACT
        Set FAC
        call RIMP2_ENERGYIJ (B32(:,:,IACT), B32(:,:,JACT), FAC, E2, ...)
      enddo
    enddo
    !$omp target exit data map(release: QVV,eij,eab,B32)
    !$acc wait
    !$acc exit data delete(QVV,eij,eab,B32)

    E2 = E2 + E2_omp
end !subroutine RIMP2_ENERGY_WHOLE ( ... )

subroutine RIMP2_ENERGYIJ( ... )
...
    !$omp target data use_device_ptr(BI,BJ,QVV)
    !$acc host_data use_device(BI,BJ,QVV)
    call DGEMM for BI(:,:), BJ(:,:), QVV(:,:)
    !$omp end target data
    !$acc end host_data
    !$omp target map(tofrom:E2_t)
    !$omp teams distribute parallel do reduction(+:E2_t) collapse(2)
    !$acc parallel loop collapse(2) reduction(+:E2_t) default(present)
    do-loop for IB      ! From 1 to NVIR
      do-loop for IA    ! From 1 to NVIR
        compute E2_t with QVV(:,:), eij(:,:), eab(:,:)
      enddo
    enddo
    !$omp end teams distribute parallel do
    !$omp end target
    E2 = E2 + FAC*E2_t
end !subroutine RIMP2_ENERGYIJ( ... )
```

offloaded arrays are directly used on the DGEMM. After that, E2_t is computed on the device via collapsed parallel loops using QVV from the DGEMM, and then it is copied back to the host.

Tables 5 and 6 show the initialization and finalization processes for cuBLAS and cuBLASXT, and they are implemented at the beginning and ending of the RI-MP2 stand-alone code, respectively. NVBLAS does not required any initialization or finalization process, since it is designed for the standard BLAS interface. Table 7 provides the syntax of the DGEMM call in RIMP2_ENERGYIJ, for NVBLAS, cuBLAS, and cuBLASXT. NVBLAS intercepts the standard BLAS DGEMM API and does not require a synchronization step since it is always based on synchronous calls for BLAS functions. The default mode of cuBLAS and cuBLASXT is as an asynchronous call; therefore, cudaDeviceSynchronize is required before starting the following computations that have dependencies of the DGEMM results, unless they can be inserted in the same CUDA stream.

Table 5. Initialization for cuBLAS and cuBLASXT

Library	Initialization before calling RIMP2_ENERGY_WHOLE(...)
cuBLAS	cublas_return = cublascreate_v2(cublas_handle)
cuBLASXT	cublas_return = cublasXtcreate(cublas_handle)
	cublasXt_deviceId(1) = 0
	cublas_return = cublasXtDeviceSelect(cublas_handle, 1, cublasXt_deviceId)
	cublas_return = cublasXtSetBlockDim(cublas_handle, 2048)

Table 6. Finalization for cuBLAS and cuBLASXT

Library	Finalization after completing RIMP2_ENERGY_WHOLE(...)
cuBLAS	cublas_return = cublasdestroy_v2(cublas_handle)
cuBLASXT	cublas_return = cublasXtdestroy(cublas_handle)

Table 7. DGEMM calls for the RI-MP2 kernel from NVBLAS, cuBLAS and cuBLASXT

Library	DGEMM call in RIMP2_ENERGYIJ(...)
NVBLAS	call DGEMM('T', 'N',&
	NVIR, NVIR, NAUXBASD, 1.0D00, &
	BI, NAUXBASD, BJ, NAUXBASD, 0.0D00, QVV, NVIR)
cuBLAS	cublas_return = CUBLASDGEMM_v2(cublas_handle, &
	CUBLAS_OP_T, CUBLAS_OP_N, &
	NVIR, NVIR, NAUXBASD, 1.0D00, &
	BI, NAUXBASD, BJ, NAUXBASD, 0.0D00, QVV, NVIR)
	cublas_return = cudaDeviceSynchronize( )
cuBLASXT	cublas_return = cublasXtDgemm(cublas_handle, &
	CUBLAS_OP_T, CUBLAS_OP_N, &
	NVIR, NVIR, NAUXBASD, 1.0D00, &
	BI, NAUXBASD, BJ, NAUXBASD, 0.0D00, QVV, NVIR)
	cublas_return = cudaDeviceSynchronize( )

5.3   Performance Results

Table 8 shows walltimes and speedups of the RI-MP2 kernel with OpenMP/OpenACC offloading with the c60 input in Fig. 2(a). As a reference, the OpenMP threading implementation linked against IBM ESSL was tested on dual IBM power9 processors with 42 threads. It is around 27 times faster than on a single core of IBM Power9 processor. The same source code using Intel MKL was tested on dual Intel Xeon Platinum 8180M Skylake processors with 112 hypre-threads, and it was around 2.63 times faster than on dual IBM Power 9 processors. OpenMP and OpenACC offloading RI-MP2 kernels linked against NVBLAS, cuBLAS and cuBLASXT were tested on a single V100 GPU on Summit. Their performance is not superior to performance of the OpenMP threading kernel on Power9 processors. According to the peak performance of a V100 GPU and two Power9 processors, the measured speedups fail to reach our expectation.

Remark 1. Since NVBLAS has cuBLASXT functions at the backend, we only test NVBLAS with OpenMP offloading to check if there is any overhead from NVBLAS. It turns out the performance difference between cuBLASXT and NVBLAS is negligible.

Remark 2. It would be interesting to see why OpenMP and OpenACC offloading implementations with NVBLAS, cuBLAS, and cuBLASXT show different performance in Table 8. However, we do not dive into the details, since their performance do not meet our expectation. In the next section, we present their optimized performance and discuss their performance difference.

Table 8. Walltimes and speedups of the RI-MP2 kernel with OpenMP/OpenACC offloading (input: c60.kern)

Directives	Math Library	Processors	Wall time (sec)	Speedup
Serial	ESSL	1 core of an IBM Power9	344.763	0.037×
OpenMP threading	ESSL	2 IBM Power9 (42 threads)	12.623	1×
OpenMP threading	MKL	2 Intel Xeon 8180M (112 threads)	4.802	2.63×
OpenMP offloading	NVBLAS	1 NVIDIA V100	11.320	1.12×
OpenMP offloading	cuBLAS	1 NVIDIA V100	9.282	1.36×
OpenMP offloading	cuBLASXT	1 NVIDIA V100	11.372	1.11×
OpenACC offloading	cuBLAS	1 NVIDIA V100	12.176	1.04×
OpenACC offloading	cuBLASXT	1 NVIDIA V100	14.548	0.87×

Figure 5 shows a NVPROF plot of the OpenMP offloading kernel with NVBLAS. The MemCopy between the host and the device looks small enough, but the compute region has a lot of short compute blocks of DGEMM and E2_t computations. Based on the plot, merging the small compute blocks could reduce kernel launching overheads on the device, and it might improve the performance of the offloading kernels.

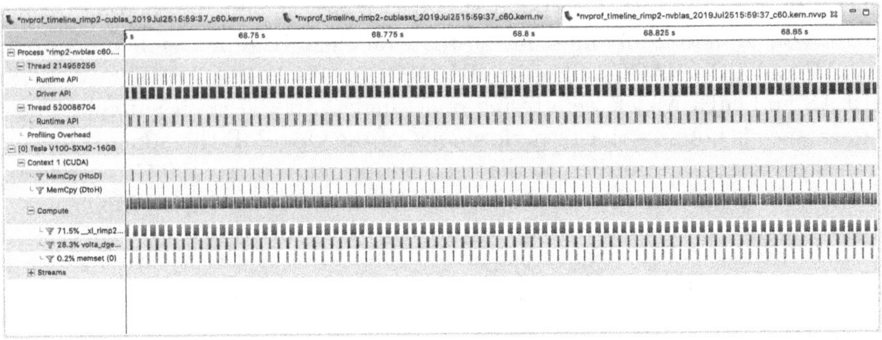

Fig. 5. NVPROF plot for the RI-MP2 kernel with NVBLAS (c60.kern), dT = 0.1 s

6   Offloading the Restructured RI-MP2 Kernel

6.1   Restructuring the RI-MP2 Kernel for an Optimized Performance on a GPU

Table 9 shows the restructured RI-MP2 kernels for a better performance on a GPU. Parts in red color represent difference from the original RI-MP2 kernel in Table 4. In order to increase the size of compute blocks for DGEMM and E2_t computations, one of arrays (i.e., B32 array, see Table 9) is merged, and is used as an input of the RIMP2_ENERGYIJ subroutine. As a result, the dimensions of inputs to DGEMM (i.e., BI and QVV arrays) in RIMP2_ENERGYIJ increase from 2D (i.e., BI(:,:), QVV(:,:)) to 3D (i.e., BI(:,:,1:JACT), QVV(:,:,1:JACT)). In addition, the inner do-loop in the RIMP2_WHOLE_ENERGY disappears, while dual do-loops for E2_t computations in RIMP2_ENERGYIJ becomes triple do-loops.

6.2   Performance Results of the Restructured RI-MP2 Kernel

Table 10 shows walltimes and speedups of the restructured RI-MP2 kernel on a V100 GPU, dual IBM Power9 processors, and dual Intel Skylake processors. The restructured RI-MP2 kernel significantly improves the performance of the OpenMP and OpenACC offloaing kernel, while it improves the performance of the OpenMP threading on CPUs slightly; as a result, the speedups of OpenMP

Table 9. The restructured RI-MP2 kernels for fewer DGEMM calls with larger matrices

```
subroutine RIMP2_ENERGY_WHOLE ( ... )
...
  do-loop for JACT      ! From 1 to NACT
    call RIMP2_ENERGYIJ (B32(:,:,1:JACT), B32(:,:,JACT), E2, ...)
  enddo
...
end !subroutine RIMP2_ENERGY_WHOLE ( ... )


subroutine RIMP2_ENERGYIJ( ... )
...
  call DGEMM for BI(:,:,1:JACT), BJ(:,:), QVV(:,:,1:JACT)
...
  do-loop for IC        ! From 1 to JACT
    Set FAC
    do-loop for IB      ! From 1 to NVIR
      do-loop for IA    ! From 1 to NVIR
        compute E2_t with QVV(:,:,IC), eij(:,:), eab(:,:)
      enddo
    enddo
    E2 = E2 + FAC*E2_t
  enddo
...
end !subroutine RIMP2_ENERGYIJ( ... )
```

and OpenACC offloading kernels with NVBLAS and cuBLASXT on a V100 GPU over OpenMP threading kernels with ESSL on dual Power9 processors become more than 7×. The speedups of OpenMP and OpenACC offloading with cuBLAS are more than 6×. They are very impressive performance on a V100 GPU, since the peak performance ratio of a V100 GPU over dual Power9 processors is a little bit higher than 7×.

In order to understand the performance difference of cuBLAS and NVBLAS /cuBLASXT, the kernels were run with NVPROF, and Fig. 6 show the NVPROF plots for the restructured RI-MP2 kernel with cuBLAS and cuBLASXT. The NVPROF plot for the kernel with NVBLAS is very similar to the plot for cuBLASXT, since NVBLAS uses cuBLASXT functions on the backend. In Fig. 6(a), the compute blocks for DGEMM calls are long and continuous. However, DGEMM blocks in Fig. 6(b) are composed of multiple small blocks, since cuBLASXT uses a tiling algorithm in Fig. 4 for better performance.

Table 10. Walltimes and speedups of the restructured RI-MP2 kernel (input: c60.kern)

Directives	Math Library	Processors	Wall time (sec)	Speedup
Serial	ESSL	1 core of an IBM Power9	342.697	0.036×
OpenMP threading	ESSL	2 IBM Power9 (42 threads)	12.231	1×
OpenMP threading	MKL	2 Intel Xeon 8180M (112 threads)	4.317	2.83×
OpenMP offloading	NVBLAS	1 NVIDIA V100	1.734	7.05×
OpenMP offloading	cuBLAS	1 NVIDIA V100	1.983	6.17×
OpenMP offloading	cuBLASXT	1 NVIDIA V100	1.728	7.08×
OpenACC offloading	cuBLAS	1 NVIDIA V100	1.905	6.42×
OpenACC offloading	cuBLASXT	1 NVIDIA V100	1.692	7.23×

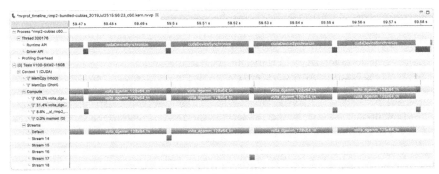

(a) w/ cuBLAS

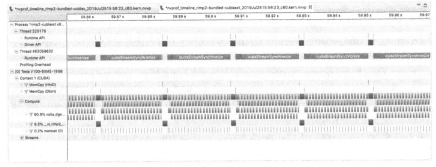

(b) w/ cuBLASXT

Fig. 6. NVPROF plot for the restructured RI-MP2 kernel with the c60 input, dT = 0.1 s

Remark 3. In this study, we employ OpenMP 4.5 from the IBM compiler and OpenACC 2.6 from the PGI compiler. Compared to the OpenMP 4.5 specification, the OpenACC 2.6 specification provides an ability to interoperate between the stream used for the DGEMM and the kernels generated by the compiler, which reduces the synchronization cost. We believe the slightly better performance of the OpenACC implementations in Table 10 is due to this difference. Codes with more frequent interoperations between GPU libraries and compiler-generated kernels may see an even greater impact. It is our hope that a future revision of the OpenMP specification will support improved interactions between the OpenMP runtime and CUDA streams to avoid unnecessary synchronization overhead. It will also help other vendor-promoted programming languages such as HIP and SYCL achieve improved interoperability with performance.

7 Performance of the Restructured RI-MP2 Kernel on Multiple GPUs via MPI+OpenMP Offloading

The restructured RI-MP2 kernel with MPI+OpenMP offloading implementation was tested on multiple GPUs on multiple nodes (upto 16 nodes) of the Summit system, as presented in Table 11. IBM Spectrum MPI version 10.3.0.1-20190611 was used on Summit. For the OpenMP offloading with cuBLAS and cuBLASXT, each MPI rank is assigned to one V100 GPU; as a result, 6 MPI ranks were assigned to one Summit node. For the OpenMP threading with ESSL on Power9 processors, each MPI employed 7 OpenMP threads; therefore, each Summit node was configured as 6 MPI ranks with 42 threads/node in total.

Table 11. Walltimes of the restructured RI-MP2 kernel on multiple GPUs (in sec): 1 GPU/MPI for cuBLAS & cuBLASXT, 7 threads/MPI for ESSL

Nodes	MPIs	w30			w60		
		cuBLAS	cuBLASXT	ESSL	cuBLAS	cuBLASXT	ESSL
1	1	2.899	2.314	86.324	87.301	72.903	2727.419
1	2	1.582	1.287	43.848	44.646	37.512	1386.807
1	4	0.899	0.759	26.768	23.181	19.67	792.305
1	6	0.664	0.643	19.333	16.08	14.074	563.707
2	12	0.447	0.397	12.626	8.845	7.999	317.892
4	24	0.402	0.379	9.358	5.383	4.921	212.748
8	48	0.337	0.308	9.347	3.722	3.687	154.441
16	96	0.358	0.332	9.349	2.923	3.169	150.704

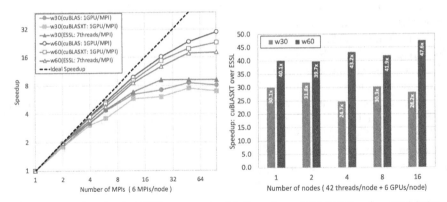

(a) Speedup of multiple GPUs over a sin-(b) Speedup of RI-MP2 w/ cuBLASXT
gle GPU   over ESSL

Fig. 7. Performance of the restructured RI-MP2 kernel with w30 and w60 inputs via
MPI+OpenMP offloading on multiple GPU nodes of the Summit system

Figure 7(a) shows the corresponding speedups of multiple GPUs over a single
V100 GPU. The RI-MP2 kernel with the w60 input shows better speedups than
with the w30 input, since the w60 input has a bigger system for computations
than the w30 input. Figure 7(b) presents speedups of the RI-MP2 kernel with
OpenMP offloading and cuBLASXT over with OpenMP threading and ESSL. It
is around 40× to 48× speedup with the w60 input, while it is 25× to 32× with
the w30 input. In summary, the RI-MP2 with the w60 input obtains more than
40× speedup via the OpenMP offloading implementation on multiple Summit
nodes. The peak performance ratio of six V100 GPUs over two Power9 processors
on a Summit node is around 43×. Therefore, this is a remarkable performance
improvement case via a directive-based offloading implementation on multiple
GPUs.

8   Concluding Remarks

The RI-MP2 kernel from GAMESS application is re-written via OpenMP
and OpenACC offloading implementations. The offloading kernels are linked
against three different math libraries for GPUs (i.e., NVBLAS, cuBLAS, and
cuBLASXT). For the first performance tests, the OpenMP/OpenACC offloading kernels are tested on a single V100 GPU. The RI-MP2 kernel with OpenMP
threading implementation is tested with vendors' optimized math libraries

(i.e., ESSL for IBM processors, and MKL for Intel processors) on a single core of IBM Power9 processor, dual-socket Power9 processors with 42 threads, and dual-socket Intel Xeon Platinum 8180M Skylake processor with 112 threads, as references.

Only offloading the math library calls themselves did not change the performance much compared to the CPU threaded version. Via restructuring the offloading kernel, the compute blocks on the GPU become big enough for the GPU; as a result, the OpenMP/OpenACC offloading RI-MP2 kernel on a single V100 GPU shows around $6\times$ to $7\times$ speedups over dual-socket Power9 processors, which is near what we expect based on peak performance ratios.

With a larger input (i.e, w60.kern), the restructured RI-MP2 kernel via MPI + OpenMP offloading implementation was tested on multiple GPUs on up to 16 Summit nodes. The MPI + OpenMP offloading kernel shows significant speedups on multiple GPUs. It shows more than $40\times$ speedup over the MPI + OpenMP threading implementation on the same number of Summit nodes.

This case study demonstrates that directive-based programming models can achieve high performance and a significant speed-up over threaded CPU-only code, with a speed-up near the theoretical speedup based on peak theoretical performance numbers. We plan to extend these directive-based offloading implementations to other kernels of GAMESS, so these kernels will be ready for coming pre-exascale/exascale US DOE machines in 2020 (i.e., Permultter) and 2021/2022 (i.e., Aurora, El Capitan, and Frontier) that have GPU accelerators provided by different vendors. Through this study, we can have a confidence about performance of directive-based programming models for accelerators.

Acknowledgment. This work was supported by the Argonne Leadership Computing Facility, which is a DOE Office of Science User Facility supported under Contract DE-AC02-06CH11357, and by the Exascale Computing Project (17-SC-20-SC), a collaborative effort of the U.S. Department of Energy Office of Science and the National Nuclear Security Administration, and by a grant from the Department of Energy Exascale Computing Project (ECP), administered by the Ames Laboratory. We also gratefully acknowledge the computing resources provided and operated by the Joint Laboratory for System Evaluation (JLSE) at Argonne National Laboratory. This research used resources of the Oak Ridge Leadership Computing Facility, which is a DOE Office of Science User Facility supported under Contract DE-AC05-00OR22725. Last but not least, we would like to thank the Exascale Computing Project (ECP) and Oak Ridge Leadership Computing Facility (OLCF) for organizing the 2019 ECP/OLCF OpenMP Hackathon in Knoxville, TN, and give special thanks our mentors, Dmytro Bykov from OLCF and Vivek Kale from BNL for their contributions to this work.

Appendix I

Table 12. Fortran wrapper for cuBLAS and cuBLASXT functions

```
module cublasf
  use, intrinsic :: iso_c_binding

  enum, bind(c) !:: cublasOperation_t
    enumerator :: CUBLAS_OP_N = 0
    enumerator :: CUBLAS_OP_T = 1
    enumerator :: CUBLAS_OP_C = 2
  end enum !cublasOperation_t

  interface

    integer(c_int) function cublasCreate_v2(handle) &
        bind(c, name="cublasCreate_v2")
      use, intrinsic :: iso_c_binding
      type(c_ptr) :: handle
    end function cublasCreate_v2

    integer(c_int) function cublasDestroy_v2(handle) &
        bind(c, name="cublasDestroy_v2")
      use, intrinsic :: iso_c_binding
      type(c_ptr), value :: handle
    end function cublasDestroy_v2

    integer(c_int) function cublasDgemm_v2(handle, &
        transa, transb, m, n, k, alpha, dA,ldda, &
        dB, lddb, beta, dC, lddc) &
        bind(c, name="cublasDgemm_v2")
      use, intrinsic :: iso_c_binding
      type(c_ptr), value :: handle
      integer(c_int), value :: transa, transb, m, n, k
      real(c_double) :: alpha, beta
      real(c_double),dimension(*) :: dA, dB, dC
      integer(c_int), value :: ldda, lddb, lddc
    end function cublasDgemm_v2

    integer(c_int) function cudaDeviceSynchronize() &
        bind(c, name="cudaDeviceSynchronize")
      use, intrinsic :: iso_c_binding
    end function cudaDeviceSynchronize

    integer(c_int) function cublasxtcreate(handle) &
        bind(c, name="cublasXtCreate")
      use, intrinsic :: iso_c_binding
      type(c_ptr) :: handle
    end function cublasxtcreate
```

```fortran
integer(c_int) function cublasXtDeviceSelect( &
    handle, nbDevices, deviceId) &
    bind(c, name="cublasXtDeviceSelect")
use, intrinsic :: iso_c_binding
type(c_ptr), value :: handle
integer(c_int), value :: nbDevices
integer(c_int),dimension(*) :: deviceId
end function cublasXtDeviceSelect

integer(c_int) function cublasXtSetBlockDim( &
    handle, blockDim) &
    bind(c, name="cublasXtSetBlockDim")
use, intrinsic :: iso_c_binding
type(c_ptr), value :: handle
integer(c_int), value :: blockDim
end function cublasXtSetBlockDim

integer(c_int) function cublasXtDgemm(handle, &
    transa, transb, m, n, k, alpha, dA, ldda, &
    dB, lddb, beta, dC, lddc) &
    bind(c, name="cublasXtDgemm")
use, intrinsic :: iso_c_binding
type(c_ptr), value :: handle
integer(c_int), value :: transa, transb, m, n, k
real(c_double) :: alpha, beta
real(c_double),dimension(*) :: dA, dB, dC
integer(c_int), value :: ldda, lddb, lddc
end function cublasXtDgemm

integer(c_int) function cublasxtdestroy(handle) &
    bind(c, name="cublasXtDestroy")
use, intrinsic :: iso_c_binding
type(c_ptr), value :: handle
end function cublasxtdestroy

end interface
end module cublasf
```

References

1. Intel Xeon Platinum 8180M Processor Information page. https://ark.intel.com/content/www/us/en/ark/products/120498/intel-xeon-platinum-8180m-processor-38-5m-cache-2-50-ghz.html
2. Intel Xeon Processor Scalable Family, Specifcation Update (2019). https://www.intel.com/content/dam/www/public/us/en/documents/specification-updates/xeon-scalable-spec-update.pdf

3. JLSE Web page. https://press3.mcs.anl.gov/jlse/
4. Summit User guide Web page. https://www.olcf.ornl.gov/for-users/system-user-guides/summit/summit-user-guide/
5. cuBLAS API Reference Guide Web page (2019). https://docs.nvidia.com/cuda/cublas
6. CUDA Toolkit Web page (2019). https://developer.nvidia.com/cuda-toolkit
7. HIP GitHub repository (2019). https://github.com/ROCm-Developer-Tools/HIP
8. IBM Engineering and Scientific Subroutine Library User guide Web page (2019). https://www.ibm.com/support/knowledgecenter/en/SSFHY8_6.1
9. IBM XL Fortran Compiler for Linux User guide Web page (2019). https://www.ibm.com/support/knowledgecenter/SSAT4T_16.1.1
10. INTEL Fortran Compiler (2019). https://software.intel.com/en-us/fortran-compilers
11. Intel Math Kernel Library User guide Web page (2019). https://software.intel.com/en-us/mkl
12. NVBLAS User guide Web page (2019). https://docs.nvidia.com/cuda/nvblas
13. PGI version 19.4 Documentation for OpenPOWER and NVIDIA Processors (2019). https://www.pgroup.com/resources/docs/19.4/openpower
14. SYCL Web page (2019). https://www.khronos.org/sycl/
15. TOP 500 list (2019). https://www.top500.org
16. Asadchev, A., Allada, V., Felder, J., Bode, B.M., Gordon, M.S., Windus, T.L.: Uncontracted Rys quadrature implementation of up to G functions on graphical processing units. J. Chem. Theory Comput. **6**(3), 696–704 (2010)
17. Asadchev, A., Gordon, M.S.: New multithreaded hybrid CPU/GPU approach to Hartree-Fock. J. Chem. Theory Comput. **8**(11), 4166–4176 (2012)
18. Bernholdt, D.E., Harrison, R.J.: Large-scale correlated electronic structure calculations: the RI-MP2 method on parallel computers. Chem. Phys. Lett. **250**(5–6), 477–484 (1996)
19. Feyereisen, M., Fitzgerald, G., Komornicki, A.: Use of approximate integrals in ab initio theory. an application in MP2 energy calculations. Chem. Phys. Lett. **208**(5–6), 359–363 (1993)
20. Gordon, M.S., Schmidt, M.W.: Advances in electronic structure theory: GAMESS a decade later, Chap. 41. In: Dykstra, C.E., Frenking, G., Kim, K.S., Scuseria, G.E. (eds.) Theory and Applications of Computational Chemistry, pp. 1167–1189. Elsevier, Amsterdam (2005). https://doi.org/10.1016/B978-044451719-7/50084-6
21. Katouda, M., Nagase, S.: Efficient parallel algorithm of second-order Møller–Plesset perturbation theory with resolution-of-identity approximation (RI-MP2). Int. J. Quantum Chem. **109**(10), 2121–2130 (2009). https://doi.org/10.1002/qua.22068, https://onlinelibrary.wiley.com/doi/abs/10.1002/qua.22068
22. NVIDIA: Nvidia Tesla v100 GPU architecture (2017). http://images.nvidia.com/content/volta-architecture/pdf/volta-architecture-whitepaper.pdf
23. Olivares-Amaya, R., Watson, M.A., Edgar, R.G., Vogt, L., Shao, Y., Aspuru-Guzik, A.: Accelerating correlated quantum chemistry calculations using graphical processing units and a mixed precision matrix multiplication library. J. Chem. Theory Comput. **6**(1), 135–144 (2009)
24. OpenACC-Standard.org: The OpenACC Application Programming Interface version 2.6 (November 2017)
25. OpenMP.org: OpenMP Application Programming Interface version 4.5, November 2015
26. Ostlund, N.S., Szabo, A.: Modern Quantum Chemistry: Introduction to Advanced Electronic Structure Theory. Macmillan (1982)

27. Schmidt, M.W., et al.: General atomic and molecular electronic structure system. J. Comput. Chem. **14**(11), 1347–1363 (1993). https://doi.org/10.1002/jcc.540141112, https://onlinelibrary.wiley.com/doi/abs/10.1002/jcc.540141112

28. Vogt, L., Olivares-Amaya, R., Kermes, S., Shao, Y., Amador-Bedolla, C., Aspuru-Guzik, A.: Accelerating resolution-of-the-identity second-order Møller-Plesset quantum chemistry calculations with graphical processing units. J. Phys. Chem. A **112**(10), 2049–2057 (2008)

29. Watson, M., Olivares-Amaya, R., Edgar, R.G., Aspuru-Guzik, A.: Accelerating correlated quantum chemistry calculations using graphical processing units. Comput. Sci. Eng. **12**(4), 40–51 (2010). https://doi.org/10.1109/MCSE.2010.29

Performance Portability for
Heterogeneous Architectures

Performance Portable Implementation of a Kinetic Plasma Simulation Mini-App

Yuuichi Asahi[1]([⊠]) [iD], Guillaume Latu[2], Virginie Grandgirard[2],
and Julien Bigot[3]

[1] National Institutes for Quantum and Radiological Science and Technology,
Rokkasho, Aomori 039-3212, Japan
asahi.yuuichi@qst.go.jp, y.asahi@nr.titech.ac.jp
[2] CEA, IRFM, Cadarache, 13108 St.Paul-lez-Durance Cedex, France
[3] Maison de la Simulation, CEA, CNRS, Univ. Paris-Sud, UVSQ,
Université Paris-Saclay, 91191 Gif-sur-Yvette, France

Abstract. Performance portability is considered to be an inevitable
requirement in the exascale era. We explore a performance portable approach for fusion plasma turbulence simulation code employing kinetic
model, namely the GYSELA code. For this purpose, we extract the
key features of GYSELA such as the high dimensionality and the semi-
Lagrangian scheme, and encapsulate them into a mini-application which
solves the similar but a simplified Vlasov-Poisson system. We implement the mini-app with a mixed OpenACC/OpenMP and Kokkos, where
we suppress unnecessary duplications of code lines. For a reference case
with the problem size of 128^4, the Skylake (Kokkos), Nvidia Tesla P100
(OpenACC), and P100 (Kokkos) versions achieve an acceleration of 1.45,
12.95, and 17.83, respectively, with respect to the baseline OpenMP version on Intel Skylake. In addition to the performance portability, we
discuss the code readability and productivity of each implementation.
Based on our experience, Kokkos can offer a readable and productive
code at the cost of initial porting efforts, which would be enormous for
a large scale simulation code like GYSELA.

Keywords: GPU · OpenACC · OpenMP · Kokkos · semi-Lagrangian

1 Introduction

The performance portability in supercomputing was not a critical issue in the past
decade, where supercomputers have been dominated by homogeneous CPU-based
clusters. A commonplace strategy has been to develop and maintain a single code
parallelized with MPI and OpenMP. If a code works well on a specific supercomputer, then it can be ported easily to other supercomputers while keeping a reasonable performance. In those days, the users and developers could focus more on
physics rather than porting and optimizing a code on several devices.

Supported by QST, Japan.

© Springer Nature Switzerland AG 2020
S. Wienke and S. Bhalachandra (Eds.): WACCPD 2019, LNCS 12017, pp. 117–139, 2020.
https://doi.org/10.1007/978-3-030-49943-3_6

The emergence of GPU (graphics processing units) computing in the HPC landscape has been changing the situation drastically. Many developers had to refactor their codes to use GPUs either by architecture specific language like CUDA or directive based approaches such as OpenMP 5.0 [19] and OpenACC [18]. Regardless of their high peak performance over the conventional multi-core CPUs, a naive porting of legacy codes often result in a poor performance on GPUs, since the optimization strategy for GPUs are different from that for CPUs. Performance portability becomes a non-trivial issue when using GPUs. Unfortunately, a high diversity in computer architectures is expected for the upcoming exascale supercomputers, including Intel/Cray CPU/GPU machine Aurora and AMD/Cray CPU/GPU machine Frontier in US and Fujitsu ARM CPU machine Fugaku in Japan. Needless to say, China and Europe will construct their own exascale systems in the early 2020s, whose details are not announced yet. In order to use these hardwares efficiently, we have to establish code refactoring approaches to easily access a good performance on different devices.

There are at least two ways to sustain the performance portability over multiple architectures: directive based approaches such as OpenMP 5.0 and OpenACC, and a higher level abstraction with performance portable framework such as Kokkos [8] and RAJA [12]. There already exist some performance analysis studies relying on different parallelization methods. D. Sunderland et al. reported the performance portability of the Unitah software with Kokkos [21]. They have focused on the 3D stencil diffusion kernel and demonstrated that the appropriate usage of Kokkos features can offer significant performance improvements by better vectorization and cache effects. T. R. Law et al. worked with a 2D unstructured hydrodynamics mini-application called BookLeaf [16]. They have implemented BookLeaf in MPI+OpenMP, MPI+CUDA, MPI+Kokkos and MPI+RAJA and assess the performance focusing on the overheads introduced by Kokkos and RAJA frameworks. They reported that the overhead introduced by the frameworks can partially be masked in memory-bound situation. P. Grete et al. combined ATHENA++, an existing magnetohydrodynamics (MHD) CPU code, with Kokkos, into K-ATHENA to allow efficient simulations on multiple architectures using a single codebase [11]. They profiled the K-ATHENA performance on different platforms including Intel Skylake CPUs, Intel Xeon Phis, and NVIDIA GPUs. They defined a performance portability metric based on the roofline analysis and it reached 83.1%.

Our goal is to explore a performance portable approach for fusion plasma turbulence simulation code employing a kinetic model such as GYSELA code [10]. The kinetic plasma simulation codes are characterized by their high dimensional feature more than 4D (see the review paper [9], for example). Since it is a huge challenge to port a whole version of the GYSELA code, we extract the key features of GYSELA and encapsulate them into a mini-app which solves a similar but simplified Vlasov-Poisson system as GYSELA. We implement the mini-app into two different portable approaches: a mixed OpenACC/OpenMP and Kokkos. The former represents the directive-based approach, where the directives are switched with macros depending on the device type, i.e. OpenACC for

GPUs and OpenMP for CPUs. A single OpenACC or OpenMP code could work on both CPUs and GPUs, but the optimization process would be too tricky. We took the mixed approach, in order to get better performance on each device. The latter represents the higher level abstraction using a single code. In both approaches, we focus on avoiding the duplications of code lines unless necessary. We assess the performance portability of a mini-app across multi-core CPU and GPU. We also discuss the readability and productivity of these two approaches based upon our experience.

This paper is organized as follows. Section 2 describes the characteristics of testbed. The CPU and GPU implementations of the GYSELA mini-app are shown in Sects. 3 and 4, respectively. The portability feature is exposed in Sect. 5. In Sect. 6, the performance portability based on each implementation is discussed. The obtained results are summarized in Sect. 7.

2   Testbed Description

In this work, the performance has been measured on JFRS-1 and Tsubame 3.0 [3] supercomputers. We employ a single socket of Intel Xeon Gold 6148 (Called "Skylake" in this work) on JFRS-1 as a conventional multicore CPU and the single Nvidia Tesla P100 GPU (called "P100" hereinafter). The hardware features are given in Table 1. On Skylake, we use 40 threads with Hyperthreading.

Table 1. Hardware description for one processor. Thermal Design Power (TDP) is extracted from vendors data-sheets [13,17]. For the STREAM bandwidth [2], we use the STREAM TRIAD value.

Processor	Intel Xeon Gold 6148 (Skylake)	Nvidia Tesla P100 (Pascal)
Number of cores	20	1792
Shared Cache [MB]	45	4
Peak performance [GFlops]	1536	5300
Peak B/W [GB/s]	127.97	732
STREAM B/W [GB/s]	80	540
B/F ratio	0.083	0.138
SIMD width	256 bit	–
TDP [W]	145	300
Manufacturing process	14 nm	16 nm
Year	2017	2016

3 GYSELA Mini-App and Baseline OpenMP Implementation

In this section, we introduce the overview of the GYSELA mini-application and its relationship to the GYSELA code [10]. The original GYSELA code is written in Fortran 90 based on the hybrid OpenMP/MPI parallelism [5,15]. However, for the sake of applying modern approaches such as Kokkos [8], we have developed the mini-app in C++. Rather than extracting a single kernel from the original GYSELA code, we have developed a mini-app which solves similar equations with the same numerical scheme as GYSELA. This way, we can easily experiment and compare different kernels and test interfaces to external libraries such as fftw and cufft. The latter is an important aspect for the performance portability and productivity.

As well as the original GYSELA code, the mini-app solves the 4D advection (Vlasov) equation with the backward semi-Lagrangian scheme. It also solves the 2D poisson equation. This mini-app solves the physically meaningful system as described in Ref. [7], but the Vlasov and Poisson equations are simplified in the mini-app. In the present work, we considered the mini-app without MPI parallelization. The GYSELA mini-app (called vlp4d) is available at https://github.com/yasahi-hpc/vlp4d.

3.1 Four-Dimensional Vlasov-Poisson System

In this subsection, we describe the four-dimensional Vlasov-Poisson system [7]. The evolution of the distribution function $f(t, \mathbf{x}, \mathbf{v})$ in phase space $(\mathbf{x}, \mathbf{v})$ is computed by solving the Vlasov and Poisson equations. The four-dimensional phase space consists of configuration space (x, y) and velocity space (v_x, v_y). The four-dimensional Vlasov equation can be written as

$$\frac{\partial f}{\partial t} + \mathbf{v} \cdot \nabla_{\mathbf{x}} f + E(t, \mathbf{x}) \cdot \nabla_{\mathbf{v}} f = 0, \tag{1}$$

with $\mathbf{x} = (x, y)$ and $\mathbf{v} = (v_x, v_y)$. The two-dimensional Poisson equation

$$\nabla_{\mathbf{x}} \cdot E(t, \mathbf{x}) = \rho(t, \mathbf{x}) - 1, \tag{2}$$

with the ion density $\rho(t, \mathbf{x}) = \int d\mathbf{v} f(t, \mathbf{x}, \mathbf{v})$ and Electric field $E(t, \mathbf{x})$. By coupling the Vlasov Eq. (1) and Poisson Eq. (2), the system can be solved self-consistently. In the following, "f^n" will denote the distribution function at time $n\Delta t$.

3.2 Algorithm

In order to avoid very expensive high dimensional interpolation, we use the Strang's operator splitting method [20] to solve the Vlasov Eq. (1). The 4D Vlasov Eq. (1) can then be split as a combination of

$$\frac{\partial f}{\partial t} + v_x \frac{\partial f}{\partial x} = 0 \text{ at } (y, v_x, v_y) \text{ fixed} \tag{3}$$

$$\frac{\partial f}{\partial t} + v_y \frac{\partial f}{\partial y} = 0 \text{ at } (x, v_x, v_y) \text{ fixed} \tag{4}$$

$$\frac{\partial f}{\partial t} + E_x \frac{\partial f}{\partial v_x} = 0 \text{ at } (x, y, v_y) \text{ fixed} \tag{5}$$

$$\frac{\partial f}{\partial t} + E_y \frac{\partial f}{\partial v_y} = 0 \text{ at } (x, y, v_x) \text{ fixed.} \tag{6}$$

The 1D advection Eq. (3) along x direction is solved with the backward semi-Lagrangian scheme as described in Algorithm 1. For the interpolation scheme, we employ the Lagrange interpolation (5th order using 6-points stencils). The 1D advection equations in each direction are solved in the same way.

Algorithm 1. 1D advection along x direction with the semi-Lagrangian Scheme

---

    for *All grid points* (y_j, v_{xk}, v_{yl}) **do**
      $\eta(x_{i=*}) \leftarrow$ Lagrange coeff. from the 1D function $f^n(x_{i=*}, y_j, v_{xk}, v_{yl})$
      for *All grid points* (x_i) **do**
        $(x_i)^* \leftarrow$ foot of characteristic for one time step Δt that ends at $(x_i, y_j, v_{xk}, v_{yl})$;
        Interpolate f^n at location $(x_i)^*$ using η coeff.;
        $f^{n+1}(x_i, y_j, v_{xk}, v_{yl}) \leftarrow$ the interpolated value;
      end for
    end for

The Poisson equation is solved in Fourier space as shown in Algorithm 2. The variable $\hat{A}$ means the Fourier representation of the variable A. Since we simply use the periodic boundary conditions in (x, y) directions, we can solve Poisson Eq. (2) with 2D FFT.

Algorithm 2. Poisson equation with 2D Fourier Transform

    Input: f^n, **Output:** E_x^n, E_y^n
    for *All grid points* (v_{xk}, v_{yl}) **do**
      $\rho^n \leftarrow \rho^n + \sum_{k,l} dv_x dv_y f^n(*, *, v_{xk}, v_{yl})$
    end for
    $\hat{\rho}^n = $ 2D FFT $[\rho^n]$ (Forward FFT in x, y directions)
    $\hat{E}_x^{\ n} = -ik_x \hat{\rho}^n / (k_x^2 + k_y^2) / \text{normalization}$
    $\hat{E}_x^{\ n} = -ik_y \hat{\rho}^n / (k_x^2 + k_y^2) / \text{normalization}$
    $E_x^n = $ 2D IFFT $\left[\hat{E}_x^{\ n}\right]$ (Inverse FFT in x, y directions)
    $E_y^n = $ 2D IFFT $\left[\hat{E}_y^{\ n}\right]$ (Inverse FFT in x, y directions)

Algorithm 3 shows the time integral scheme used in the mini-app. As shown, we call the 1D advection along x and y directions twice and the other kernels once in each time step.

Algorithm 3. One time step

Input: f^n, **Output:** f^{n+1}
1D advection along x direction for $\Delta t/2$
1D advection along y direction for $\Delta t/2$
Velocity space integral: Compute $\rho^{n+1/2}$
Field solver: Compute $E_x^{n+1/2}, E_y^{n+1/2}$
1D advection along v_x direction for Δt
1D advection along v_y direction for Δt
1D advection along y direction for $\Delta t/2$
1D advection along x direction for $\Delta t/2$

3.3   Baseline OpenMP Implementation

The baseline version is implemented with OpenMP. Listing 1.1 shows the 1D advection along x direction as an example. In order to manage high dimensional array, we built an in-house view class which mimics the view class in Kokkos (See Subsect. 4.1 for detail). Contrary to the Kokkos implementation, our view can hold the data in row-major layout only.

Listing 1.1. 1D advection (x direction) with the semi-Lagrangian scheme

```
1   #define LAG_ORDER 5
2   #define LAG_OFFSET 2
3   #define LAG_PTS 6
4   double inv_dx = 1./dx;
5   #pragma omp for schedule(static) collapse(2)
6   for(int ivy = 0; ivy < nvy; ++ivy) {
7     for(int ivx = 0; ivx < nvx; ++ivx) {
8       const double vx = vx_min + ivx * dvx;
9       const double depx = dt * vx;
10      for(int iy = 0; iy < ny; ++iy) {
11        for(int ix = 0; ix < nx; ++ix) {
12          const double x = x_min + ix * dx;
13          const double xstar = x_min + fmod(Lx + x − depx − x_min, Lx);
14          int ipos1 = floor((xstar − x_min) * inv_dx);
15          const double d_prev1 = LAG_OFFSET
16                          + inv_dx * (xstar − (x_min + ipos1 * dx));
17          ipos1 −= LAG_OFFSET;
18          double coef[LAG_PTS];
19          lag_basis(d_prev1, coef);
20          double ftmp = 0.;
21          for(int k = 0; k <= LAG_ORDER; k++)
22            ftmp += coef[k] * fn[ivy][ivx][iy][(nx + ipos1 + k) % nx];
23          fnp1[ivy][ivx][iy][ix] = ftmp;
24        }
25      }
26    }
27  }
```

We simply parallelize along the outermost directions (v_x, v_y) with "for collapse (2)" pragma. All the 4D loops appeared in the 1D advections, and integral kernels are also parallelized in the same way. The Lagrange bases are computed by the inline function "lag_basis" (line 19). As found in Listing 1.1, the memory accesses for each grid point are read operation from the 4D array f^n and write operation to the 4D array f^{n+1}. The indirect memory access due to the integer operations on "ipos1" is found in line 22. It should be noted that the OpenMP parallel region "omp parallel" is declared outside of this kernel, so there is only "omp for" inside.

3.4   Characteristics of Kernels

It turned out that more than 95 % of the costs come from the advection kernels in Vlasov solver and the integral kernel in Poisson solver. Thus, in the present work, we only measure the performance of these kernels. The characteristics of the kernels are summarized in Table 2. Although the advection kernels seem to be very similar, they perform interpolations along different directions. This gives a critical difference in performance on cache-based architecture like CPUs as discussed in Subsect. 6.1. As an intrinsic nature of the semi-Lagrangian scheme, these kernels are sharply curbed by indirect memory accesses. The integral kernel reduces the 4D array into 2D array, which is a little more complicated than simply reducing an array into a scalar.

Table 2. Features of the kernels. The advection kernels are characterized by indirect memory access patterns, while the integral kernel requires the reduction over velocity space. The Flop/Byte is measured in average considering a perfect and unlimited cache.

Kernel	advect_x (advect_y)	advect_vx (advect_vy)	Integral
Memory accesses	1 load + 1 store	1 load + 1 store	1 load
Access pattern	Indirect access	Indirect access	Reduction by row
Flop/Byte (f/b)	67/16	65/16	1/8

4   GPU Implementation of GYSELA Mini-App

Since the GPU acceleration is an important aspect of our work, we have ported the code to GPU environment. We have employed Kokkos as a higher level abstraction approach and OpenACC as a directive-based approach.

4.1   Kokkos Implementation of GYSELA Mini-application

Kokkos is an open source performance portable library based on C++11 [8]. The higher level abstractions available in Kokkos include "Memory Spaces", "Memory Layout", "Memory Traits", "Execution Patterns", "Execution Spaces", and

"Execution Policies". The three former abstractions are relevant to the memory management and the three latter abstractions focus on the parallel operations.

Listing 1.2. Example of Kokkos views

```
1  #include <Kokkos_Core.hpp>
2  #include <Kokkos_Complex.hpp>
3  typedef double float64;
4  typedef Kokkos::complex<double> complex64;
5  typedef Kokkos::DefaultExecutionSpace execution_space;
6  typedef Kokkos::View<float64*, execution_space> view_1d;
7  typedef Kokkos::View<float64**, execution_space> view_2d;
8  typedef Kokkos::View<float64***, execution_space> view_3d;
9  typedef Kokkos::View<float64****, execution_space> view_4d;
10 typedef Kokkos::View<complex64*, execution_space> complex_view_1d;
11 typedef Kokkos::View<complex64**, execution_space> complex_view_2d;
```

Abstract Memory Management in Kokkos. Kokkos offers the multidimensional array support called "views". Views allow an abstract memory management which can provide efficient memory access patterns for the given device. The memory access patterns are particularly important when accessing the high dimensional array. For multicore CPUs, it is preferable to apply the thread-level parallelization to the outermost loop(s) and each thread performs some computations over the innermost loop(s) in a SIMD (Single Instruction, Multiple Data) manner. In contrast, on GPUs, it is important to assign threads to the innermost loop to access memory contiguously (coalesced way).

Listing 1.3. Velocity space integral in Poisson eq. (2) using C++11 lambda

```
1  Kokkos::parallel_for(nx*ny, KOKKOS_LAMBDA (const int ixy) {
2    int ix = ixy%nx, iy = ixy/nx;
3    float64 sum = 0.;
4    for(int ivy=0; ivy<nvy; ivy++) {
5      for(int ivx=0; ivx<nvx; ivx++) {
6        sum += fn(ix, iy, ivx, ivy);
7      }
8    }
9    rho(ix, iy) = sum;
10 });
```

Listing 1.4. 1D advection (x direction) in Eq. (3) using a functor

```
1    struct advect_1D_x_functor {
2      Config* conf_;
3      view_4d fn_, fnp1_;
4      ...
5      advect_1D_x_functor(Config*conf, const view_4d fn, view_4d fnp1, float64 dt)
6        : conf_(conf), fn_(fn), fnp1_(fnp1), dt_(dt) {
7        const Domain *dom = &(conf_->dom_); // Initialize class members
8        ...
9      }
10
11     KOKKOS_INLINE_FUNCTION
12     void operator()( const int &i ) const {
13       int4 idx_4D = Index::int2coord_4D(i, nx_, ny_, nvx_, nvy_);
14       int ix = idx_4D.x, iy = idx_4D.y, ivx = idx_4D.z, ivy = idx_4D.w;
15       // Compute Lagrange bases (same as lines 12−19 in Listing 1.1)
16       ...
17       float64 ftmp = 0.;
18       for(int k=0; k<=LAG_ORDER; k++) {
19         int idx_ipos1 = (nx_ + ipos1 + k) % nx_;
20         ftmp += coef[k] * fn_(idx_ipos1, iy, ivx, ivy);
21       }
22       fnp1_(ix, iy, ivx, ivy) = ftmp;
23     }
24   }
25
26   Kokkos::parallel_for(nx*ny*nvx*nvy, advect_1D_x_functor(conf, fn, fnp1, dt));
```

We define 1D to 4D views in the header file as shown in Listing 1.2. By defining the views with "Kokkos::DefaultExecutionSpace" (lines 6–9, 10–11), the "Memory Space" and "Memory Layout" are specified to fit with the given architecture. For example, the data are located on the device space for CUDA backend. For CUDA (resp. OpenMP) backend, the multidimensional array is mapped to the memory in column major (resp. row major). The former corresponds to Fortran Layout and the latter corresponds to C layout. A view only keeps the *metadata* such as data shape, "Memory Space" and "Memory Layout", and the actual *data* are located on the host or device specified by the "Memory Space". "Memory traits" specify how the data is accessed, but we have not tested this feature in the present work. It is also worth noting that there is the official support for the complex data defined in "Kokkos_Complex.hpp" (line 2).

Listing 1.5. Helper for index computation

```
1   namespace Index {
2   #if ! defined( KOKKOS_ENABLE_CUDA )
3       // For Layout right (C layout)
4       KOKKOS_INLINE_FUNCTION
5       int4 int2coord_4D(int i, int n1, int n2, int n3, int n4) {
6           int j234 = i%(n2*n3*n4), j1 = i/(n2*n3*n4);
7           int j34 = j234%(n3*n4), j2 = j234/(n3*n4);
8           int j4 = j34%n4, j3 = j34/n4;
9           return make_int4(j1, j2, j3, j4);
10      }
11  #else
12      // For Layout left (Fortan layout)
13      KOKKOS_INLINE_FUNCTION
14      int4 int2coord_4D(int i, int n1, int n2, int n3, int n4) {
15          int j123 = i%(n1*n2*n3), j4 = i/(n1*n2*n3);
16          int j12 = j123%(n1*n2), j3 = j123/(n1*n2);
17          int j1 = j12%n1, j2 = j12/n1;
18          return make_int4(j1, j2, j3, j4);
19      }
20  #endif
21  }
```

Abstract Parallel Operations in Kokkos. In order to perform parallel operations in an abstract way, Kokkos offers three types of "Execution Patterns" including "parallel_for", "parallel_reduce" and "parallel_scan". The "Execution Space" specifies where the parallel operations are performed either GPUs or CPUs. The "Execution Policy" determines how an execution pattern is performed. A user can transmit a kernel to an execution pattern in either C++11 lambdas or functors. Listing 1.3 shows the velocity space integral operation in Eq. (2) given by a lambda function. In this kernel, the 4D view "fn" is reduced to the 2D view "rho" inside a 1D flatten parallel loop (line 1). Functors would be preferable for a kernel with many lines, which improves code reusability (see Subsect. 5.4 for adding a new range policy without reimplementing the entire operation). Listing 1.4 shows the kernel to compute 1D advection along x direction given by a functor. The functor in Listing 1.4 is then fed to the "parallel_for" with a naive 1D range policy as shown in the bottom line of the Listing 1.4 Here, the "parallel_for" is operated over a single index which covers the entire four-dimensional loops. In order to unpack the single index to the multidimensional indices, we have prepared a helper for the index computations (line 22) as defined in Listing 1.5, where memory accesses are contiguous for the given device. Here, the execution space is identified using the macro "KOKKOS_ENABLE_CUDA". As discussed in Subsect. 5.4, the naive 1D policy harms the performance particularly on CPUs, since it conflicts with the vectorization on CPUs.

4.2   OpenACC Implementation of GYSELA Mini-application

Since a multidimensional indices support of our in-house view class is relying on the C++11 standard library, our view class is unavailable in the accelerated region (lines 7–26). Thus, we just use the 1D raw pointer in the accelerated region as found in Listing 1.6 (lines 1–2).

Listing 1.6. 1D advection (x direction) in OpenACC

```
1   float64 *dptr_fn = fn.raw(); // Raw pointer to the 4D view fn
2   float64 *dptr_fnp1 = fnp1.raw();
3
4   const int n = nx * ny * nvx * nvy;
5   #pragma acc data present(dptr_fn[0:n],dptr_fnp1[0:n])
6   {
7     #pragma acc parallel loop collapse(3)
8     for(int ivy = 0; ivy < nvy; ivy++) {
9       for(int ivx = 0; ivx < nvx; ivx++) {
10        for(int iy = 0; iy < ny; iy++) {
11          #pragma acc loop vector independent
12          for(int ix = 0; ix < nx; ix++) {
13            // Compute Lagrange bases (same as lines 12−19 in Listing 1.1)
14            ...
15            float64 ftmp = 0.;
16            for(int k=0; k<=LAG_ORDER; k++) {
17              int idx_ipos1 = (nx + ipos1 + k) % nx;
18              int idx = idx_ipos1 + iy*nx + ivx*nx*ny + ivy*nx*ny*nvx;
19              ftmp += coef[k] * dptr_fn[idx];
20            }
21            int idx = ix + iy*nx + ivx*nx*ny + ivy*nx*ny*nvx;
22            dptr_fnp1[idx] = ftmp;
23          }
24        }
25      }
26    }
27  }
```

The raw pointers to 4D views "dptr_fn" and "dptr_fnp1" are required for the data to be allocated on GPUs with "#pragma acc enter data create" at the initialization stage. In order to maximize the loop body size, the outermost three loops are collapsed (lines 8–10), whereas the innermost loop is vectorized with "#pragma acc loop vector independent". In OpenACC, it is of great importance to inform compilers about the locations of data (line 5) by using the OpenACC data-clause. Without this, the host to device data transfers arise when entering the accelerated region (line 7) and the performance degrades significantly.

5   Portable Implementation of GYSELA Mini-App with OpenACC/OpenMP and Kokkos

In this section, we present a portable implementation of the GYSELA mini-app based on OpenACC/OpenMP and Kokkos. The former approach uses a single code and changes the directives depending on architecture with C macros. We separate the directives since we are willing to use OpenMP and OpenACC for GPUs (e.g. managing multiple GPU cards with OpenMP threads.) In the latter approach, we just use the single code based on Kokkos. Either using OpenACC or Kokkos, we first write codes on GPUs and made some tests on them. Once we have checked that the code works correctly, we make the CPU versions while keeping the GPU capability and avoiding the code duplications. For OpenACC and Kokkos GPU version, we used pgi and gcc compilers, respectively. For the rest, we used Intel compilers. The details are listed in Table 3.

Table 3. Compilers and compiler flags used for each version.

Version	Compiler	Compiler flags
Skylake (Kokkos)	Intel compiler 18.0.2	-O3 -fopenmp -xCORE-AVX512
Skylake (OpenMP)	Intel compiler 18.0.2	-O3 -fopenmp -xCORE-AVX512
P100 (Kokkos)	cuda/8.0.61	-O3 -std=c++11 -mrtm -arch=sm_60
P100 (OpenACC)	pgi compiler 19.1	-O3 -ta=nvidia:cc60

5.1   Portable Implementation with Kokkos

It is straight forward to write a CPU version in Kokkos: just change the compiler flags "KOKKOS_DEVICES" from "Cuda" to "OpenMP" and "KOKKOS_ARCH" from "Pascal60" to "SKX" in our case. Listing 1.7 shows the Kokkos implementation of Poisson solver in Fourier space. Since we use cufft to perform 2D FFT on GPUs, we have to prepare the fftw version to perform 2D FFT on CPUs, which is probably the most demanding part. We have prepared a FFT wrapper class which manages the 2D FFT using the domain specific FFT libraries as backends (lines 1, 32–34). The backend is switched depending on the macro "KOKKOS_ENABLE_CUDA". Except for this wrapper, the same code works on both GPUs and CPUs without any modifications. As for the parallel part in lines 6–30, the coalesced memory accesses are allowed for GPUs along "ix1" index. At the same time, the thread level parallelization is applied on CPUs along "ix1" index. Since the 2D view has a column-major layout on GPUs and a row-major layout on CPUs, the 'ix1' dimension is the innermost (resp. outermost) direction on GPUs (resp. CPUs). It should be noted that the shallow copies (lines 3–4) are needed to capture these class members by "KOKKOS_LAMBDA" (this matters when compiled with nvcc 8.0.64).

Listing 1.7. Kokkos implementation for Poisson solver

```
1   fft_->rfft2(rho_.ptr_on_device(), rho_hat_.ptr_on_device());
2
3   complex_view_2d ex_hat = ex_hat_, ey_hat = ey_hat_, rho_hat = rho_hat_;
4   view_1d filter = filter_;
5   float64 normcoeff = 1./(nx*ny);
6   Kokkos::parallel_for(nx1h, KOKKOS_LAMBDA (const int ix1) {
7     float64 kx = ix1 * kx0;
8     int ix2 = 0;
9     ex_hat(ix1, ix2) = −kx * I * rho_hat(ix1, ix2) * filter(ix1) * normcoeff;
10    ey_hat(ix1, ix2) = 0.;
11    rho_hat(ix1, ix2) = rho_hat(ix1, ix2) * filter(ix1) * normcoeff;
12
13    for(int ix2=1; ix2<nx2h; ix2++) {
14      float64 ky = ix2 * ky0;
15      float64 k2 = kx * kx + ky * ky;
16
17      ex_hat(ix1, ix2) = −(kx/k2) * I * rho_hat(ix1, ix2) * normcoeff;
18      ey_hat(ix1, ix2) = −(ky/k2) * I * rho_hat(ix1, ix2) * normcoeff;
19      rho_hat(ix1, ix2) = rho_hat(ix1, ix2) / k2 * normcoeff;
20    }
21
22    for(int ix2=nx2h; ix2<nx2; ix2++) {
23      float64 ky = (ix2−nx2) * ky0;
24      float64 k2 = kx*kx + ky*ky;
25
26      ex_hat(ix1, ix2) = −(kx/k2) * I * rho_hat(ix1, ix2) * normcoeff;
27      ey_hat(ix1, ix2) = −(ky/k2) * I * rho_hat(ix1, ix2) * normcoeff;
28      rho_hat(ix1, ix2) = rho_hat(ix1, ix2) / k2 * normcoeff;
29    }
30  });
31
32  fft_->irfft2(rho_hat.ptr_on_device(), rho_.ptr_on_device());
33  fft_->irfft2(ex_hat.ptr_on_device(), ex_.ptr_on_device());
34  fft_->irfft2(ey_hat.ptr_on_device(), ey_.ptr_on_device());
```

5.2   Portable Implementation with OpenACC/OpenMP

It is more problematic to replace OpenACC directives with OpenMP directives. We use the in-house macro "ENABLE_OPENACC" to switch OpenACC and OpenMP directives. Listing 1.8 shows the OpenACC/OpenMP implementation of Poisson solver in Fourier space (roughly the same one as Listing 1.7). As found in Listing 1.8, we have to add the data-clause directives for OpenACC (lines 2, 6, 23). Clearly, this kind of macro heavy implementation degrades the readability. It may be worth commenting on the layout issue in this version. Since the array layout is always row-major in this version, the memory access pattern cannot be ideal for both GPUs and CPUs. In this case, the performance issues arise on the CPUs where the thread level parallelization is applied to the inner most direction (along "ix1" index).

Listing 1.8. OpenACC/OpenMP implementation for Poisson solver

```
1   #if defined( ENABLE_OPENACC )
2      #pragma acc data present(dptr_rho,dptr_ex,dptr_ey,...)
3      {
4   #endif
5      #if defined( ENABLE_OPENACC )
6         #pragma acc host_data use_device(dptr_rho, dptr_rho_hat)
7      #endif
8      fft_->rfft2(dptr_rho, dptr_rho_hat);
9      #if defined( ENABLE_OPENACC )
10        #pragma acc parallel loop
11     #else
12        #pragma omp for schedule(static)
13     #endif
14     for(int ix1=0; ix1<nx1h; ix1++) {
15        int idx = ix1; float64 kx = ix1 * kx0;
16        dptr_ex_hat[idx] = -kx * I * dptr_rho_hat[idx] * dptr_filter[ix1] / (nx1*nx2);
17        dptr_ey_hat[idx] = 0.;
18        dptr_rho_hat[idx] = dptr_rho_hat[idx] * dptr_filter[ix1]/ (nx1*nx2);
19        for(int ix2=1; ix2<nx2h; ix2++) { /* Similar computations ... */ }
20        for(int ix2=nx2h; ix2<nx2; ix2++) { /* Similar computations ... */ }
21     }
22     #if defined( ENABLE_OPENACC )
23        #pragma acc host_data use_device(dptr_rho,...)
24        {
25     #endif
26        fft_->irfft2(dptr_rho_hat, dptr_rho);
27        // Inverse FFTs for dptr_Ex_hat and dptr_Ey_hat
28     #if defined( ENABLE_OPENACC )
29        }
30     #endif
31  #if defined( ENABLE_OPENACC )
32     }
33  #endif
```

5.3 Performance Comparison of Baseline Versions

In this subsection, we compare the performance of the baseline versions. The problem size is $(N_x, N_y, N_{v_x}, N_{v_y}) = (128, 128, 128, 128)$ and the number of iterations is 128. Figure 1 shows the obtained performance of the baseline version on each device of Table 1. In the original implementation, OpenACC version outperforms the Kokkos version for advection kernels. For the integral kernel, Kokkos version is a bit faster. Performance of Kokkos CPU version is a bit disappointing, since it is two to three times slower than the OpenMP version.

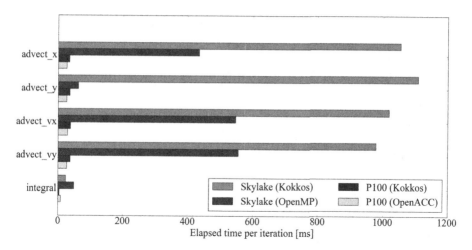

Fig. 1. The baseline performance of the OpenACC/OpenMP and Kokkos versions.

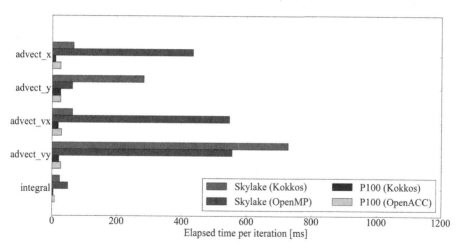

Fig. 2. The improved performance of the OpenACC/OpenMP and Kokkos versions.

5.4   3D MDRange Policy

In order to improve the performance of Kokkos version, we have modified the execution policy from the naive 1D (bottom line in Listing 1.4) to 3D policy as shown in Listing 1.9. The first and second arguments of this 3D policy specifies the start and end indices in each dimension. The third argument gives the tiling dimensions. Correspondingly, we have added a new operator to the functor in Listing 1.4 for this 3D range policy as shown in Listing 1.10. Contrary to the flattened version in Listing 1.4, 3D loops over "ix", "iy" and "ivx" are managed in the more preferable way for each architecture in Listing 1.10. In this version, we no longer need the index unpacking helper in Listing

1.4. In addition, the loop along v_y direction is kept inside the operator (line 6) which makes a room for vectorization on CPUs. As expected, the kernels benefit from the vectorization on CPUs. On CPUs, the tile sizes are set as $(TX, TY, TZ) = (16, 1, 1), (1, 32, 4), (1, 1, 8)$ and $(1, 1, 16)$ for the 1D advection kernels along x, y, v_x and v_y directions, respectively. The best tile sizes are chosen by manual tile size scan. On GPU, we use $(TX, TY, TZ) = (32, 4, 2)$ only to fit with the warp size of 32.

Listing 1.9. 3D MDRangePolicy

```
1  typedef typename Kokkos::Experimental::MDRangePolicy<
2    Kokkos::Experimental::Rank<
3    3, Kokkos::Experimental::Iterate::Default, Kokkos::Experimental::Iterate::Default>
4  > MDPolicyType_3D;
5  MDPolicyType_3D mdpolicy_3d( {{0,0,0}}, {{nx,ny,nvx}}, {{TX,TY,TZ}} );
6  Kokkos::parallel_for("md3d_advection_x", mdpolicy_3d,
7    advect_1D_x_functor(conf, fn, fnp1, dt));
```

Listing 1.10. 3D operator for 1D advection (x direction)

```
1  KOKKOS_INLINE_FUNCTION
2  void operator()(const int ix, const int iy, const int ivx) const {
3    // Compute Lagrange bases (same as lines 12−19 in Listing 1.1.)
4    ...
5
6    for(int ivy=0; ivy<nvy; ivy++) {
7      float64 ftmp = 0.;
8      for(int k=0; k<=LAG_ORDER; k++) {
9        int idx_ipos1 = (nx_ + ipos1 + k) % nx_;
10       ftmp += coef[k] * fn_(idx_ipos1, iy, ivx, ivy);
11     }
12     fnp1_(ix, iy, ivx, ivy) = ftmp;
13   }
14 }
```

This example indicates that the careful settings of execution policies can offer significant performance improvements particularly on CPUs. Figure 2 shows the performance of updated version, where Kokkos version outperforms for advections along x and v_x directions. As we have noted, the 4D array Layouts in Skylake (Kokkos) and Skylake (OpenMP) are different. Therefore one can expect significant difference in terms of performance using OpenMP versus Kokkos. The innermost direction is v_y direction in Skylake (Kokkos) and it is x direction in Skylake (OpenMP). The advection along innermost direction shows low performance on Skylake, since the innermost loop cannot be well vectorized due to the indirect memory accesses.

6   Performance Portability, Readability and Productivity

In this section, we present the absolute performance in Flops and summarize the acceleration against the OpenMP baseline version. We also discuss the code readability and productivity [6] of each implementation, which are also important ingredients in a modern parallel computing framework.

6.1   Performance Evaluation

In this subsection, we evaluate the achieved performance with each implementation. As a reference, we estimated the ideal performance by the Roofline model [22] as follows.

$$\text{Attainable GFlops/s} = \min(F, B \times f/b), \tag{7}$$

where F is the Peak Floating Point Performance in GFlops, B is the Peak Memory Bandwidth in GBytes/s and f/b is the operational intensity. Figures 3 and 4 show the Roofline models for Skylake and P100. The red line shows the Roofline estimated by Eq. (7), and the achieved performance of each kernel is marked with the star (See Table 2 for the details of kernels).

Kokkos and OpenMP Performance on Skylake. Comparing Figs. 3 (a) and (b), the advection kernels along x and v_x directions show almost the ideal performance in the Kokkos implementation, while the advection kernel along y direction shows the highest performance in OpenMP implementation. The difference can be explained by the difference in memory layouts, where the innermost direction is v_y (resp. x) direction in Kokkos (resp. OpenMP) implementation. Thus, the interpolation along v_y (resp. x) direction bothers vectorization in Kokkos (resp. OpenMP) due to the irregular accesses to memory (indirect memory accesses). The best performance is obtained in the advection along the second innermost direction, where the indirect memory access to that direction benefits from local L2 cache and the SIMD vectorization along the innermost direction is still feasible. In the current problem size of 128^4 grid points, the pressure to the local cache at each step for accessing the innermost two directions is estimated as $(n_x \times n_y)$ or $(n_{v_x} \times n_{v_y}) = 128^2$, which requires 0.125 MB for storing double precision numbers. This size fits with the local L2 cache on Skylake (1 MB). The good performance in Kokkos for the interpolation along x direction (the outermost direction) can be interpreted as the benefit of tiling and good use of the shared L3 cache. We foresee the same performance as Kokkos if we redesign the OpenMP version with a tiling and loop reordering. A recent proposal to add tile directives to OpenMP will make ease this kind of optimizations in OpenMP [14].

Kokkos and OpenACC Performance on P100. Comparing Figs. 4 (a) and (b), the advection kernel along x direction in Kokkos shows almost the ideal performance. This originates from good caching effects of GPUs. By explicitly using the texture memories, we may expect substantial speedups [4], but it is too architecture specific and does not fit with the philosophy of performance portability. The low performance of integral kernel in the OpenACC implementation may be improved by specifying correctly the thread group size, which remains as a future task.

Table 4 shows the achieved performance and upper ceilings for each kernel. The Kokkos version of integral kernel achieves a higher bandwidth than

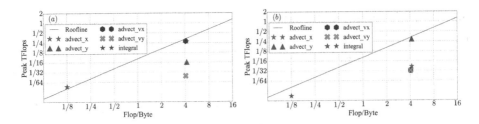

Fig. 3. Roofline Model for 1D advection kernels and integral kernel on Skylake with (a) Kokkos and (b) OpenMP. The kernels close to the upper ceiling indicate a good performance.

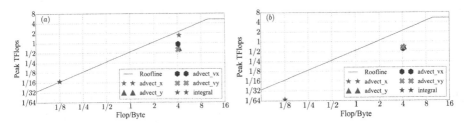

Fig. 4. Roofline Model for 1D advection kernels and integral kernel on P100 with (a) Kokkos and (b) OpenACC. The kernels close to the upper ceiling indicate a good performance.

STREAM TRIAD bandwidth. As shown in Listing 1.3, this kernel is quite similar to STREAM2 SUM [1] which gives a higher bandwidth than STREAM TRIAD bandwidth on Skylake and P100. The final performance of the entire mini-app is summarized in Table 5. These results demonstrate that the Kokkos versions can outperform the OpenMP or OpenACC versions, unless we make device specific optimizations. However, we have to state that we paid development efforts on the Kokkos implementation, especially on the 3D range policy discussed in Subsect. 5.4.

6.2   Readability

In this subsection, we discuss the code readability for the given implementation.

OpenMP. The directive-based OpenMP version is probably the most straight forward and readable. In the OpenMP implementation, we only have to insert pragmas to the loops to parallelize, which does not harm code readability.

OpenACC. Although it is directive-based, the OpenACC version is little more complicated than the OpenMP version, mainly due to the existence of data-clause. In OpenACC, it is of critical importance to minimize the data-transfer between CPUs and GPUs, which can be controlled by the data-clause. If the

Table 4. Achieved performance on single Skylake and P100. The ideal performance is estimated by the Roofline model in Eq. (7), where the upper ceiling is given by the STREAM bandwidth in each case. The achieved GB/s to the STREAM bandwidth are presented in the parentheses.

	Kernel	f/b	Ideal performance [GFlops]	Achieved performance	
				GFlops	Bandwidth [GBytes/s]
Skylake (Kokkos)	advect_x	67/16	335	271.7	64.9 (81.1%)
	advect_y	67/16	335	63.5	15.2 (19.0%)
	advect_vx	65/16	325	278.5	68.6 (85.7%)
	advect_vy	65/16	325	24.0	5.90 (7.4%)
	integral	1/8	10	11.4	91.6 (114.5%)
Skylake (OpenMP)	advect_x	67/16	335	41.8	9.98 (12.5%)
	advect_y	67/16	335	291.1	69.51 (86.9%)
	advect_vx	65/16	325	31.94	7.86 (9.8 %)
	advect_vy	65/16	325	31.5	7.74 (9.6%)
	integral	1/8	10	5.5	43.7 (54.7%)
P100 (Kokkos)	advect_x	67/16	2261.3	1737.9	415.0 (76.9%)
	advect_y	67/16	2261.3	704.4	168.2 (31.1%)
	advect_vx	65/16	2193.8	935.7	230.3 (42.7%)
	advect_vy	65/16	2193.8	638.6	157.2 (29.1%)
	integral	1/8	67.5	68.7	550.0 (101.9 %)
P100 (OpenACC)	advect_x	67/16	2261.3	710.8	169.8 (31.4%)
	advect_y	67/16	2261.3	695.6	166.1 (30.8%)
	advect_vx	65/16	2193.8	605.2	149.0 (27.6%)
	advect_vy	65/16	2193.8	657.5	161.8 (30.0%)
	integral	1/8	67.5	16.9	134.9 (25.0%)

Table 5. The elapsed time of the entire mini-app with 128 iterations. The acceleration with respect to the baseline OpenMP version, that is Skylake (OpenMP), is also shown.

Version	Time [s]	Acceleration
Skylake (OpenMP)	278.197	1.0
Skylake (Kokkos)	192.079	1.45
P100 (OpenACC)	21.476	12.95
P100 (Kokkos)	15.600	17.83

code is written in C++, we need special treatments to manage data locations of class members. In addition, we have to pay some attentions to call external libraries such as cufft inside class methods (See Subsect. 5.2).

Kokkos. Once the code is made based upon Kokkos, the Kokkos code would be quite readable. Moreover, we can make a single code that works on both CPUs and GPUs without duplicating the code. Some sort of optimizations like tiling can be applied without changing the kernel as explained in Subsect. 5.4.

OpenACC/OpenMP. The merged version loses a bit of readability due to the intensive macros (see Subsect. 5.2). If we separate the OpenMP and OpenACC codes, the code can be simplified at the cost of huge duplications of the code.

6.3   Productivity

If a code is small (e.g. less than 5k lines of codes) and written in C++, there may be not much difference in productivity either using OpenACC/OpenMP or Kokkos. The challenge using Kokkos for the production code, however, lies in the refactoring of data and loop structures and possibly language over the entire code. When it comes to the GYSELA code, we have to refactor more than 50k lines of code written in Fortran 90 [10] into C++ besides changing data and loop structures. In contrast, we can keep the code structure and language if we rely on OpenACC and OpenMP. The initial investments to port the production code with Kokkos would be enormous, but this approach may suppress the maintenance and further development costs in the upcoming CPU and accelerator based supercomputers. A directive with supports for memory layout and access pattern managements (such as a tiling support in OpenMP [14]) would be a true game-changer.

7   Summary

This paper presents a case study on the performance portability of kinetic plasma simulation code with the semi-Lagrangian scheme, namely the GYSELA code. The kinetic simulation codes are characterized by their high-dimensionality, more than four dimensional. Although the optimization strategy of this kind of code on conventional multicore CPUs is established, it is still questionable to port the code to GPU environment without harming the performance. In the present work, we extract the key features of GYSELA and encapsulate them into a mini-app which solves a similar but simplified Vlasov-Poisson system as GYSELA. The GYSELA mini-app is implemented in a mixed OpenACC/OpenMP and Kokkos focusing on the performance portability, productivity and readability. The mixed OpenACC/OpenMP approach represents the directive-based approach, whereas the Kokkos approach represents the higher level abstraction using a single codebase. In both approach, we focus to avoid the duplications of code lines unless needed.

In the mixed OpenACC/OpenMP approach, the OpenMP code can be ported with OpenACC without any difficulty. The outstanding feature of OpenACC is that we can generate GPU codes just by inserting few lines of pragmas. If we suppress the extra data transfer between CPUs and GPUs, the OpenACC version gives a speed-up of around $10\times$ compared the baseline OpenMP version. Unfortunately, by merging OpenMP and OpenACC directives, the code will soon lose the readability due to the intensive macro usage. The lack of memory layout abstraction can lead to inappropriate memory access patterns, which may result in a performance bottleneck.

In the Kokkos approach, we have to pay initial porting costs for refactoring the code. For example, we have to declare arrays as views and replace parallel loops by appropriate "parallel_patterns". Once the porting is done, the code can run on both CPUs and GPUs without any modifications. At first, we employed a 1D naive range policy which covers the entire 4D loops and found a relatively low performance on CPUs. The 1D flattened loop impairs performance, probably interfering with the vectorization of the innermost loop. By introducing the 3D range policy, the performance of CPU version has improved dramatically and achieved a speed-up of 1.45 with respect to the baseline OpenMP version. The Kokkos GPU version is 17 times faster than the baseline OpenMP CPU version.

Finally, we summarize the obtained results from the view point of performance portability, readability and productivity. The mixed OpenACC/OpenMP approach is the most promising in terms of productivity. Relying on OpenACC directives, we can port the GYSELA code without changing language from Fortran 90 to C++. In contrast, we have to rewrite the code in C++ in Kokkos approach, where the porting costs would be enormous for a large scale code like GYSELA consisting of more than 50k lines. At the cost of huge initial refactoring efforts, Kokkos will offer a readable and productive code which may suppress the maintenance and further development costs in the upcoming supercomputers.

Acknowledgement. This work was carried out using the JFRS-1 supercomputer at Computational Simulation Centre of International Fusion Energy Research Centre (IFERC-CSC) in Rokkasho Fusion Institute of QST and Tsubame 3.0 supercomputer at Tokyo Tech. This work was partly supported by JHPCN projects jh180081-NAHI and jh190065-NHI, 102515-15 the MEXT, Grant for HPCI Strategic Program Field No. 4: Next-Generation Industrial Innovations, and Grant for Post-K priority issue No. 6: Development of Innovative Clean Energy.

References

1. The STREAM2 Home Page. http://www.cs.virginia.edu/stream/stream2/. Accessed 09 Oct 2019
2. Sustainable Memory Bandwidth in High Performance Computers. https://www.cs.virginia.edu/stream/. Accessed 09 Oct 2019
3. TSUBAME Computing Services TSUBAME3.0. http://www.t3.gsic.titech.ac.jp/en

4. Asahi, Y., Latu, G., Ina, T., Idomura, Y., Grandgirard, V., Garbet, X.: Optimization of fusion kernels on accelerators with indirect or strided memory access patterns. IEEE Trans. Parallel Distrib. Syst. **28**(7), 1974–1988 (2017). https://doi.org/10.1109/TPDS.2016.2633349

5. Asahi, Y., Latu, G., Bigot, J., Maeyama, S., Grandgirard, V., Idomura, Y.: Overlapping communications in gyrokinetic codes on accelerator-based platforms, concurrency and computation: practice and experience. https://doi.org/10.1002/cpe.5551

6. Asanović, K., et al.: The landscape of parallel computing research: a view from Berkeley. Technical report. UCB/EECS-2006-183, EECS Department, University of California, Berkeley (2006). http://www2.eecs.berkeley.edu/Pubs/TechRpts/2006/EECS-2006-183.html

7. Crouseilles, N., Latu, G., Sonnendrücker, E.: A parallel Vlasov solver based on local cubic spline interpolation on patches. J. Comput. Phys. **228**(5), 1429–1446 (2009). https://doi.org/10.1016/j.jcp.2008.10.041, http://www.sciencedirect.com/science/article/pii/S0021999108005652

8. Edwards, H.C., Trott, C.R., Sunderland, D.: Kokkos: enabling manycore performance portability through polymorphic memory access patterns. J. Parallel Distrib. Comput. **74**(12), 3202–3216 (2014). https://doi.org/10.1016/j.jpdc.2014.07.003, http://www.sciencedirect.com/science/article/pii/S0743731514001257

9. Garbet, X., Idomura, Y., Villard, L., Watanabe, T.H.: Gyrokinetic simulations of turbulent transport. Nucl. Fusion **50**, 043002 (2010). https://doi.org/10.1088/0029-5515/50/4/043002

10. Grandgirard, V., et al.: A 5D gyrokinetic full-f global semi-Lagrangian code for flux-driven ion turbulence simulations. Comput. Phys. Commun. **207**, 35–68 (2016). https://doi.org/10.1016/j.cpc.2016.05.007, http://www.sciencedirect.com/science/article/pii/S0010465516301230

11. Grete, P., Glines, F.W., O'Shea, B.W.: K-athena: a performance portable structured grid finite volume magnetohydrodynamics code. CoRR abs/1905.04341 (2019). http://arxiv.org/abs/1905.04341

12. Hornung, R.D., Keasler, J.A.: The RAJA Portability Layer: Overview and Status. Technical report, Lawrence Livermore National Lab. (LLNL), Livermore, CA, USA. https://doi.org/10.2172/1169830

13. Intel: intel® xeon® glod 6148 processor (27.5 m cache, 2.40 Ghz). https://ark.intel.com/content/www/us/en/ark/products/120489/intel-xeon-gold-6148-processor-27-5m-cache-2-40-ghz.html

14. Kruse, M., Finkel, H.: A proposal for loop-transformation pragmas. CoRR abs/1805.03374 (2018). http://arxiv.org/abs/1805.03374

15. Latu, G., ASAHI, Y., Bigot, J., Fehér, T., Grandgirard, V.: Scaling and optimizing the Gysela code on a cluster of many-core processors. In: SBAC-PAD 2018, WAMCA Workshop, SBAC-PAD 2018 Proceedings, Lyon, France, September 2018. https://hal.inria.fr/hal-01719208

16. Law, T.R., et al.: Performance portability of an unstructured hydrodynamics mini-application. In: Proceedings of 2018 International Workshop on Performance, Portability, and Productivity in HPC (P3HPC). ACM, New York (2018). https://doi.org/10.1109/CLUSTER.2018.00078

17. Nvidia: NVIDIA Tesla P100. https://images.nvidia.com/content/pdf/tesla/whitepaper/pascal-architecture-whitepaper.pdf

18. OpenACC: OpenACC 2.7 API Reference Card (2019). https://www.openacc.org/sites/default/files/inline-files/API%20Guide%202.7.pdf. Accessed 20 Aug 2019

19. OpenMP: OpenMP 5.0 Reference Guide (2019). https://www.openmp.org/wp-content/uploads/OpenMPRef-5.0-0519-print.pdf. Accessed 20 Aug 2019
20. Strang, G.: On the construction and comparison of difference schemes. SIAM J. Num. Anal. **5**(3), 506–517 (1968). https://doi.org/10.1137/0705041
21. Sunderland, D., Peterson, B., Schmidt, J., Humphrey, A., Thornock, J., Berzins, M.: An overview of performance portability in the Uintah runtime system through the use of Kokkos. In: 2016 Second International Workshop on Extreme Scale Programming Models and Middlewar (ESPM2), pp. 44–47 (2016). https://doi.org/10.1109/ESPM2.2016.012
22. Williams, S., Waterman, A., Patterson, D.: Roofline: an insightful visual performance model for multicore architectures. Commun. ACM **52**(4), 65–76 (2009). https://doi.org/10.1145/1498765.1498785

A Portable SIMD Primitive Using Kokkos for Heterogeneous Architectures

Damodar Sahasrabudhe[1(✉)], Eric T. Phipps[2], Sivasankaran Rajamanickam[2], and Martin Berzins[1]

[1] Scientific Computing and Imaging Institute, University of Utah,
Salt Lake City, UT, USA
{damodars,mb}@sci.utah.edu
[2] Center for Computing Research, Sandia National Laboratories,
Albuquerque, NM, USA
{etphipp,srajama}@sandia.gov

Abstract. As computer architectures are rapidly evolving (e.g. those designed for exascale), multiple portability frameworks have been developed to avoid new architecture-specific development and tuning. However, portability frameworks depend on compilers for auto-vectorization and may lack support for explicit vectorization on heterogeneous platforms. Alternatively, programmers can use intrinsics-based primitives to achieve more efficient vectorization, but the lack of a GPU back-end for these primitives makes such code non-portable. A unified, portable, Single Instruction Multiple Data (SIMD) primitive proposed in this work, allows intrinsics-based vectorization on CPUs and many-core architectures such as Intel Knights Landing (KNL), and also facilitates Single Instruction Multiple Threads (SIMT) based execution on GPUs. This unified primitive, coupled with the Kokkos portability ecosystem, makes it possible to develop explicitly vectorized code, which is portable across heterogeneous platforms. The new SIMD primitive is used on different architectures to test the performance boost against hard-to-auto-vectorize baseline, to measure the overhead against efficiently vectroized baseline, and to evaluate the new feature called the "logical vector length" (LVL). The SIMD primi-

The authors thank Sandia National Lab and Department of Energy, National Nuclear Security Administration (under Award Number(s) DE-NA0002375), for funding this work. Sandia National Laboratories is a multimission laboratory managed and operated by National Technology and Engineering Solutions of Sandia, LLC., a wholly owned subsidiary of Honeywell International, Inc., for the U.S. Department of Energy's National Nuclear Security Administration under contract DE-NA-0003525. The authors are grateful to Sandia and also Center for High Performance Computing, University of Utah for extending the resources to run the experiments. This paper describes objective technical results and analysis. Any subjective views or opinions that might be expressed in the paper do not necessarily represent the views of the U.S. Department of Energy or the United States Government.

Electronic supplementary material The online version of this chapter (https://doi.org/10.1007/978-3-030-49943-3_7) contains supplementary material, which is available to authorized users.

© Springer Nature Switzerland AG 2020
S. Wienke and S. Bhalachandra (Eds.): WACCPD 2019, LNCS 12017, pp. 140–163, 2020.
https://doi.org/10.1007/978-3-030-49943-3_7

tive provides portability across CPUs and GPUs without any performance degradation being observed experimentally.

Keywords: Portability · Vectorization · CUDA · SIMD Primitive · KNL · ARM

1 Introduction

Many different new computer architectures are being developed to potentially improve floating point performance such as those being developed for exascale. For example, Intel Haswell, Knights Landing (KNL), and Skylake processors support vector processing with a vector length of 512 bits. ARMv8.2-A processors have a vector length of 2048 bits [29]. Nvidia, Intel and AMD GPUs may be part of upcoming supercomputers [6,23]. Multiple performance portability frameworks are being developed to avoid architecture-specific tuning of programs for every new architecture. Such portability frameworks as Kokkos [5] and RAJA [12] provide uniform APIs to shield a programmer from architectural details and provide a new performant back-end for every new architecture to achieve the performance portability. The Kokkos [5] library achieves performance portability across CPUs and GPUs through the use of C++ template meta-programming.

Many pre-exascale and proposed exascale CPU and many-core architectures increasingly rely on Vector Processing Units (VPUs) to provide faster performance. VPUs are designed with Single Instruction Multiple Data (SIMD) capabilities (Vector capabilities) that execute a single instruction on multiple data elements of an array in parallel. SIMD constructs can enhance the performance by amortizing costs of instruction fetch, decode, memory reads and writes [7]. The process of converting a scalar code (which processes one element at a time) into a vector code (which can handle multiple elements of an array in parallel) is known as the "Vectorization" or "SIMD transformation". Thus, effective vectorization becomes very important for any performance portability tool, including Kokkos, to extract the best possible performance on CPUs.

Another important class of supercomputers uses GPUs as accelerators (e.g., Summit, Sierra). The Single Instruction Multiple Threads (SIMT) execution model of NVIDIA'S CUDA divides iterations of a data parallel kernel among multiple CUDA blocks and threads. A warp, a group of 32 CUDA threads, runs in the SIMD mode *similar* to the VPU (an exception: the latest Volta GPUs allows out of sync execution of warp threads). Any portable solution to vectorization should allow both styles of vectorization without considerable effort from application programmers. Furthermore, it is essential to distinguish between the physical vector length (PVL) in the hardware and the logical vector length (LVL) as needed by the application usage. For example, Fig. 1(a) shows how Kokkos' uniform APIs, Team, Thread and Vector [5], provide three levels of parallelism, and how they are mapped to CPUs and Nvidia GPUs. At the third level, user-provided C++11 lambda is called and loop indexes are passed to the lambda.

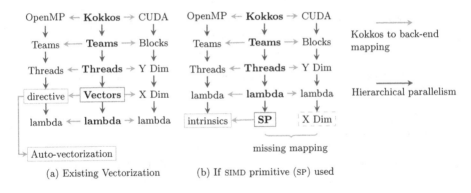

(a) Existing Vectorization   (b) If SIMD primitive (SP) used

Fig. 1. Kokkos APIs and mapping to CPU and CUDA

On Nvidia GPUs, the CUDA threads can be arranged in a three-dimensional grid. Each thread is identified by a triplet of ids in three dimensions which are accessed using "threadId.<x or y or z>". Consider the number of teams, threads and vectors requested by a user are L, T and V, respectively. In this case, GPUs, "L" Kokkos Teams are mapped to "L" CUDA blocks. The CUDA block id is mapped to the Kokkos team id. Each CUDA block is of the size VxTx1. The CUDA threads within a block can be logically divided among T partitions of size V (not to be confused with CUDA-provided Cooperative Groups). Each partition is assigned with a unique threadIdx.y ranging from 0 to T-1. Kokkos maps these partitions to Kokkos threads and the Kokkos thread id to CUDA threadIdx.y. The threads within a partition are assigned a unique threadIdx.x ranging from 0 to V-1. Kokkos Vectors get mapped to V threads within each partition. On a CPU, the Kokkos Teams and Kokkos Threads are mapped to OpenMP thread teams and OpenMP threads. Using the Kokkos Vector augments the user code with the compiler directives, which helps the compiler in auto-vectorization. This Kokkos design enables efficient SIMT execution on GPUs. However, successful automatic vectorization on CPUs depends on a lack of loop dependencies, minimal execution path divergence in the code, and a countable number of iterations, i.e., the number of iterations should be known before the loop begins execution [14]. Traditionally, compilers auto-vectorize loops that meet these criteria but fail to auto-vectorize outer loops or codes having complex control flows, such as nested if conditions or break statements. This problem can be addressed by using SIMD primitive libraries that encapsulate architecture-specific intrinsic data types and operators to achieve explicit vectorization without compromising portability across CPUs. Several such libraries exist for CPUs [17,20,27,32]. However, using SIMD primitive libraries would break the portability model as shown in Fig. 1(b). Instead of calling the Kokkos-provided **Vector**, programmers directly call the **lambda** from a **Thread**, and in turn invoke any SIMD primitive libraries, which would map user data types and functions to platform specific intrinsics. This explicit vectorization can generate more efficient code where compilers do a poor job. However, as far as the authors are aware no portable SIMD primitive library provides a GPU back-end, except OpenCL, which supports vector data types on all devices [24]. Using such primitive libraries with Kokkos, however, leads to compilation errors due to missing CUDA back-end for the primitive. *As a result, programmers are forced to make a compromise - either achieve portability at the cost of non-optimal* CPU *performance through the compiler auto-vectorization or achieve the optimal* CPU *performance using* SIMD *primitives, but maintain a separate version of code for* GPU *without using* SIMD *primitive, thereby compromising portability. Maintaining a different code for* GPU*s defeats the purpose of using Kokkos i.e., "performance portability".* In order to remedy the situation, this work makes the following contributions:

Heterogeneous Performance Portability: The primary contribution of this work is to add a new CUDA back-end to the existing SIMD primitive in Kokkos and make the SIMD primitive portable across heterogeneous platforms with Nvidia GPUs, for the first time. (More back-ends can be added to Kokkos and to the primitive to support a wider range of heterogeneous platforms.) The CUDA back-end is developed with the exact front-end interfaces as those built for the CPU back-end. Using these uniform interfaces, the application programmers can now achieve efficient vectorization on the CPU *without maintaining a separate* GPU *version of the code*, which was not possible before. Thus, the new SIMD primitive provides GPU portability and requires only a few hundred lines of new code for the GPU back-end.

Using the new portable SIMD primitive gives a speedup up to 7.8x on Intel KNL and 2.2x on Cavium ThunderX2 (ARMv8.1) for kernels that are hard to auto-vectorize. A comparison of the primitive with *existing SIMD code* (either auto-vectorized CPU code or equivalent CUDA code) shows no overhead due to the primitive. The portable primitive provides explicit vectorization capabilities, without the need to maintain a separate GPU code. As the outer loop may now be easily vectorized using the new primitive, more efficient code can be generated than auto-vectorization of the inner loop.

Logical Vector Length (LVL): Another feature of the new primitive is the Logical Vector Length (LVL). Application developers can pass the desired vector length as a template parameter (LVL) without considering underlying physical vector length. The LVL can be used to write codes agnostic of physical vector length (PVL), as explained in Sect. 3. Vectorizing the outer loop coupled with the LVL automatically introduces the "unroll and jam [3]" transformations, without any burden on programmers. These transformations can exploit instruction level parallelism and data locality to provide speedups up-to 3x on KNL and 1.6x on CUDA than the auto-vectorized/SIMT code.

Easy Adoption: Introducing the portable SIMD type needs less than a 10% change in user's loop. Once the primitive is introduced, the code can be explicitly vectorized on CPUS and also ported to GPUs without any further changes.

Applicability to Use Cases: The new portable SIMD data type supports a wide variety of computational science use cases, such as PDE assembly for complex applications, 2D convolution, batched linear algebra, and ensemble sparse matrix-vector multiplication as will be shown below.

2   Related Work

Vectorization has been studied from multiple perspectives: tools to identify vectorization opportunities [9]; portability frameworks using intermediate representations (IR) [26]; data parallel programming models [21] and data layout transformations [8]. Existing methods for improving vectorization include compiler directives, framework-based methods, tools to assist compilers [9], and language extensions [21]. Compilers provide directives that help auto-vectorization, e.g., the Intel compiler's #pragma vector directive instructs the compiler to override efficiency heuristics. Intel's #pragma simd can be used to force vectorization (although it has been deprecated in the 2018 version). #pragma ivdep instructs the compiler to ignore assumed loop dependencies. OpenMP provides #pragma omp simd, which is similar to #pragma simd. Even after specifying these directives, complex control structures in a loop may prevent auto-vectorization. The LLVM community is gradually developing more advanced vectorization capabilities such as outer loop vectorization [30]. OpenCL [24], a portable parallel programming standard, provides vector data types on all the supported devices. The maximum length of a vector data type in OpenCL is limited to 16, which may be problematic for architectures with larger PVLs. On the other hand, the LVL implemented in this work can be passed as a template argument and offers more flexibility to users. In addition to Kokkos, there are other recently developed performance portable libraries such as RAJA[12], Alpaka [33] and OCCA[22]. The SIMD vectorization support in RAJA is limited to using the execution policy RAJA::simd_exec, which adds #pragma omp simd to the code and relies on compiler auto-vectorization [15]. Alpaka refactors user code to help the compiler in auto-vectorization. OCCA also provides hints to enable auto-vectorization but lacks any explicit SIMD support at present.

Multiple implementations of a SIMD primitive for CPUs such as the Vc vectorization library [20], the Unified Multi/Many-Core Environment (UME) framework [17], and the Generic SIMD Library [32] enable an explicit vectorization using architecture-specific SIMD intrinsics and operator overloading. KokkosKernels [19] is a library that implements computational kernels for linear algebra and graph operations using Kokkos. KokkosKernels uses a SIMD data type for its batched linear algebra kernels [18]. Embedded ensemble propagation [27] using the Stokhos package in Trilinos [28] for uncertainty quantification uses another version of SIMD primitives that allows flexible vector lengths. Furthermore, Phipps [27] addressed portability of this "ensemble type" to SIMT architectures. Pai [26] addressed SIMT portability using Intermediate Representations (IR).

While all these efforts are successful, they do not yet provide the full range of portability shown in this work.

3   Portable SIMD Primitive

The portable SIMD primitive developed here sits on top of Kokkos, which provides basic performance portability across a range of architectures. Figures 2, 3 and 4 present pseudo code of the portable SIMD primitive.

```
// PVL: physical vector length
// LVL: logical vector length
// EL: element per vector lane

#define PVL ... //detect architecture-specific PVL

using namespace std;

// advanced declarations
template<typename T, int LVL, int EL=LVL/PVL>
struct simd_cpu; //for cpu

template<typename T, int LVL, int EL=LVL/PVL>
struct simd_gpu; //for gpu

template<typename T, int LVL, int EL=LVL/PVL>
struct gpu_temp;

// conditional aliases for Primitive and Temp
template<typename exe_space, typename T, int LVL>
using simd = typename conditional<
  is_same<exe_space, OpenMP>::value,
  simd_cpu<T, LVL>, simd_gpu<T, LVL> >::type;

template <typename exe_space, typename T, int LVL>
using Portable_Temp = typename std::conditional<
  is_same<exe_space, OpenMP>::value,
  simd_cpu<T, LVL>, gpu_temp<T, LVL>>::type;
```

Fig. 2. Common declarations used in SIMD primitive

```
template<int LVL, int EL>
struct simd_cpu<double, LVL, EL>{

  __m512d _d[EL];  // knl instrinsic for 8 doubles

  Portable_Temp<exe_space, double, LVL> operator+ (const simd &x){
    Portable_Temp<exe_space, double, LVL> y;
#pragma unroll(EL)
    for(int i=0; i<EL; i++)
      y._d[i] = _mm512_add_pd( _d[i], x._d[i]);
    return y;
  }
  //more operators and overloads ...
};
```

Fig. 3. SIMD primitive: KNL specialization for double

Common Declarations: Figure 2 shows some common declarations used to achieve portability. The PVL macro definition derives platform-specific vector length, i.e., physical vector length (PVL). "simd_cpu" and "simd_gpu" are forward declarations for CPU and CUDA primitives, respectively. They need a data type and the logical vector length (LVL) as the template parameters. An alias "simd" is created using std::conditional, which assigns "simd_cpu" to "simd" if the targeted architecture (or the execution space in the Kokkos nomenclature)

```
template <typename T, int LVL, int EL>
struct gpu_temp{
    T a[EL];
    //more operators and overloads ...
};

template<typename T, int LVL, int EL>
struct simd{

  T _d[LVL];

  Portable_Temp<exe_space, T, LVL> operator+ (const simd &x){
    Portable_Temp<exe_space, T, LVL> y;
#pragma unroll(EL)
    for(int i=0; i<EL; i++){
        int tid = i * blockDim.x + threadIdx.x;
        y._d[i] = _d[tid] + x._d[tid]
    }
    return y;
  }
  //more operators and overloads ...
};
```

Fig. 4. SIMD primitive: CUDA definition

```
using namespace Kokkos;
typedef View<double*> dView;
void add_scalar(dView &A, dView&B, int n){
  parallel_for(..., [&](team_member t){//team loop
    parallel_for(..., [&](int tid){//thread loop
    //calculate "start" and "end" for the thread
    for(int i=start; i<end; i++)
      for(int j=0; j<n; j++)
        if(B[i] < 1.0)
          B[i] += A[j];
  });
 });
}

typedef simd<exe_space, double, SIMD_LVL> Double;
typedef Kokkos::View<Double*, KernelSpace> SimdView;

void add_vector(dView &A, dView&B_s, int n){
  SimdView B(reinterpret_cast<Double *>(B_s.data()));
  parallel_for(..., [&](team_member t){//team loop
    parallel_for(..., [&](int tid){//thread loop
    //calculate "start" and "end" for the thread
    for(int i=start; i<end/SIMD_LVL; i++)
      for(int j=0; j<n; j++)
        B[i] = if_else( (B[i]<1.0), (B[i]+A[j]), B[i]);
  });
 });
}
```

Fig. 5. Example usage of the SIMD primitive: conditional addition of arrays without (top) and with SIMD primitive.

is OpenMP and "simd_gpu" if the execution space is CUDA. The simd template expands into respective definitions at compile time depending upon the execution space. As a result, both execution spaces can be used simultaneously, thus giving portable and heterogeneous execution. The "Portable_Temp" alias and "gpu_temp" type are used as a return type and are explained later.

CPU Back-end: The CPU back-ends containing architecture-specific SIMD intrinsics are developed for Intel's KNL and Cavium ThunderX2. Template specializations are used to create different definitions specific to a data type as shown in Fig. 3 (which is a specialization for double on KNL). Overloaded operators invoke architecture-specific intrinsics to facilitate standard arithmetic operations, math library functions, if_else condition (as shown in the example later). The new primitive can support bitwise permutation operations such as shuffle and has been verified with some preliminary experiments. One such example of an overloaded operator is shown in Fig. 3. The operator+ calls the intrinsic function "_mm512_add_pd", which performs the addition of eight doubles stored in the intrinsic data type __mm512 in a simd manner. The return data type of the operator+ is "Portable_Temp". When the execution space is OpenMP, Portable_Temp is set to "simd_cpu" itself, which simply returns an intrinsic data type wrapped in the primitive. The KNL specific back-end from Kokkos::Batched::Vector is reused, and the functionalities of the LVL and alias definition based on the execution space are added on top of it. A new back-end was added for ThunderX2 using ARMv8.1 intrinsics.

Logical Vector Length: Users can pass the desired vector length as the template parameter "LVL". The LVL iterations are evenly distributed among the physical vector lanes by the primitive. As shown in operator+ (Fig. 3), each vector lane iterates over EL iterations, where "EL=LVL/PVL", e.g., if PVL=8 and LVL=16, then EL=2, i.e. each vector lane will process two elements. Thus LVL, allows users to write vector length agnostic code. In use cases, such as the 2D convolution kernel presented in this work later, using LVL improved performance up to 3x.

CUDA Back-end and Portable_Temp: Finally, a new CUDA back-end is added with the same front-end APIs as used in the CPU back-end, making the primitive portable, as shown in Fig. 4. The common front-end APIs present a unified user interface across heterogeneous platforms, which allows users to maintain a single portable version of the code and yet achieve effective vectorization. The portability of the primitive avoids the development of two different versions as required prior to this work. The common front-end APIs include structures "simd" and "Portable_Temp", declared in Fig. 2, along with their member functions. Whenever a programmer switches to the CUDA execution space, "simd" alias refers to "simd_gpu" and expands into an CUDA definition of the SIMD primitive. To emulate the CPU execution model of SIMD processing, the GPU back-end contains an array of "logical vector length" number of elements (double _d [LVL]). These elements divided among the PVL number of CUDA threads along the x dimension. (The PVL is auto-detected based on a platform.) CUDA assigns unique threadIdx.x to each thread ranging from 0 to PVL-1 (as explained in Sect. 1.) Each CUDA thread within operator+ (Fig. 4) adds different elements the array _d indexed by "tid = i * blockDim.x + threadIdx.x". (In this case blockDim.x represents the number CUDA threads along x dimension, which is set to PVL.) Together, the PVL number of CUDA threads process a chunk of PVL number of elements in a SIMT manner. Each CUDA thread execute EL number of iterations (loop variable i). Thus, the primitive processes LVL=PVL*EL number of elements within array _d. Offsetting by threadIdx.x allows coalesced access and improves the memory bandwidth utilization.

However, the CUDA back-end needed an additional development of gpu_temp to be used as a return type. Consider a temporary variable of a type "SIMD" used in the CPU code. The declaration is executed by the scalar CPU thread and the elements of the variable are automatically divided among CPU vector lanes by the intrinsic function. Thus each vector lane is assigned with only "EL=LVL/PVL" number of elements. However, when used inside a CUDA kernel, each CUDA thread i.e., each vector lane, declares its own instance of the SIMD variable. Each instance contains LVL elements and results into allocating PVLxLVL elements. The problem can be fixed by setting the alias Portable_Temp to the type "gpu_temp". "gpu_temp" holds only EL elements - exactly those needed by the vector lane. Thus, the total number of elements is still LVL. As a result, the CUDA implementation of the SIMD primitive needs combinations of operands: (SIMD, SIMD), (SIMD, Portable_Temp), (Portable_Temp, SIMD) and (Portable_Temp, Portable_Temp).

Two alternatives to avoid Portable_Temp were considered. The PVL can be set to 1 (or EL). One can even use CUDA-supported vector types such as float2 and float4. Both options will solve the return type problem mentioned earlier as each vector lanes processes 1/2/4 elements and returns the same number of elements as opposed to elements getting shared by vector lanes. Using CUDA vector types can slightly improve the bandwidth utilization due to vectorized load and store. CUDA, however, lacks any vectorized instructions for floating point operations, and the computations on these vector types get serialized. Thus, using either of these options will remove the third level of parallelism (i.e., Kokkos Vector). Hence, the Portable_Temp construct was chosen.

Example Usage: Figure 5 shows an example of vectorization using the portable SIMD primitive and Kokkos, but without showing Kokkos-specific details. Kokkos View is a portable data structure used to allocate two arrays, A and B. Elements of A are added into each element of B until B reaches 1. The scalar code (add_scalar function) does not get auto-vectorized due to a dependency between if(B[i]<1.0) condition and addition. (Of course, adding #pragma simd or interchanging loops helps in this example, but may not always work.) The add_vector function, a vectorized version of add_scalar, shows how the SIMD primitive can vectorize the outer loop. Array A is cast from double to simd<double>, the number of iterations of the outer loop is factored by the LVL, and the "if" condition is replaced by an if_else operator. The statement calls four overloaded operators, namely, <, +, if_else and =. Vectorizing across the outer loop works because the outer loop iterations are not dependent on each other. If the LVL is increased to

2*PVL, the loop gets unrolled by a factor of two and each vector lane processes on two iterations consecutively. As the main computations usually take place in the innermost loop, the unrolled outer loop automatically gets jammed with the inner loop. Users can simply set LVL = nxPVL and the primitive unrolls the outer loop by a factor of n. Because the iterations of the outer loop are independent of each other, the transformation can exploit instruction level parallelism.

4   Experiments

Experimental Platforms: A node of Intel KNL with 64 cores, 16 GB of High Bandwidth Memory (or MCDRAM) configured in flat quadrant mode and 192 GB RAM was used to test the CPU version. Each KNL core consists of two VPUs with a vector length of 512 bits. Thus, using the double precision floating point numbers allows a vector length of 8. The codes were compiled with the Intel compiler suite 2018 with the optimization flags -O3 -xMIC-AVX512 -std=c++11 -fopenmp.

Tests were also run on a single node of the Astra cluster at Sandia National Laboratories. Each Astra node provides 128 GB of high bandwidth memory and two Cavium ThunderX2 CN99xx processors with 28 cores each. Cavium ThunderX2 is an ARMv8.1-based processor with a vector length of 128 bits. It can execute two double precision operations with a single SIMD instruction. The GNU 7.2.0 compiler suite was used to compile applications with the flags -O3 -std=c++11 -mtune=thunderx2t99 -mcpu=thunderx2t99 -fopenmp.

The NVIDIA P100 GPU with Compute Capability 6.0, 3584 CUDA cores, 16GB of High Bandwidth Memory and 48 KB of shared Memory per SM was used to

Table 1. Summary of use cases, goals and expectations.

Use case	Goal	Baseline	Expected performance	
			CPU	GPU
PDE	CPU: achieve effective Vectorization for the complex, hard to vectorize code; GPU: find out the overhead for a performance sensitive portable kernel	CPU: not vectorized; GPU: Ported to CUDA	Near ideal speedup	No extra speedup. No new overhead
2dConv	Evaluate the benefit of LVL by comparing it with a baseline already running in SIMD mode	CPU: auto-vectorized; GPU: ported to CUDA	Small extra speedup due to LVL	Small extra speedup due to LVL
GEMM	Find out the overhead of the primitive by comparing it with a baseline already running in SIMD mode efficiently	CPU: auto vectorized; GPU: ported to CUDA	No extra speedup. No new overhead	No extra speedup. No new overhead
SpMV				

†Baselines are written using Kokkos for two reasons: first to make the code portable and second to measure the overhead of the primitive *only*. If the baseline is written using raw CUDA or OpenMP, then the performance measurements will include the overhead of both Kokkos and the primitive.

Algorithm 1. CharOx Loop Structure, Holmen [10]

1: **for all** patches
2:   **for all** Gaussian quadrature nodes
3:   **Kokkos::parallel_for** cells in a patch //**Can cells loop be vectorized?**
4:       Compute reaction constants.
5:       **Nested loops** over reactions and species.
6:       **Multiple loops** over reactions and species.
7:       **Nested loops** over reactions and species.
8:       **while** residual < threshold **do** //**indefinite number of iterations**
9:           **Multiple loops** over reactions.
10:           **Nested loops** over reactions and species.
11:           Compute a matrix inverse.
12:           **Multiple loop** over reactions.
13:       **end while**
14:       **Loop** over reactions.
15: **end Kokkos::parallel_for**

---

test the GPU performance. The applications were compiled using gcc v4.9.2 and nvcc (from CUDA v 9.1) with the optimization flags -O3 -std=c++11 –expt-extended-lambda –expt-relaxed-constexpr.

Use Cases and Experimental Setup: The primary aim of the portability libraries such as Kokkos is to enable "performance portable" programming. The portable code gets compiled and executed on the heterogeneous platforms without making any platform-specific changes and also provides performance close to the native implementations (such as using raw CUDA or using vector intrinsics). However, it is essential to understand that Kokkos or the SIMD primitive is not a magic construct to provide an extra performance boost. *When the baseline itself is efficiently vectorized or has an efficient CUDA implementation, using Kokkos or the primitive can provide portability, but will not provide extra speedup.* Considering these factors, different use cases are chosen to test the performance of the SIMD primitive for different scenarios. Table 1 summarizes the four different kernels used in the evaluation. Of the four use cases, first two are not efficiently vectorized and are chosen to demonstrate the effectiveness of the primitive, whereas last two are efficiently vectorized and are chosen to measure the overhead of the primitive.

Use cases were implemented using Kokkos - first without using the SIMD primitive and then using it. A typical transformation from scalar code to vectorized code using the portable SIMD primitive needs casting of legacy data structures and variables and updating any conditional assignments. Some algorithm specific use cases need a special handling, e.g., the while loop discussed in Sect. 4.1. All the arithmetic operations and math library functions remain untouched. *For all four kernels, less than 10% of the lines of code were modified to introduce the SIMD primitive* and this did not require any complex code transformations or new data structures, which is typically needed to auto-vectorize a complex code. The use of Kokkos and the SIMD primitive allows the same code to be compiled on the different target platforms. Various combinations of the number of threads were tested and the best timing was chosen. Each experiment was repeated at least 100 times, and the averages timings were used to compute the speedups.

4.1   PDE Assembly

Uintah [2] is a massively parallel asynchronous multi-task runtime that can be used to solve complex multi-physics problems. It is being used for the multi-scale and multi-physics combustion simulation of a coal boiler under DoE's PSAAP II project and has been successfully scaled to 256k cores on Titan and 512k cores on MIRA [2]. One of the longest running kernels within Uintah is CharOx. It simulates the char oxidation of coal particles by modeling multiple chemical reactions and physical phenomenon involved in the process [1,11,25]. The CharOx kernel consists over of 350 lines of code, reads around 30 arrays, updates five arrays, and performs compute-intensive double precision floating point arithmetic operations, such as exponentials, trigonometric functions, and divisions in nested loops about 300 to 500 times for every cell. As shown in Algorithm 1, the main cell iterator loop contains different loops over reactions and species, each with multiple levels of nesting. The Newton Raphson Solve loop has an undetermined number of iterations and contains more nested loops. The iterations of the cell iterator loop are not dependent on each other. Hence, vectorizing the cell iterator loop can potentially give a maximum speedup.

Auto-Vectorization: On the KNL platform, the Intel compiler auto-vectorizes some of the innermost loops only. Vectorization of the cell iterator loop can be forced by adding the "#pragma simd" directive. However, *this provides only 4.3x speedup,* whereas the ideal speedup for the double precision on KNL is 8x, assuming the majority of the code is scalar. (Unfortunately, the pragma is deprecated in Intel compilers from 2018 onwards, and its replacement "#pragma vector" fails to "force" vectorize the cell loop.) An inspection of the vectorization report and assembly code shows gather/scatter instructions generated for every read/write to the global arrays. These gather and scatter instructions are the reason for the speedup of 4.3x. To maintain the halo region, Uintah internally offsets *all* elements in its data structures with a *constant* value. All cells have the *same* offset. Thus the stride between elements is always one, but the compiler cannot deduce this and generates gather instructions. However, using the SIMD primitive calls SIMD intrinsics that explicitly generate move instructions rather than gather and makes vectorization efficient.

The GNU compilers used on the ThunderX2 platform did not vectorize the cell iterator loop even after adding vectorization hint directives.

On the GPU, the size and the complexity of the kernel substantially increases register usage. Profiling shows that 255 registers are used by every thread within a block, thereby preventing the simultaneous execution of multiple blocks on a single Streaming Multiprocessor (SM). This results in poor occupancy of the SMs (only up to 12%). Hence, the SIMD primitive must not add additional overhead in terms of registers, memory, or execution dependency, and the GPU performance must not be compromised to gain CPU performance. Apart from casting data structures and variables to those based on the portable SIMD primitive, the Newton-Raphson solver [10] used to solve oxidation equations for every cell needed special handling. The solver iterates until the equations converge. In the vectorized version, the vector of cells iterates until all cells within the vector converge. Although the technique needs extra iterations for a few cells, it works faster than executing solver iterations sequentially in a scalar mode.

The experiments were carried out using a total of 64 patches with two patch sizes - 16^3 and 32^3. The CharOx kernel is invoked five times for every patch. With 64 patches, the kernel is executed 320 times in every timestep. The simulation was run for 10 timesteps, and the average loop execution time over 3200 calls was recorded. The shear complexity of this loop appears to provide a distinctive and unusual challenge for performance portability.

Goal: This use case shows a particular instance where the compiler does a poor job in auto-vetorizing the code on the CPU, but the CUDA code works efficiently on the GPU. *It is thus important to ensure that improving CPU performance using the primitive does not degrade GPU performance.* The kernel is large and complex enough to cause a register spill on the GPU even without using the SIMD primitive. Thus, adding SIMD will help us to understand the performance of sensitive kernels on GPU and associated overhead, if any.

Expectation: The code performs double precision floating point operations. Hence, the speedups close to 8x and 2x are expected on KNL and ThunderX2, respectively. These are the ideal speedups for double precision computations on these platforms considering the respective vector lengths of 512 bits and 128 bits. The GPU code already runs in a SIMT mode, and hence the new primitive will provide portability without a performance boost. However, portability should not cause any significant overhead either. Ideally, GPU performance should remain the same with and without SIMD.

4.2 2D Convolution

Algorithm 2. Algorithm for a 2D Convolution Kernel

1: **for** b in 0:mini-batches
2:   **for** co in 0:output filters
3:    **for** i in 0:M //image rows
4:     **for** j in 0:M //image columns
5:      **for** ci in 0:input channels
6:       **for** fi in 0:F //filter rows
7:        **for** fj in 0:F //filter columns
8:         out(b, co, i, j) += in(b, ci, i-F/2+fi, j-F/2+fj) * filter(co, ci, fi, fj)

2D convolution [4] (as shown in Algorithm 2) is a heavily used operation in deep neural networks. The algorithm multiplies a batch of images (*in*) with a filter (*filter*) by sliding the filter over the image to accumulate the result (*out*). The operation is repeated for multiple filters. This algorithm has a high arithmetic intensity. Using the SIMD primitive provides an opportunity to exploit the

Table 2. Sparse matrices used for ensemble SpMV and comparison of the baseline Kokkos version with Intel's mkl and Nvidia cusparse libraries for ensemble size = 64.

Name	Rows	Columns	Nonzeros	Execution time (ms)			
				mkl	baseline	cusparse	baseline
				KNL	KNL	P100	P100
HV15R	2017169	2017169	283073458	275	147	160	123
ML_Geer	1504002	1504002	110686677	105	44	54	37
RM07R	381689	381689	37464962	46	25	23	14
ML_Laplace	377002	377002	27582698	34	11	13	9

spatial locality for all three variables: When the "i" loop is parallelized across the Kokkos threads and the "j" loop across the SIMD lanes, every "filter" element is reused for the "LVL" number of "j" iterations. Also, two levels of parallelism help reusing elements in different rows "in" and "out" (similar to a stencil block). Of course, these improvements can be obtained manually without using the primitive. However, using the primitive introduces these transformations implicitly and improves the programmability, portability and the maintenance of the code.

The mini-batch loop in the original code is parallelized across OpenMP threads/CUDA blocks. The code is then auto-vectorized across the j loop using the directive #pragma simd on CPU and mapping the x dimension CUDA threads across the j loop on a GPU. #pragma unroll was used to unroll the full lengths of the fi and fj loops. The code was then converted into a SIMD primitive code instead of using #pragma simd. Different combinations of mini batch sizes (3584 and 7168), filter sizes (3×3, 5×5 and 7×7), number of input (3, 5 and 10) and output channels (3, 5 and 10) were tested for different values of the LVL.

Goal: Evaluate the effectiveness of the LVL against the vectorized baseline.

Expectation: As the baseline is efficiently auto-vectorized, using SIMD primitive with LVL=PVL will not perform any better. However, setting LVL=2*PVL or 4*PVL should give speedups on both CPU and GPU due to instruction level parallelism and data reuse.

4.3 Compact GEMM

The general matrix-matrix multiplication (GEMM) on a batch of small, dense, matrices is widely used within scientific computing and deep learning. Thread-parallel GEMM operations over collections of matrices organized in an interleaved fashion can be made efficient and portable using the SIMD primitive [18]. This approach is implemented within KokkosKernels, and used in a large-scale CFD code called SPARC [13]. The KokkosKernels' batched GEMM kernel achieves performance comparable or sometimes better than vendor provided libraries such as Intel's math kernel library (mkl) and Nvidia's cuBLAS [18,31]. KokkosKernels maintains two versions of batched GEMM - the CPU version which uses an intrinsics-based SIMD primitive, and a CUDA version, which does not have a SIMD primitive. The only change needed in the kernel to utilize the portable SIMD primitive was to map the matrix dimension to the SIMD dimension by casting matrices from Kokkos views of doubles to Kokkos views of the SIMD primitive. Thus, each CPU thread (or a section of a CUDA warp) carried out each operation on the LVL number of matrices in SIMD fashion. Both kernels had the same tiling optimizations with tile sizes of 3×3 and 5×5 to extract spatial and temporal locality among matrix elements. Experiments were carried out using four matrix sizes: 3×3, 5×5, 10×10 and 15×15 using a batch of 16,384 matrices on all three platforms.

Goal: The goal is to compare the performances of the new SIMD primitive and the existing high performance explicitly vectorized code on CPU. Any performance degradation will reveal the associated overheads, if any.

Expectation: The SIMD primitive should perform as well as the code without the SIMD primitive on both CPU and GPU. Neither a performance boost nor any extra overhead is expected.

4.4   Embedded Ensemble Propagation

This kernel is heavily used in the uncertainty quantification of predictive simulations which, involve evaluation of simulation codes on multiple realizations of input parameters. The efficiently auto-vectorized baseline kernel multiplies a sparse matrix by an ensemble of vectors with matrix rows distributed across threads and vectors distributed across SIMD lanes. Vectors are arranged in an interleaved fashion similar to batched GEMM. This design, introduced by Phipps [27], allows the reuse of matrix values across all vectors and provides up-to 4x speedups over traditional batched sparse matrix-vector multiplication. Instead of repeating Phipps' experiments, the vectorized ensemble version itself is used as a baseline. Compared to the vendor-provided libraries, i.e., Intel's mkl and Nvidia's cusparse, the baseline kernels exhibit 1.8x to 3x speedup on KNL and 1.3x to 1.6x on P100, respectively (See Table 2). These observations are in line with Phipps' experiments. This baseline kernel is converted to use our SIMD type by casting data structures from double to those using the SIMD primitive and setting the LVL equal to the ensemble length. Hence, any performance degradation from baseline can show the shortcomings in the LVL implementation.

Goal: The goal is to find out any overhead associated with the SIMD primitive by evaluating its performance against the highly optimized baseline that implements the same design and parallelism pattern but without using the primitive.

Expectation: The code with the SIMD primitive should perform as well as the baseline on CPU and GPU. No performance boost and no overhead is expected.

5   Results and Performance Analysis

The rows in Fig. 6 show the results of four use cases, and the columns indicate three platforms. Each plot shows execution time along with the speedup compared to the baseline. The baseline is either the auto-vectorized code (AV) or the code with no SIMD primitive (NSP) colored in cyan. Results of using the SIMD primitive with different values of the LVL are represented by "SP". As mentioned earlier, the experiments have three goals: a) Find out performance improvement when the code is not efficiently vectorized (PDE and 2dConv cases), b) Ensure that performance improvement on one platform, does not hamper the performance on another platform (PDE), and c) Measure the overhead of the new primitive against the efficiently vectorized baseline, where the expected speedup is 1x (GEMM and SpMV). The performance of each use case is analyzed below.

The vectorized code (AV and SP) both executes fewer instructions than the scalar code, but the vector instructions execute more slowly than the scalar counterparts, consuming more cycles. Hence, the Instructions Per Cycle (IPC) count does not reflect the exact speedup. Similarly, KNL hardware counters do not accurately measure floating point operations (FLOPs), and numbers often get skewed while measuring floating point instructions (FLIPs) [16]. Hence, simple counts such as the total number of instructions and cache hits are used here for performance analysis. The performance metrics and events are collected using Intel vtune amplifier, Nvidia nvprof, and the PAPI library.

5.1   PDE Assembly

The KNL plot in Fig. 6(a) shows the SP version that achieves 5.7x and 7.8x speedups over AV for mesh patch sizes of 16^3 and 32^3, respectively. Analysis of the 16^3 patch problem shows the number of instructions (INST_RETIRED.ANY) executed reduced from 1273 million for the AV code to 204 million for the SP code (Table 3). Similarly, L1 cache data misses (PAPI_L1_DCM) decreased from 2.4 million for AV to 1.2 million for the SP. In this case, some of the cache lines are evicted over the course of one iteration due to the complex operations and the 30+ different arrays used in the kernel. When the next iteration starts, at least some of the memory is missing from the L1 cache due to earlier evictions. However, the vectorized code can take advantage of entire cache lines, and all eight double elements from the 64 bytes cache lines can be read by eight vector lanes, thus fully utilizing data fetched in a cache line. The increased cache line efficiency along with vectorization provides near optimal speedup.

The P100 results show the NSP and SP both performing equally well. As the NSP running on the GPU runs in SIMT mode, the SP does not provide any extra level of parallelism and cannot provide an extra boost. These results showing 1x speedup are important in showing that the SP does not create any overhead on a GPU, even when the NSP kernel causes register spilling. All the metrics collected by nvprof showed similar values in this case. Increasing the value of LVL to 2xPVL slowed down the performance by 1.5x, because the increased LVL increased register spilling (evident from increased local memory accesses).

The SP version of CharOx kernel boosted performance by 2.2x and 2.3x for patch sizes of 16^3 and 32^3, respectively, on ThunderX2. The ThunderX2 metrics show a similar trend as that observed on KNL. The total number of instructions executed are reduced from 4253.8 million for the NSP to 1823.1 million for the

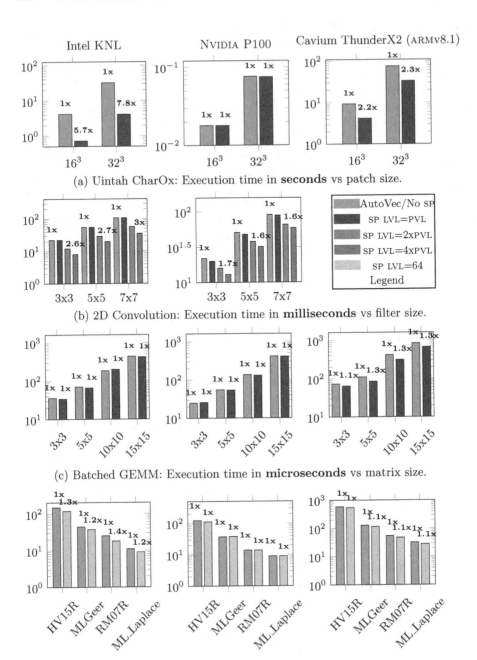

(a) Uintah CharOx: Execution time in **seconds** vs patch size.

(b) 2D Convolution: Execution time in **milliseconds** vs filter size.

(c) Batched GEMM: Execution time in **microseconds** vs matrix size.

(d) Ensemble SpMV: Execution time in **milliseconds** vs data sets

Fig. 6. Comparison of execution times along with speedups for different kernels on different architectures. Speedup "1x" indicates zero new overhead due to the new primitive.

SP. Again, vectorization reduced the number of cache misses from 5.7 million to 1.5 million, which provided super-linear speedups up to 2.3x where the PVL supported by the hardware for double precision is only 2.

Table 3. Performance metrics for CharOx. (counts in millions)

	Intel KNL		Cavium ThunderX2	
	Number of instructions	L1 cache data misses	Number of instructions	L1 cache data misses
No SIMD primitive	1273	2.4	4253	5.7
SIMD primitive	204	1.2	1823	1.5

5.2 2D Convolution

Figure 6(b) shows speedups up to 3x on KNL and 1.6x on P100 for the 2D Convolution kernel shown in Algorithm 2. The input image size, the number of input and output channels were set to 64x64, 3 and 10, respectively. The image was padded by filter size/2 number of cells. The baseline NSP and the SP with LVL=PVL perform equally well as both get efficiently vectorized. Setting LVL=2xPVL and 4xPVL gives better results on both KNL and P100.

Line number 8 of Algorithm 2 multiplies "in" with "filter" and accumulates the result in "out". Vectorizing the j loop coalesces accesses for "in" and "out". "filter" is independent of the j dimension, and hence the value is reused across all vector lanes. When the LVL is set to 2xPVL (or 4xPVL), the same filter value gets reused across twice (or four times) the PVL elements. An assembly instruction inspection shows the register containing "filter" was reused across multiple fma operations. All these fma operations are independent of each other and can exploit instruction level parallelism. This "unroll and jam" transformation can be introduced by simply increasing the value of LVL. Using LVL in this case can save developers having to manually perform "unroll and jam" - especially for larger codes - and maintain readability of the code.

Table 4. Performance metrics for 2DCov. (counts in billion)

	Intel KNL		Nvidia P100		
	Number of instructions	Number of memory loads	Number of instructions	Number of memory loads	L2 cache hit rate
No SIMD primitive	6.2	3	9.8	1.3	25%
SIMD primitive	2.6	2	6.8	0.8	83%

The reuse of the "filter" values across the j iterations reduced the number of memory loads from 3 billion for the NSP to 2 billion for the SP with LVL=4xPVL on

KNL and from 1.3 billion to 0.8 billion on the P100. The number of instructions executed reduced by 2.3x and 1.4x on KNL and P100 platforms, respectively. The L2 cache hit rate improved on the P100 from 25% to 83%. Additionally, the number of control flow instructions executed was reduced by a factor of 3.5 on the P100 due to outer loop unrolling (see Table 4). The effectiveness of the primitive and LVL can be judged from the fact that the naive code in Algorithm 2 with the SIMD primitive and LVL=4xPVL was only 20% slower than the highly tuned cuDNN library by Nvidia as shown in Table 5. A small fix to use GPU's constant memory to store the filter gave additional boost and the naive code performed equally well as the cuDNN library. Thus, the primitive can help application programmers who may focus on the algorithms and applications rather than spending time on specialized performance improvement techniques such as tiling, loop unrolling, using shared memory, etc.

Table 5. Performance comparison with Nvidia cuDNN. Execution time in milliseconds

Filter size	cuDNN	simd primitive LVL=4XPVL	simd primitive LVL=4XPVL with constant memory
3×3	11	13	11
5×5	24	31	25
7×7	49	59	47

Unfortunately, experiments for 2D Convolution could not be conducted on ThunderX2 because the Astra cluster was moved to a restricted domain by Sandia National Laboratories.

5.3 Compact GEMM

Figure 6(c) shows that the NSP and SP versions perform equally well on the KNL and P100 (speedup is 1x) and that the SP does not create any overhead. These results are as expected because KokkosKernels (the NSP version) contains explicitly vectorized code for KNL and Kokkos code tuned explicitly for GPUs. These observations are confirmed by the same number of instructions executed by the NSP and SP versions - 23 million on KNL and 20 million on P100.

However, the ThunderX2 results show an improvement of up to 1.3x. The architecture-specific intrinsic back-end for ThunderX2 had not yet been updated in the KokkosKernels, and it falls back to an emulated back-end using arrays and "for" loops. Although this NSP version gets auto-vectorized by the compiler, the SP leads to more efficient vectorization. The NSP version executes 146 million instructions whereas the SP version executes 114 million instructions on ThunderX2.

5.4   Embedded Ensemble Propagation

The kernel is evaluated using 13 matrices from the University of Florida sparse matrix collection. However, results from only four matrices (listed in Table 2) that represent the general trend are presented for the sake of brevity. Sparse matrix-vector ensemble multiplication results on the GPU shown in Fig. 6(d) indicate both versions, NSP and SP, perform equally on the P100 GPU. Both the versions are efficiently ported to the SIMT model and use the same ensemble logic for data reuse. Therefore, the matching GPU performance for both versions meets our expectation and indicates that the primitive does not cause any overhead.

More surprising were speedups up to 1.3x on KNL and and 1.1x ThunderX2. Profiling showed about 10% to 20% reduction in the number of instructions executed for different sparse matrices and different ensemble sizes. While the FLOPs were, of course, the same for both versions, an assembly code inspection revealed the reason behind the speedups. The result of matrix - vector ensemble multiplication is also a vector ensemble. The design by Phipps et al. [27] fetches a matrix element and multiplies all vectors with it to avoid repeated accesses to matrix elements, which are costly when the sparse matrix is stored in the "compressed row storage" format. Although the Phipps design performs faster than the traditional batched multiplication, it has to repeatedly fetch elements from the resultant vector ensemble to do the accumulation. In the NSP version, the compiler generates three vector instructions for every vector operation: (i) a fetch of the result ensemble from memory to a vector register, (ii) a vectored fused-multiply-add (fma) on the result stored in a vector register with a vector from memory and a matrix element stored in vector register, and (iii) a store of the result from the vector register in the memory. When the SP is used, the ensemble length is mapped to the LVL. This mapping helps the compiler to deduce the array length and number of registers. Hence, for N = 64, all result elements get loaded into eight vector registers only once, and fma operations are repeated on these registers. Hence, using the SP eliminates the need to transfer the result back and forth from the memory and takes only one store to move the accumulated result from the vector registers to the memory. Thus, one load and one store are saved for every fma operation, resulting in a more efficient code.

6   Assigning the Optimal LVL Value

The LVL value depends on register availability and levels of parallelism, both dictated by the algorithm and hardware. If the LVL is set to 2xPVL or 4xPVL, the compiler can usually allocate the structure into registers. Then the code can take advantage of instruction level parallelism, if supported by the hardware, as observed in the cases of 2DCov and SpMV. When, however, the LVL was set to 8xPVL, the compiler allocated the structure into memory instead of registers and so hampered the performance of 2DCov with extra loads and stores. The CharOx kernel is very complicated and register spilling happens even in the NSP. Therefore, setting LVL = 2xPVL, increased the register pressure further and resulted in slower execution in contrast to other use cases. The second factor in choosing the right LVL is the number of levels of parallelism an algorithm can offer. If the both levels of parallelism, thread level and SIMD level, are applied to the same loop (as in GEMM or CharOx), then increasing the LVL effectively increases the workload per thread and decreases the degree of parallelism available, which can cause a load imbalance among cores. The GEMM kernels were hand-tuned to unroll and jam along matrix rows and columns. The optimization gave enough workload to fully exploit available instruction level parallelism. As a result, increasing the LVL did not provide any further advantage.

7   Conclusion and Future Work

This study describes a portable SIMD data type whose primary benefit is to achieve vectorization in a portable manner on architectures with VPUs and GPUs. This capability has a potential to be useful for massive applications that use Kokkos to extract performance from future architectures (including exascale architectures), without explicitly tuning the user code for every new architecture. The largest benefits the SIMD primitive were observed in the most complex kernel, which was hard to auto-vectorize. Performance boosts of up to 7.8x on KNL and 2.2x on Cavium ThunderX2 can be observed for double precision kernels (PDE). For the kernels which are vectorized/ported to GPUs, the new SIMD primitive results in the speedups up-to 3x on KNL, 1.6x on P100 and 1.1x on ThunderX2 due to more efficient vectorization (SpMV), cache reuse (2dConv), instruction level parallelism (2dConv) and loop unrolling (2dConv and SpMV). The comparison with efficiently vectorized kernels showed minimal overhead for PDE and zero overhead for GEMM and SpMV kernels. The new primitive makes outer loop vectorization easier (as shown with CharOx, SpMV and 2dConv). The PDE example proved that performance on one platform can be improved without compromising the performance on another platform.

The Kokkos-based design will make it easier to port this SIMD primitive to future GPU exascale architectures such as A21, and Frontier. The Kokkos profiling interface can possibly be extended to profile the primitive-based code in the future. Preliminary experiments showed that the new primitive can be easily extended to both OpenACC and OpenMP 4.5. It will be interesting to compare the performance of OpenACC, OpenMP 4.5/5.0 (in the future), and Kokkos.

Data Availability Statement

Summary of the Experiments Reported

The performance comparison of the portable SIMD primitive (the main contribution) was done using four different problems on Intel's KNL, Nvidia's P100 and Cavium ThunderX2. Bowman, White and ASTRA clusters from Sandia National Laboratory were used to conduct the experiments along with some machines available at SCI Institute, University of Utah and kingspeak cluster at CHPC,

University of Utah. The problems used in experiments include: CharOxidation kernel from Uintah framework, 2d convolution used in deep neural networks, batched general matrix multiplication and ensembeled sparse matrix - vector multiplication. More details about each problem are described in the research paper.

Artifact Availability

Software Artifact Availability: All author-created software artifacts, details regarding the baseline experimental setup, and modifications made for the paper are maintained in a public repository under an OSI-approved license and can be accessed using the following DOI:

List of URLs and/or DOIs where artifacts are available:
10.6084/m9.figshare.11553012

Artifact Evaluation

Verification and Validation Studies: The result from all four baselines (without SIMD primitive) were compared to the modified version (using the SIMD primitive) and the exact match was ensured between both values to ensure accuracy of the code.

Accuracy and Precision of Timings: The execution timings from all four baselines (without SIMD primitive) were compared to the modified version (using the SIMD primitive) to evaluate the performance. Each experiment was repeated at least 100 times and the average of the timings is used to calculate speedups.

References

1. Adamczyk, W., et al.: Application of LES-CFD for predicting pulverized-coal working conditions after installation of NOx control system. Energy **160**, 693–709 (2018)
2. Berzins, M., et al.: Extending the Uintah framework through the petascale modeling of detonation in arrays of high explosive devices. SIAM J. Sci. Comput. **38**, 101–122 (2016). http://www.sci.utah.edu/publications/Ber2015a/detonationsiam16-2.pdf
3. Carr, S.: Combining optimization for cache and instruction-level parallelism. In: Proceedings of the 1996 Conference on Parallel Architectures and Compilation Technique, pp. 238–247. IEEE (1996)
4. Cope, B., et al.: Implementation of 2D Convolution on FPGA, GPU and CPU. Imperial College Report, pp. 2–5 (2006)
5. Edwards, H., Trott, C., Sunderland, D.: Kokkos: enabling manycore performance portability through polymorphic memory access patterns. J. Parallel Distrib. Comput. **74**(12), 3202–3216 (2014)
6. U.S. Department of Energy: U.S. Department of Energy and Cray to Deliver Record-Setting Frontier Supercomputer at ORNL. https://www.energy.gov/articles/us-department-energy-and-cray-deliver-record-setting-frontier-supercomputer-ornl (2019)

7. Espasa, R., Valero, M.: Exploiting instruction-and data-level parallelism. IEEE Micro **17**(5), 20–27 (1997)
8. Henretty, T., Stock, K., Pouchet, L.-N., Franchetti, F., Ramanujam, J., Sadayappan, P.: Data layout transformation for stencil computations on short-vector SIMD architectures. In: Knoop, J. (ed.) CC 2011. LNCS, vol. 6601, pp. 225–245. Springer, Heidelberg (2011). https://doi.org/10.1007/978-3-642-19861-8_13
9. Holewinski, J., et al.: Dynamic trace-based analysis of vectorization potential of applications. ACM SIGPLAN Not. **47**(6), 371–382 (2012)
10. Holmen, J.: Private communication (2018)
11. Holmen, J.K., et al.: Portably improving uintah's readiness for exascale systems through the use of kokkos. SCI Institute (2019). http://www.sci.utah.edu/publications/Hol2019a/UUSCI-2019-001.pdf
12. Hornung, R., Keasler, J.: The RAJA portability layer: overview and status. Technical report, Lawrence Livermore National Laboratories (LLNL), Livermore, CA, United States (2014)
13. Howard, M., et al.: Employing multiple levels of parallelism for CFD at large scales on next generation high-performance computing platforms. In: 2018 Proceedings of the Tenth International Conference on Computational Fluid Dynamics (ICCFD 10), Barcelona, 9–13 July 2018
14. Intel: Requirements for Vectorizable Loops (2012). https://software.intel.com/en-us/articles/requirements-for-vectorizable-loops
15. Jacob, A., et al.: Towards performance portable GPU programming with RAJA. In: Workshop on Portability Among HPC Architectures for Scientific Applications (2015)
16. Jeffers, J., Reinders, J., Sodani, A.: Intel Xeon Phi Processor High Performance Programming: Knights Landing Edition. Morgan Kaufmann, Burlington (2016)
17. Karpiński, P., McDonald, J.: A high-performance portable abstract interface for explicit SIMD vectorization. In: Proceedings of the 8th International Workshop on Programming Models and Applications for Multicores and Manycores. ACM (2017)
18. Kim, K., et al.: Designing vector-friendly compact BLAS and LAPACK kernels. In: Proceedings of the International Conference for High Performance Computing, Networking, Storage and Analysis, p. 55. ACM (2017)
19. Kim, K., et al.: KokkosKernels v. 0.9, Version 00 (2 2017). https://www.osti.gov//servlets/purl/1349511
20. Kretz, M., Lindenstruth, V.: Vc: a C++ library for explicit vectorization. Softw. Pract. Exp. **42**(11), 1409–1430 (2012)
21. Leißa, R., Hack, S., Wald, I.: Extending a C-like language for portable SIMD programming. ACM SIGPLAN Not. **47**(8), 65–74 (2012)
22. Medina, D., St-Cyr, A., Warburton, T.: OCCA: A unified approach to multi-threading languages. arXiv preprint arXiv:1403.0968 (2014)
23. IT Peer Network: Think Exponential: Intel's Xe Architecture. https://itpeernetwork.intel.com/intel-xe-compute#gs.emsehp (2019)
24. Opencl, K., Munshi, A.: The openCL specification version: 1.0 document revision: 48, 23 (2008). https://www.khronos.org/registry/OpenCL/specs/opencl-1.0.pdf
25. Pedel, J., Thornock, J., Smith, S., Smith, P.: Large eddy simulation of polydisperse particles in turbulent coaxial jets using the direct quadrature method of moments. Int. J. Multiph. Flow **63**, 23–38 (2014). https://doi.org/10.1016/j.ijmultiphaseflow.2014.03.002

26. Pai, S., Govindarajan, R., Thazhuthaveetil, M.: PLASMA: portable programming for SIMD heterogeneous accelerators. In: Workshop on Language, Compiler, and Architecture Support for GPGPU, held in conjunction with HPCA/PPoPP (2010)
27. Phipps, E., D'Elia, M., Edwards, H., Hoemmen, M., Hu, J., Rajamanickam, S.: Embedded ensemble propagation for improving performance, portability, and scalability of uncertainty quantification on emerging computational architectures. SIAM J. Sci. Comput. **39**(2), C162–C193 (2017)
28. Phipps, E., Tuminaro, R., Miller, C.: Stokhos: trilinos tools for embedded stochastic-galerkin uncertainty quantification methods. Technical report, Sandia National Laboratories (SNL-NM), Albuquerque, NM, United States (2008)
29. Stephens, N., et al.: The ARM scalable vector extension. IEEE Micro **37**(2), 26–39 (2017)
30. Tian, X., et al.: LLVM compiler implementation for explicit parallelization and SIMD vectorization. In: Proceedings of the Fourth Workshop on the LLVM Compiler Infrastructure in HPC, p. 4. ACM (2017)
31. Trott, C.R.: Kokkos: the C++ performance portability programming model. Technical report, Sandia National Laboratories (SNL-NM), Albuquerque, NM, United States (2017)
32. Wang, H., Wu, P., Tanase, I., Serrano, M., Moreira, J.: Simple, portable and fast SIMD intrinsic programming: generic simd library. In: Proceedings of the 2014 Workshop on Programming Models for SIMD/Vector Processing. ACM (2014)
33. Zenker, E., et al.: Alpaka-an abstraction library for parallel kernel acceleration. In: 2016 IEEE International Parallel and Distributed Processing Symposium Workshops (IPDPSW), pp. 631–640. IEEE (2016)

Author Index

Printed in the United States
By Bookmasters